Married to Tolstoy

CYNTHIA ASQUITH

dy Cynthia Mary Evelin (Charteris) Asquith

MARRIED

to

TOLSTOY

*The unhappy lonely wives of great men are
the wives of whom posterity makes Xantippes*

DIARY OF COUNTESS TOLSTOY

Illustrated with photographs

GREENWOOD PRESS, PUBLISHERS
NEW YORK

Reprinted with the permission of the Houghton Mifflin Company

First Greenwood Reprinting, 1969

Library of Congress Catalogue Card Number: 69-13803

PRINTED IN THE UNITED STATES OF AMERICA

To
Mary Herbert

Contents

CONTENTS

Illustrations

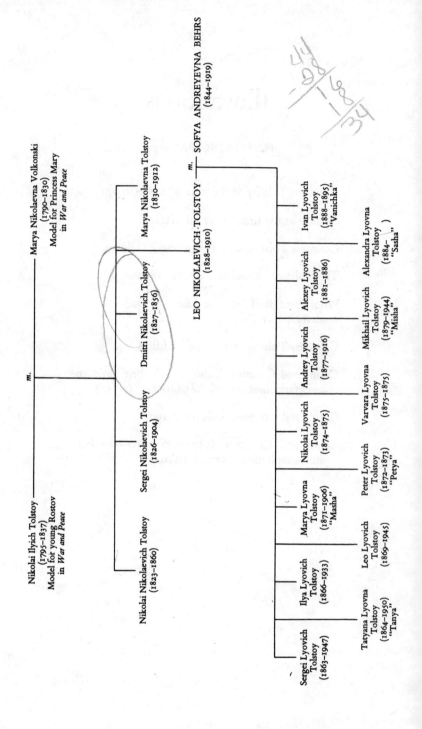

Nikolai Ilyich Tolstoy
(1795–1837)
Model for young Rostov
in *War and Peace*

m.

Marya Nikolaevna Volkonski
(1790–1830)
Model for Princess Mary
in *War and Peace*

Nikolai Nikolaevich Tolstoy
(1823–1860)

Sergei Nikolaevich Tolstoy
(1826–1904)

Dmitri Nikolaevich Tolstoy
(1827–1856)

Marya Nikolaevna Tolstoy
(1830–1912)

LEO NIKOLAEVICH TOLSTOY
(1828–1910)

m.

SOFYA ANDREYEVNA BEHRS
(1844–1919)

Sergei Lyovich
Tolstoy
(1863–1947)

Tatyana Lyovna
Tolstoy
(1864–1950)
"Tanya"

Ilya Lyovich Tolstoy
(1866–1933)

Leo Lyovich
Tolstoy
(1869–1945)

Marya Lyovna
Tolstoy
(1871–1906)
"Masha"

Peter Lyovich
Tolstoy
(1872–1873)
"Petya"

Nikolai Lyovich
Tolstoy
(1874–1875)

Varvara Lyovna
Tolstoy
(1875–1875)

Andrey Lyovich
Tolstoy
(1877–1916)

Mikhail Lyovich
Tolstoy
(1879–1944)
"Misha"

Alexey Lyovich
Tolstoy
(1881–1886)

Alexandra Lyovna
Tolstoy
(1884–)
"Sasha"

Ivan Lyovich
Tolstoy
(1888–1895)
"Vanichka"

Foreword

Marriage with a genius can seldom be easy; to be married to one as immense and as self-contradictory as Tolstoy was proportionately difficult. In Romain Rolland's words, his writings had 'disturbed the conscience of the world', and his desperate struggles to put his published principles into practice had drawn a searchlight of scrutiny on to his home life. His wife was consequently exposed to ceaseless and often hostile observation. Few women have had to live in such a glare of publicity; none has been more the victim of over-simplification.

For years the drama of the Tolstoys' married life had been played before a world audience. In 1910 it flared into melodrama. Every newspaper blazoned the news that, at the age of eighty-two, Tolstoy had staggered out into the snow in the middle of the night and fled from his much-loved home. To escape from what or whom? From the woman to whom he had been married for forty-eight years!

Ten days later followed the news of his death at an obscure railway station. The world mourned the great writer; his miserable wife was blamed for his death.

Tolstoy's motives for leaving home were complex. Quite apart from domestic strife, he had long wanted to withdraw from the world and end his days in solitude and contemplation. That his ill wife's hysterical behaviour precipitated his flight is indisputable. But the attendant circumstances were not given to the public. Because it was not known that several doctors had recently pronounced her so ill as virtually to be out of her mind, she was almost universally condemned. So much for the contemporary verdict. The verdict of posterity has been little kinder.

No marriage has been more densely documented than the Tolstoys'. In the last nightmare year no fewer than seven onlookers were writing copious diaries about their relationship. Worse, husband and wife themselves both had the lifelong habit

13

of keeping diaries; all of them should have been private (Tolstoy's of the last phase was headed 'For Myself Alone') but nearly
all have been published; some, thanks to the deleting of certain
passages, with a definite bias against Countess Tolstoy. In the last
fifty years innumerable biographies of Tolstoy have been written,
most of them, naturally, by his votaries. Consequently, what his
wife always dreaded has largely come about: her haunting fear
that, labelled a Xantippe, she would be remembered only as the
woman who tormented a genius husband by not allowing him
to live according to his principles. Today most people remember
only the tragic end of her marriage, forgetting the forty-eight
arduous years through which she had shared Tolstoy's life, had
borne and brought up their huge family, managed his business
affairs, and slaved for him in countless ways. Advocates she has
undoubtedly had, but they have tended to put themselves out of
court by overstating the case for the defence, notably Bernard
Shaw in his entertaining but irresponsible indictment of the
'practical' side of Tolstoy's life:

> 'No English old maid of county family, living in a Cathe-
> dral town, could have made more absurd attempts to start an
> ideal social system by private misconduct than he. He tried to
> ignore money as Don Quixote did. He left his own skilled
> work to build houses that could hardly be induced to stand,
> and to make boots that any army contractor would have been
> ashamed of. He let his property drift to the verge of insol-
> vency like the laziest Irish squire because he disapproved of
> property as an institution. He connived at all sorts of evasions.
> He would not own property or copyrights; but he would
> make them over to his wife and children and live in their
> country house at Yasnaya Polyana, and their house in Moscow
> very comfortably, only occasionally easing his conscience by
> making things as difficult for them as possible.'

Countess Tolstoy would have been the first indignantly to
repudiate Shaw's extravagant over-simplification. Except in distraught moments, or when as was her avowed habit, deliberately
using her diary as a safety-valve, she never herself accused Tolstoy
of insincerity. Realizing his intellectual integrity, she respected his
ideals, theoretically even sympathizing with many of them. But

as a reformer she thought that he tunnelled too fast and too deep. Furthermore, wifehood was not her only rôle in life. Far from it. She was very much a mother and could not think it right to impose upon children ideals, as yet unrecognized by society, which they could not understand. Above all, like Turgenev, who deplored what he called the 'intellectual suicide of the greatest writer in the world', she so much feared that the preacher in Tolstoy might kill the artist. That is why, as other women fight drink in their husbands, she in hers fought didacticism.

Countess Tolstoy herself would have been the last to deny that she had faults, and that they became more pronounced with the years. Far from self-blinded, she was miserably aware of her later failures. Witness her pitiful outburst after her husband's death: 'How deeply I loved him, and how blunderingly!' That she also had many remarkably good qualities is equally undeniable, and indeed the question arises whether any woman could have done much better in her place?

To be married to Tolstoy was surely to have to walk a tightrope without the power of balance, to carry a burden beyond any woman's endurance. That Countess Tolstoy had not broken down years before she did shows her to have been a woman of exceptional strength of character as well as of constitution. Imagine the mere physical strain of her life. Thirteen children in twenty-three years! Unending difficulties as housekeeper and hostess in a home become a Mecca, to which, though its owner had come to disapprove of servants, innumerable guests had still to be welcomed to meals. Wife, mistress, sick-nurse to Tolstoy, she toiled, too, as his unflagging secretary, copying out literally miles of manuscripts; and on the top of all this, when twenty years after marriage Tolstoy decided that to take money for writing was wrong—a form of prostitution—all the immense business of the publication of his books was shovelled into her already over-full hands.

By a not uncommon irony Countess Tolstoy's lot would have been easier had she been a lesser woman. An adoring, completely compliant nonentity might have lived in peace with Tolstoy; whereas, gifted with beauty and charm, and justifiably possessed of literary and artistic as well as social ambitions, she, far from being one of nature's consorts, was in her own right a remarkable woman. More sense of humour might have made things easier both for herself and for others. In that conciliating sense there seems little doubt that she was somewhat deficient. But the young, charming and happy do not need much sense of humour either to reconcile themselves to life or to reconcile other people to them. In her youth Countess Tolstoy made a delightful impression on everyone. Even the very discerning thought her an admirable wife for a writer. Turgenev praised her to the skies. 'How well you did to marry your wife!' he said to Tolstoy. 'She is a woman of the kind that alas no longer exists.'

It was indeed generally admitted that many years of the Tolstoys' life together were very happy. And, after all, by what criterion is a marriage of nearly fifty years to be judged? Not, surely, by the chance 'curtain' to the too-long dragging drama? By the measure of happiness shared? The Tolstoys had enjoyed great happiness. By the severity of the sufferings inflicted and incurred? Seldom can a man and woman have made one another suffer more. But that was because neither ever lost the appalling power each had to hurt the other, a power that would inevitably have diminished had it not been for the love between them; a love that, though sorely strained, could never die. Thirty years after marriage Countess Tolstoy wrote in her diary: 'I can still say with all my heart, I thank Thee, God!'; and at very much the same time Tolstoy wrote to his brother: 'It is as though our honeymoon had only just begun, and I think there is only one man in a million as lucky as I.'

The wife of a great man for ever stands on trial. No verdict is final. This book, written by a self-appointed Counsel for the Defence, will attempt with sympathy, but without bias, to tell the story of the woman whose opportunity, glory, and doom was to be married to Tolstoy.

I

Courtship

THE prologue to the drama of the long heaven and hell shared by the Tolstoys was played on a summer's day of 1856. The scene was a country villa near Moscow, where a bright-eyed, rosy-cheeked little girl was dancing and clapping her hands with excitement at the prospect of seeing the author of her favourite book, *Childhood*. Count Leo Tolstoy was coming to visit her mother, a great friend of his boyhood. Lyubov Behrs had told her excited daughter that besides being a famous writer their expected visitor was a hero of Sebastopol. He was, she said, so recklessly brave that he would almost certainly have got himself killed had he not been ordered out of the firing line by the Czar, Alexander II, who after reading and weeping over his books *Childhood*, *Boyhood*, and *Sebastopol in December*, had declared: 'That young man's life must be saved!'

The eleven-year-old girl had heard too of Count Leo Tolstoy's fame as the progressive landowner who had tried to free his serfs before the agitation that led to their liberation in 1861. She had also been told that he was a great athlete, and such a crazy gambler that one luckless night he had lost so much money that he had had to sell his house.

Count Leo Tolstoy arrived. Little Sofya was presented to him by her mother. Trembling from head to foot, she made a deep curtsey; then, spellbound, sat gazing at him with her beautiful dark eyes, memorizing every word he said. Could this soldier really be the author of the book she loved so much that she had learnt pages of it by heart? Yes, erect, impeccably smart in his uniform, there he sat in her home, radiating his immense vitality, and—for at that time the future pacifist was a keen soldier—telling her mother about Sebastopol.

His rugged forcible face struck the little girl as almost ugly, but

17

it was strikingly expressive—the eyes, steel-grey, glinting, were unforgettable. 'I know nothing,' wrote Turgenev, 'more disturbing than Tolstoy's eyes. They look straight into your heart and search for your God.'

The dazzling visitor stayed to dinner, and the little girl was allowed to wait on him, her hands shaking as she handed the dishes. Directly he left she tied a red ribbon to the chair on which he had sat, so that she should always know which had been so signally honoured. She then copied several passages from his second book, *Boyhood*, and carried them hidden in her dress, close to her heart.

Tolstoy's diary briefly recorded this first meeting with his future wife: 'Dined at Pokrovskoye. The children waited on us. What dear, merry little girls!'

Other visits followed, and whenever Tolstoy came he told the 'dear, merry little girls' enthralling stories, and invented games, organized picnics, galvanizing the whole family into feeling more alive than ever. 'He fits all ages. He can understand everything, and everything can be said to him,' was the unanimous verdict.

These first meetings were followed by an interlude of several years. Tolstoy was either abroad or engrossed in Utopian schemes for his estate. Among various activities he taught at his school for the peasant children, and brought out an educational magazine called, after his home, *Yasnaya Polyana*.

In 1861 he again became a frequent visitor to the Behrs family. Meanwhile the dark-eyed Sofya Andreyevna, now seventeen, had blossomed into a slender, graceful girl, light of step and—seemingly—light of heart. She had been extremely well brought up, and an air of innocence veiled her tempestuous emotions and restlessly energetic mind. Both she and her younger sister, Tanya, had a sparkling liveliness that delighted Tolstoy, who at first fell in love with the whole family and its atmosphere of fondness, laughter and tears. (The devoted, merry, susceptible Rostov family in *War and Peace* was admittedly drawn from his wife's.)

Sofya's mother's maiden name had been Lyubov Irtenev. She had been brought up in the province of Tula at Krasnoye, the home of her father, Alexander Islenev, a member of the very old Russian nobility. Her mother had been Countess Sophia, daughter of Count Savodsky, famous statesman and favourite of Catherine the Great. Against her will Countess Sophia had been married very young to a Count Kozlov. After the early break-up of that unhappy marriage, she fell in love with Alexander Islenev and lived with him for the rest of her days. He regarded her as his wife; she took his name; a priest even performed a secret marriage ceremony; but as her drunken husband could never be persuaded to divorce her, she was, though socially accepted, never really married, and their six children could not be legitimatized. They were therefore given the name of Irtenev, instead of Islenev. Lyubov, Sofya's mother, was the youngest daughter of this union. Krasnoye was within easy reach of the Tolstoys' home, Yasnaya Polyana, and the children of the two families had been play-fellows.

When Lyubov was fifteen she fell dangerously ill with what was then called inflammation of the brain. The doctor, Andrey Behrs, who was called in, saved her life, and during the seven weeks he attended her they fell in love. Her father protested against their marriage because Dr. Behrs, though of Russian nationality, was of German origin, his grandfather, a Captain Ivan Behrs, having been one of four officers of the Horse Guards sent by the King of Prussia to St. Petersburg at the request of the Empress of Russia, who needed instructors for new cavalry regiments, then being formed. Both Ivan Behrs and his son had, however, married Russian wives, so Dr. Andrey Behrs, Sofya's father, was only one-eighth part German. When Lyubov Irtenev was sixteen, and he thirty-four, they were married. He became Court Physician, was given a comfortable Government apartment in the Kremlin, and later acquired a country villa of his own. They had thirteen children, ten sons and three daughters, Ilsa, Sofya, and Tanya.

Sofya had been educated at home. She loved literature, wrote short stories, showed talent for painting and music, and at sixteen passed a university examination that gave her a diploma as a teacher. Her essay was declared the best of the year. It was remembered, too, for hearing of her engagement, the professor wrote to Tolstoy: 'This is just the wife for you. She has a great flair for literature.'

When Tolstoy resumed his visits to the Behrs family he was in a perceptibly saddened mood. His beloved elder brother, Nicholas, had died. His attempts to better the lives of the peasants at Yasnaya Polyana had disappointed him, and his political activities were incurring the suspicions of the Government. His pallor and brooding disillusioned air enthralled Sofya, who, despite a fleeting Natasha Rostov-like engagement to a military cadet called Polivanov, had never ceased to dream of the soldier-writer, whom she still pictured, his sword in one hand, his pen in the other. 'My fondest memory is of him,' she wrote in her first diary.

Tolstoy's frequent visits made Dr. Behrs and his wife hope and believe that he was seriously interested in their eldest daughter, Lisa, whom he had often met in Moscow society and who was in love with him. Fondness for his old friend Lyubov Behrs and approval of the way in which she brought up her daughters—she had taught them to sew, to keep house and to teach their younger brothers—made him say to his sister, Countess Marya Tolstoy: 'If I ever marry, it will be one of the Behrs girls.' This remark, circulated in Moscow gossip, fortified the hopes of the Behrs and their large circle of friends. Tolstoy did consider Lisa as a possible wife, but any inclination he may have felt not being nearly strong enough, he came to the convenient conclusion that he was much 'too old' for her. After all, he told himself, he was only two years younger than her mother!

In the summer of 1862 he continually turned up at the Behrs' country villa, Pokrovskoye, usually walking the eight miles from Moscow. But at first this was without any thought of marriage. He was merely basking in the atmosphere of happy family life, entering with his amazing perceptiveness into all its concerns, and delighting in the high spirits and artless instinctive coquetry of Sofya and her younger sister Tanya. The frequency of his visits revived the parental hopes of Dr. Behrs and his wife. Surely Leo Tolstoy was now going to do the correct—and convenient— thing, and propose to their eldest daughter, Lisa, a beautiful, clever, yet, when compared with her spirited sisters, rather dull girl. But—unwelcome fact the parents were slow to recognize— it soon became clear that it was their second daughter, Sofya, who was now the magnet. She had a lovely complexion, dazzlingly white teeth; and the look of wonder in her brilliant, wide-open, very dark eyes gave a peculiar charm to her vivacious face. Moreover, both she and Tanya had an attraction lacked by the beautiful and intellectual Lisa. In the words of Tolstoy's friend, the lyric poet, Fet: 'Despite the watchful supervision of their mother and their own *irreproachable modesty*, they had that attractive quality which the French call *'du chien'*.

One day, while Sofya and Tolstoy were on one of their frequent country walks, she shyly confessed that she had written a novel. He begged her to show it to him. Visibly embarrassed, looking almost guilty, she refused. Tolstoy, disconcerted, and alarmed by his rising emotions, told himself that this glimmering girl could not possibly be for his old (he was not yet thirty-four) and sullied self. He decided to stop coming. Day after day Sofya waited for him in vain.

But when they were back in Moscow he came to dinner. He looked ill and had a bad cough. That evening the bright, wide-open eyes of Sofya's favourite sister, the fifteen-year-old Tanya, noticed that, sitting beside Tolstoy, her eldest sister, Lisa, smiled incessantly and talked in the soft unnatural voice she affected when she wanted to be particularly charming. Evidently she was, in Rostov family parlance, 'sugaring up' to him. That night, when the sisters went to bed, Tanya saw that Sofya looked sad and subdued. She knelt longer than usual over her prayers. Intently watching, Tanya remained silent, but, at last, unable to contain herself, softly called her name: 'Sofya,' she asked, 'you love the Count?'

'I don't know,' quietly answered her sister.

Apparently the question did not surprise her.

'Oh, Tanya,' said Sofya, after a little pause, 'two of his brothers have died of consumption!'

Sofya lay long awake. Her sister heard her sigh, saw her brush away tears. That whispered 'I don't know' had been more eloquent than a passionate protestation of love.

Tanya, still a child, remembered Sofya's young lover, Polivanov. Is it possible, then, to love two people at once? she wondered. Or has a new love supplanted the old?

At the beginning of August, Tolstoy dined with the Behrs in Moscow. When his hostess told him that they were about to stay with her father at Ivitzky, Tolstoy made her promise that on their way they would spend a night or two at his home, where she had not been since childhood. This prospect thrilled Sofya. She had always been attracted by the name Yasnaya Polyana (Clear Glade) and longed to see where Tolstoy had spent his boyhood. When the time came, Sofya, her mother, and her two sisters travelled to the city of Tula, where for the last time they

changed horses, and then, under an immense sky, drove south-
ward through vast undulating country, past miles and miles of
unfenced cornland, to Yasnaya Polyana. This typical small
Russian village had one street of straw-thatched huts made of
mud-and-wattle, a communal pump, and a minute church. Two
rounded white-painted brick towers stood at the entrance to the
park, and the house was approached by a lovely avenue of birch
trees. To Tolstoy's grief and remorse the home of his ancestors in
which he had spent his childhood, a fine many-columned, bal-
conied white house of forty rooms, was no longer there. This,
with its estate of about 5,400 acres and some 350 male serfs and
their families, he had in 1847 inherited at the age of nineteen; but,
sold to pay for his gambling losses, the much-loved house had
been bodily removed by its purchaser. After this loss, the thought
of which still made him grind his teeth, Tolstoy had moved into
an adjacent two-storeyed wooden building, done up in the
simplest possible way.

The Behrs family were warmly welcomed by their anxious
host and the two old ladies who lived with him—his beloved
aunt, Tatyana Ergolsky, the 'guardian angel', as he called her, of
his orphaned boyhood, and her companion, Natalya Petrovna,
also a relative of his.

The hospitality at Yasnaya Polyana was simple in the extreme.
The guests were shown into a vaulted room on the ground floor
with the iron rings, from which home-smoked hams and horses'
saddles used to be slung, still screwed into its stone ceiling. There
was very little furniture: one unpolished table made out of birch
wood by the estate carpenter, and wooden sofas painted white
with hard-cushioned seats covered in coarse striped blue-and-
white canvas. The host took his guests into the kitchen garden to
eat raspberries, in the dusk, and Sofya was greatly enjoying herself, but when it grew dark her mother sent her indoors to unpack
their luggage, and while she and Dynyasha, one of the chamber-
maids, were preparing the beds, the owner of the house suddenly
strode into the room. Dynyasha told her master that she could
arrange three beds on the sofas but there was no room for a
fourth. 'Why not try the long armchair?' suggested Tolstoy, and
fumblingly began to unfold a sheet.

Long afterwards Sofya wrote a description of this momentous
visit to her future home:

'I felt a little embarrassed, but at the same time there was something delightful and intimate in the way in which Lev Nikolaevich helped us to make our beds. . . . The drawing-room door led on to a little balcony which I have loved ever since. It gives me joy to this day. I took a chair and going out on to the balcony, I admired the beauty. I shall never forget the emotions I felt that evening, though I shall never be able to describe them. Was it the influence of the country, of nature, of the sense of spaciousness? Was it a presentiment of what was to happen, when before long I became the mistress of the house? Was it simply a farewell to the freedom of girl-hood? I cannot tell. But there was something new and signifi-cant in my mood that evening, something rapturous, hitherto unexperienced. Lev Nikolaevich came to call me to supper:

"No, thank you, I don't want to eat," I said. "It's so lovely out here."

Lev Nikolaevich returned to the dining-room, but before finishing his supper he came back to the balcony. I can't re-member all we talked about: I only remember how he said to me, "How serene and simple you are!" . . . I liked that very much.

I slept well in the long chair Lev Nikolaevich had prepared for me. At first I tossed about, for the two arms made it a little narrow and uncomfortable; but my heart was full of joy and laughter as I thought of Lev Nikolaevich preparing my bed for me, and I soon fell asleep, with a new feeling of joy in my whole being.'

Next morning Sofya awoke to a sense of exhilaration and a 'longing to run round the place, look at everything, talk to every-body'. It was a lovely day. Tolstoy proposed that she should ride his grey horse, Belogubka. The name delighted her. She longed to be on its back. 'But I've no riding habit,' she said, pointing at her yellow dress with its black velvet buttons and belt. 'That doesn't matter,' laughed Tolstoy. 'There are no villas here. No one except the trees will see you.' He lifted her into the saddle. Then he mounted his own white horse and they galloped into the Zaseka Forest. The rest of the party tamely followed in the jolting droshky, a peculiar home-made conveyance, shaped like an Irish car, in which twelve people could sit back to back, six on either side.

They stopped to picnic in a meadow where there was a very inviting haystack, and again and again the future Countess Tolstoy climbed to its top and rolled down it with peals of laughter. After their meal, seated on the haystack, and led by Tolstoy's powerful voice, they all sang choruses.

A long magic day, and all the time Sofya could feel his eyes looking at her.

Next day Sofya drove with her family from Yasnaya Polyana to Ivitsky, to stay with her grandfather, Istenev. He was delighted to hear that they had been visiting Leo Tolstoy, of whom he was very fond. Ivitsky was a large house, but apparently no more luxurious than Yasnaya Polyana. Sofya's diary uncomplainingly described her room as containing no table, only one wooden chair, and a 'bed behind the cupboard'.

She had little time to discover how much she missed Tolstoy, for the very day after her departure from Yasnaya Polyana he unexpectedly turned up at Ivitsky. On the spur of the moment he had mounted his horse and ridden the forty miles between the two homes.

The house was filled with guests, and in the evening the young people decided to dance. The music struck up. Sofya pirouetted with excitement. A young man bore her off. Tolstoy, having pronounced himself too old to dance, stood against the wall, wistfully watching her. Flushed, her dark eyes glittering, she swirled round the room in her pretty crinoline dress with lilac ribbons fluttering from the shoulders—a fashion of those days archly called '*Suivez-moi, jeune homme*'.

For some time Tolstoy tried to repress the emotion he was struggling not to recognize as love. Later in the evening, for a few tingling minutes, chance left him and Sofya by themselves, so they supposed, in the drawing-room. They had an involuntary eavesdropper. 'The Imp', as Tolstoy called Tanya, who had been asked to sing, had hidden herself under the piano, and when her sister and Tolstoy, both looking so much wrought up, came into the room she did not dare show herself. Then occurred the extraordinary scene years later almost exactly described in *Anna Karenina* where Levin proposes to Kitty.

'Sofya,' Tolstoy suddenly blurted out, 'can you read a sentence which I'll write in initials only?'

Dumbly, Sofya nodded. Snatching up a piece of white chalk,

he scribbled a long row of letters on the green baize card-table: 'Y.y.a.y.d.f.h.r.m.t.k.o.m.o.a.a.o.m.i.f.h.' Sofya, half guessing, half telepathizing, and only once prompted by him, somehow made out the message: 'Your youth and your desire for happiness remind me too keenly of my old age and of my incapacity for happiness.'

Encouraged by Sofya's astounding intuitiveness, Tolstoy, his strong expressive face twisting as he wrote, initialled another sentence: 'A wrong idea exists in your family as to me and your sister Lisa. Won't you and Tanya protect me?'

Again, almost magically, Sofya grasped his meaning. Her diary gives her explanation of what seems inexplicable:

'My heart began to throb violently, and I seemed suddenly to have lost all sense of time and reality. At that moment I felt as if I could grasp everything; conceive the inconceivable. . . . I read without hesitating for a second. Lev Nikolenka wasn't even surprised. Our state of mind was so tense and exalted that nothing seemed to surprise us.'

Sofya had scarcely finished deciphering Tolstoy's message when she heard her mother's peremptory voice: 'Sofya, will you please go to bed at once!'

'I felt,' wrote Sonya, 'that something serious had taken place between us—something that couldn't stop there. But for various reasons I checked my thoughts.'

Even after that queerly veiled declaration, Sofya dared not let herself be sure of Tolstoy's love, but hope fluttered. At all events it was clearly not for her sister that this wonderful being visited them. And Tolstoy? Strange! He, who in his novels shows such astounding power to read women's hearts—to divine and depict their thoughts and emotions in every possible vicissitude—was at this moment in his own life so much blinded by passion and fears that he could not see that this young woman—child, as he called her—was quiveringly in love with him.

It was more than two months before this singular incident had its sequel. Tolstoy could no longer question his passionate love for the child. She had taken utter possession of his heart. 'I did not believe,' he wrote in his diary, 'I could ever be so much in love. If this goes on much longer I'll go mad, I'll shoot myself!'

Doubts about his own emotions were now replaced by a terror of refusal. He did not dare propose. Another feeling, more delicate than fear, helped to restrain him:

> Love that so desires would fain keep her changeless;
> Fain would fling the net, and fain have her free.

'Whenever I am in love,' he had written in his diary, 'it seems to me that the woman I love is garmented in bronze.'

Later in the summer, when the Behrs family returned to their country villa, Tolstoy, then living in Moscow, came to visit them almost every day and would often stay until long after the evening meal. On wonderful moonlit nights he and Sonya would stroll in the garden and talk. She found his deep, vibrant, almost hoarse voice, strangely stirring. 'It sounded so tender,' she wrote; 'as though it were coming from a distance.' When one evening he suddenly exclaimed 'What a mad, mad night!' her heart beat fast. Was he going to say something important? But the silence remained unbroken. 'Everything,' wrote Sonya of that slow enchanted summer, 'seemed so lovely and free of care. I had no desires and the future seemed of no importance.' Yet she had a sense of something momentous impending, and though happy, was often grave, even sad, for, as her diary declared, to her, love could never be 'an emotional game, but always something akin to suffering'.

At times high spirits would seize them both. One day Sofya, reclining with mock dignity in her father's carriage from which the horses had just been unharnessed, luxuriously drawled out to Tolstoy: 'When I'm an Empress I'll be driven about in a grander carriage than this!' Tolstoy, putting himself between the shafts, bowled the carriage at a rattling speed round and round the yard, shouting out: 'This is how my Empress shall travel!' Sofya recalled this jest in the first letter she ever wrote to Tolstoy, one of congratulations on his thirty-fourth birthday:

> 'If I were an Empress, I would send you on your birthday a most gracious mandate; but being a simple mortal, I merely congratulate you on having come into God's world, and I hope that you will look on it for a very long time, and, if possible, always with the same eyes as now.'

Meanwhile Sofya was very worried about her sister Lisa's feelings for Tolstoy, and her parents' assumption that it was she he was in love with. Deciding one evening to try to enlighten her mother, she tiptoed into her bedroom.

'Well, Sofya?' asked Lyubov Behrs, guessing that her daughter had something to confide. 'Tell me all about it, my dear.'

'Listen, Mother,' said Sofya timidly. 'I know people think that it isn't *me* that Lev Nikolaevich wants to marry, and yet I do believe he does love me.'

To her astonishment, her usually sympathetic mother, hating to hear her own stifled fears expressed, tartly told her to go away and 'not to think nonsense'. 'Don't imagine everyone is in love with *you*,' she added. Deeply hurt, Sofya fled from the room and did not mention the matter again.

After long demurring, Sofya at last allowed Tolstoy to read her novel. Perhaps she hoped it would precipitate a declaration. It had precisely the reverse effect. No wonder she had blushed when he had first asked to see it; for, thinly disguised as fiction, her book was largely a study of her relationship with him. He could not possibly fail to recognize himself in the erratic Prince Dublitzky of the 'perpetually changing ideals'. The heroine was attracted by Dublitzky's personality, and recognized his genius, but she thought him ugly, and arranged for him to marry her elder beautiful, but rather frigid, sister. This revived all Tolstoy's earlier misery about his looks. Unable to see the charm in his own expression, he was convinced that he was repulsively ugly. He hated his jutting nose, long convex upper lip, large ears, and bristling hair: 'I believed there could be no happiness for a man with such a broad nose, thick lips and small eyes as mine, and I implored God to perform a miracle—to grant me good looks. For a beautiful face I would have bartered all I had! That night he wrote in his diary: 'You disgusting mug, don't poke your snout where there are poetry, youth, beauty, and love. . . . Hard work—the spiritual monastery are all that remains for you!' He also wrote: 'She let me read her story. What a powerful sense of truth and simplicity!' But to the young authoress he said nothing at all, and chagrined, she burned her book. 'An immense pity,' declared her sister, Tanya, 'because in this novel, as though in a rough copy for *War and Peace*, Countess Rostov and her daughters were all clearly portrayed.' The heroine was a beauti-

ful girl with large black eyes, her elder sister a cold charmless
blonde, her younger sister (actually called Natasha) slender, en-
chanting, high-spirited.

Tolstoy now seemed frozen into silence. Dr. Behrs grew indignant with him for coming so often and making no proposal
of marriage. He even began to suspect that it was not his daughter,
but his wife, Tolstoy was in love with!

Every moment Tolstoy loved Sofya more and more. Her
dewy freshness haunted him. Compared with her, all other girls,
he complained, seemed 'mere dried-up things in crinolines'. 'That
I could love so madly, I would never have believed,' he wrote.
'If it goes on like this I *shall* shoot myself! . . . She is adorable in
every way. But I am the repulsive Dublitzky! Yet may I not be
made beautiful by love?'

Jealousy, too, now tormented Tolstoy, not only of the handsome young military cadet, Polivanov, but also of another older
admirer of Sofya's, Professor Popov.

How could he, asked his diary, ever have hoped that this
innocent girl could be for his sullied self? Yet, he argued: 'She
blushes. She seems all emotion.' Hope battled with despondency.
He decided to propose. Day after day he came with that resolve,
but paralysed by fear, could never bring himself to utter the
words. At last, at four o'clock one morning, desperation drove
him to write a proposal of marriage.

'I've written a letter,' records his diary. 'I'll give it to her
tomorrow. God, how I fear to die! Happiness, and such happiness,
seems to me impossible. My God, help me!'

Even then he dared not give the letter to Sofya. It was Tanya's
lovely contralto voice that at last broke the spell. Years afterwards
her book of memoirs, *Tolstoy As I Knew Him*, described the long-
awaited climax of her brother-in-law's courtship. When he appeared that evening she at once noticed how overwrought he
was. She felt sure that something was about to happen. Would it
be a proposal? Or goodbye for ever? She had no idea. Unable to
keep still, Tolstoy asked Sofya to play the piano. Affected by his
tension, she was too agitated to play properly and called to Tanya
to come and sing the words of the song 'Il Bacio' (The Kiss) that
she was murdering. Tanya knew that Tolstoy resented her joining them, but feeling herself in good voice, she refused to be put
off, and began to sing. Her young voice filled the room. Sofya's

trembling fingers stumbled so badly that Tolstoy silently slid into her place on the piano stool, and his playing of the accompaniment at once gave fresh life to Tanya's voice and new meaning to the words. Carried away by the melody, Tanya sang as she had never sung before, and when she reached the finale with its passionate yearning, her voice triumphantly soared to the very high last note. The second the song ended, Tolstoy sprang to his feet, and with tears in his eyes and voice, exclaimed: 'How *wonderfully* you sing tonight!' The next moment he thrust into Sofya's hand the letter he had carried about for days.

Unwittingly Tanya had done the trick. How or why she did not then know, but later Tolstoy confessed that, while accompanying her, he had been, so to speak, tossing up for it: 'If she takes the high note well I must deliver the letter today,' he had sworn to himself. 'If she fails, I must *not* deliver it. . . .'

The instant the envelope was in her hand, Sofya flashed out of the room, sped to her bedroom, and locked herself in to read her love-letter, in which, after describing the torment of his fears, Tolstoy at last came to the point:

'Tell me, as an *honest person*, and with hand on heart, without haste, *for God's sake without haste*—do you wish to be my wife? If you say "yes" boldly with all your heart, then say it: but if you have the faintest shadow of doubt say "no". For Heaven's sake think it over carefully. I'm terrified to think of a "no", but I'm prepared for it and will be strong enough to bear it . . .'

The letter ended on an alarming note of warning: 'But it will be *terrible* if I am not loved by my wife as much as I love you.'

Tolstoy did not have long to wait in suspense. The ecstatic girl allowed herself no time to read the letter properly. Skipping the preamble, her eyes merely skimmed the lines until they came to 'Do you wish to be my wife?'

At that, 'light as a feather' (her own words) she 'flew' to him.

'Well?' he asked, taking her by both hands.

'Of course—yes!'

In his terse diary that night Tolstoy wrote: 'Have told her. And she? Yes—like a wounded bird.'

2

Betrothal

THE happiness to which Sofya awoke next morning did
not remain untroubled. To begin with, there was her disappointed sister, who had long been growing more and
more obviously unhappy, and last night had not been able to
leave Sofya in peace even to read her love-letter, but banging on
the door of the bedroom they both shared with Tanya, had
screamed out: 'Sofya! Open the door. Open it at once!'

Reluctantly the door had been inched open.

'Sofya, what has he written to you? I *must* know!'

'He has proposed to me,' Sofya had raptly answered,
frightened but really too excited, too happy, to think about
anyone but herself and Lev Nikolaevich.

'Refuse him at once!' Lisa had screamed.

Clutching the precious letter, Sofya had merely brushed past
her sister on her birdlight flight to her lover.

But now that her own happiness seemed secure, her heart
ached for Lisa. She had never been able to love her as she loved
Tanya—she found her too cool, disdainful and reserved—yet
family affection was strong.

Sofya had at once told her mother of her engagement, and
this morning the atmosphere was thunderous. Dr. Behrs was very
angry. Not only did he grieve for Lisa's feelings, he was affronted
because at that time, in Russia, it was regarded as a slur on the
elder sister if the younger married first. He refused to give his
consent. His wife, a wise family psychologist, appealed to Lisa to
bring her father round, and Lisa, who had recovered her self-
control, now behaved extremely well. Sofya and Leo Tolstoy,
she assured her father, were destined for one another; and now
that she knew that her sister really loved him she would soon be

able to readjust her own relationship with him; her only wish was for them both to be happy. Proud of Lisa's dignified behaviour, and touched by Sofya's tears, the father calmed down and consented to the marriage.

Despite all that Lisa might say, the atmosphere between the sisters was still strained. Nor was it improved by an unfortunate misunderstanding that afternoon. It was the 'Name Day' of both Lyubov Behrs and of Sofya, and friends streamed in to congratulate them.

'You must also congratulate us on our daughter's engagement to Count Leo Tolstoy,' said the hostess to her guests; and to the general embarrassment several people enthusiastically congratulated Lisa.

Before the company had recovered from this disconcerting incident, Polivanov, the hero of Sofya's boy-and-girl romance (depicted by Tolstoy in *War and Peace* as Denisov) appeared. He had for some time been away from Moscow, and a letter written by Sofya to tell him of her change of heart had never reached him. At sight of her old sweetheart—young, handsome, resplendent in his Guards uniform—Sofya blushed painfully, while Tolstoy scowled. Lyubov Behrs did not dare tell Polivanov of the betrothal, but one of her sons drew him into another room and broke the news to him. The poor boy's eyes filled with tears. Shortly afterwards Sofya, looking agonized, slipped out of the room to have a word with her childhood's love.

'I knew,' said Polivanov sadly but unreproachfully, 'that you would not stick to me. I felt it.'

Sofya assured him that for no other man in the world than Leo Tolstoy would she ever have forsaken him.

Polivanov wanted to leave at once, but to Tolstoy's visible rage, Dr. Behrs persuaded him to stay to dinner, immediately after which he hurried away. Jealousy of Polivanov was not Tolstoy's only trouble. Though he did not feel himself to blame, the thought of Lisa distressed him. 'Lisa,' he wrote in his diary, 'pitiable and painful, she must have hated me.'

If Tolstoy had been an unconscionable time over his wooing, his native impetuosity reasserted itself the instant he was engaged. The marriage, he declared, must take place exactly one week from the day he had been accepted. Lyubov Behrs protested. At first, indeed, she would not consider such unconventional haste. 'Her trousseau has to be made,' she objected.

'Trousseau!' exclaimed Tolstoy. What did such flummery matter? 'Sofya has plenty of clothes. What *can* she want with more?'

Finally the mother had to yield to his stubbornness, and the wedding was fixed for September 23rd. The bridegroom asked the bride where she would like to spend their first weeks together. In Moscow? Abroad? He was delighted when she said she would prefer to go straight to Yasnaya Polyana. He warned her that they would not have the house to themselves. His old aunt and her companion, both permanent inmates, would be there. She did not mind. She wanted to begin her married life in her husband's home.

Short as was the engagement, it gave Tolstoy time for his first mistake. Belief in the necessity of complete candour impelled him to make his bride read his diary in which, besides setting down all his heart-searchings, aspirations and self-denunciations, he had unfortunately also recorded the many now bitterly repented moral lapses—'debaucheries' he called them—of his bachelor days. His wife, he felt, ought to know the worst of him. These confessions came as a shattering revelation to Sofya, whose upbringing had been particularly sheltered, and who shied away from what she no doubt called 'all that side of life'. She had looked upon Tolstoy as the personification of virtue. 'You have never been in love before, have you?' she had even asked him. Hideously shocked, she cried all night, and came down with embarrassingly reddened eyelids.

Distress over her bridegroom's sins of the flesh probably prevented her from being scared by other revelations which girls of today might well find more alarming. To eyes less innocent, Tolstoy's perpetual moral book-keeping, and the somersaults—ethical, intellectual, and spiritual—which, without his ever quite landing on his feet, he was for ever turning, would have been more disquieting reading than his moral lapses. Undoubtedly, too, this extraordinary diary made it clear that whoever married Tolstoy would take on no easy job. Would not a man who set himself so high a standard expect moral perfection in his wife? Flagrant inconsistencies alarmed Sofya too. Still more, perhaps, his impulsiveness, of which various extraordinary instances were given: 'If three days pass without my doing a good deed I shall shoot myself,' he wrote on one day, and on the fourth gave away his horse to the first man he met. Yet, for all the crazy impulsiveness, Sofya was struck by symptoms of a seemingly incongruous calculation. One statement particularly chilled her: 'I have come to Moscow with three aims: 1. To gamble; 2. To obtain a post; 3. To marry.'

If Tolstoy's hypersensitivity was a perpetual torment to himself, to the girl who was to marry him his declared ambition to thicken his skin must have been more alarming. Lamenting his inability to rid himself of 'the terrible yoke of the fear of ridicule', his diary hankers after 'the priceless trait of complete indifference to other people's feelings'—a state of mind scarcely conducive to happy family life. Nor did Sofya like the many bitter indictments of women; for example, among innumerable rules made for himself: 'Regard feminine society as a necessary evil, and as far as you can avoid it. From whom indeed do we learn voluptuousness, frivolity in everything, and many another vice, if not from women?'

A pleasing understatement stood out: 'There is something in me which compels me to believe that I was not born to be like everybody else'; and indeed this disarming diary of a young man assuredly not born to be like everybody else abounds in comic avowals. One day the austere idealist, who thinks waste of time a crime, and struggles to live by the most rigid time-table, has to confess that he has spent two entire days playing cards with himself! Twin faults, respectively called 'pride' and 'lack of pride' are frequently deplored; the quaintest examples of them given: 'After dinner spent the evening prowling about and experiencing *voluptuous desires . . .*' (the italics are his). 'I fell into despair because my left moustache came down lower than my right, and I spent two hours trying to level them with scissors.'

The shocks and fears of the reader might well have dissolved into laughter, but the bride of eighteen was in no mood to laugh. It is difficult to believe that the passage about his moustache could have been read without a smile, but reading with widening eyes about her lover's carnal sins, the distressed Sofya had little attention for less curdling themes.

No doubt it was as well for the bride's peace of mind that the shortness of the engagement spared her many love-letters. If

Valérie Arsenev, the only other girl to whom Tolstoy had become anywhere near to being engaged, had married him, she
could not have pleaded that she had not been warned. His so-
called love-letters to her were among the queerest ever penned.
At best they were sermons—excelsior exhortations to Valérie to
improve herself, not only spiritually, but in the most practical
matters. He even ordered her to put on her stockings for herself,
and scolded her for enjoying the coronation festivities. He was
glad, he wrote, that her 'current-pattern' dress had been crumpled.
Valérie loved him, and so put up with his chidings; but she must
have found it difficult to bear his threats as to what would happen
to *him* should he not find complete happiness in marriage. Such a
calamity, he declared, would ruin everything, even his talent for
writing! And if he should lack the courage to cut his throat, then
he would become a gambler, a drunkard and even (curious effect
on a well-to-do man) a thief. 'You know my nasty suspicious
changeable character,' ended one of these *billets doux*, 'and God
knows if there is anything that could alter it. Perhaps strong love,
which I have never felt, and in which I do not believe.'

As though such letters were not enough, Tolstoy told Valérie
of the far worse ones he had refrained from posting.

If Sofya was fortunate in missing her quota of love-letters her
betrothed's diary was bad enough. Indeed, it did irreparable
harm. On that point there can be no doubt. For one thing, it
sowed the seeds of the groundless jealousy of other women that
was all her life to torment her. Years and years later she wrote:

> 'I don't think I've ever got over the horror I experienced
> when I read Leova's diary before our marriage, and I doubt
> whether the sharp sting of jealousy and my bewilderment at
> the thought of such filth and debauchery has ever disappeared.
> May God preserve all young souls from such wounds, for
> they will never heal.'

Sofya's last week in her home was extremely exhausting—a
turmoil of visitors, endless tryings-on, constraint between herself
and Lisa, heartache over Polivanov.

At last the twenty-third of September came. The wedding
was to be at eight o'clock in the evening in the Court Church of
the Kremlin, famous for its wonderful invisible choir. To the

general consternation, in the middle of the morning, when everything was in confusion, Tolstoy, violating every convention,
defying every superstition, burst his way into the house. Told by
Tanya of his arrival, Lyubov Behrs, astonished and displeased,
hurried to her daughter's room to find the bride and bridegroom
seated side by side on a packed and corded trunk. And the bride
was weeping bitterly! No wonder. Tolstoy, who had not been
able to sleep all night, had been tormenting her with questions.
Was she absolutely sure that she loved him? Was she troubled
by memories of Polivanov? If she had any doubts whatsoever,
far better be honest, admit them and agree to part. Does he want
to be out of it for his *own* sake? wondered Sofya in sudden dreadful misgiving.

'A nice time you've chosen to upset her and make her cry!'
scolded the indignant mother. Abashed, the bridegroom slunk
away. The qualms of that morning were recorded in his diary.
'On the morning of the marriage, fear, disbelief, and dislike of
the ceremony.'

At six o'clock the harassed bride began to dress. Everyone
seemed conspiring to upset her. The needlewomen, kneeling on
her toes, with pins and threads of cotton in their mouths, sniffled.

'What *shall* we do without our little Countess?' whimpered
her old Nannie.

'I'll die of loneliness without you!' Tanya kept on saying, and
their little brother Petya gazed at her with tears in his large black
eyes.

At length the last hook in the bride's billowing white dress
was fastened; the long tulle veil and the flowers pinned to her
dark head. The family party now waited for the best man to
come to tell them that the bridegroom was in the church. The
minutes ticked past. No news. A whole hour went by. Sofya
could not forget the state Leo had been in only that morning. A
petrifying thought shot into her mind. Was it conceivable that
he had run away . . .?

At last, not the expected best man, but Tolstoy's agitated valet
arrived to explain the delay. His master had no dress-shirt to put
on. By mistake it had been packed with his other things and sent
in his luggage to the bride's house. It was Sunday and all the shops
were shut! A trunk was unpacked, a shirt found, and the valet
hurried away. At last news came. The bridegroom was waiting

in the aisle. Strained, exhausted, the bride wept all the way to the church.

The gorgeous wedding ceremony is unforgettably described in *Anna Karenina* with Levin and Kitty as the bridegroom and bride. So, too, is the conflict in the bridegroom's mind.

The usual wedding reception was given at the Behrs' home. Corks popped, champagne sparkled, toasts were drunk. The hour of departure arrived. The new dormeuse (sleeping coach) with its six horses, a cockaded coachman, and a postillion, drew up at the door, and in accordance with the old Russian custom everyone sat still in silence for a few moments before the departure of the bride and bridegroom. At last they set out on the 130-mile drive to Yasnaya Polyana. Here in her own words are the bride's emotions on bidding goodbye to the home of a happy childhood:

'Lev Nikolaevich was in a hurry to get off. For the first time I suddenly fully realized that I was going away for ever from those I had loved all my life. Struggling to repress my tears, I began to say goodbye. It was terrible! When I said goodbye to my father, I burst into tears. As I kissed Lisa goodbye, I looked into her eyes. She too was weeping. Tanya sobbed loudly like a child and so did Petya. Then I went downstairs and blessed with the sign of the cross little Vyacheslav, who was fast alseep. I said goodbye to my nurse. Throwing her arms around me, she hugged me passionately. Finally came the last moment specially saved for my beloved mother. I flung myself round her neck. We both sobbed. And our sobs expressed our mutual gratitude for all the love and kindness we had given one another; forgiveness for whatever pain we had involuntarily caused one another, and our grief at parting. When at last, wrenching myself away, I took my place in the carriage, she gave a piercing cry which I shall remember for the rest of my life. Never could I forget that cry. It seemed torn straight from my mother's heart. The autumn rain was pouring down, and the puddles reflected the dim lights of the street lanterns. Lev Nikolaevich shut the carriage door with a bang. The horses' feet began to splash through the puddles and we drove away. Tired, heartbroken, huddled up in my corner of the carriage, I kept on weeping.

Lev Nikolaevich seemed surprised, dismayed. "If leaving my family was such sorrow I evidently didn't love him very much," he said. He did not realize then that if I was capable of so much love for my family, I would be able to transfer it to him and to our children, which indeed, was what happened.'

Forty-eight hours later the bride and bridegroom arrived at Yasnaya Polyana, where, according to the old Russian custom, they were ceremoniously welcomed at the door by 'Auntie Tatyana', bearing an icon of the Mother of God, and Tolstoy's brother, Sergei, holding the traditional bread and salt. In silence the married pair bowed low, crossed themselves and embraced 'Auntie Tatyana'. Thus Sofya was received into the home where, in the overwhelmingly full life awaiting her, she was to be so rapturously happy; so desperately unhappy.

3
Yasnaya Polyana

'INCREDIBLE HAPPINESS!' exclaimed Tolstoy's diary at the beginning of the forty-eight years of his married life, and shortly after came the entry: 'No one has had or will have such happiness. . . . She is so incredibly good, so pure and harmonious. Something tortures me—jealousy for the man who could be fully her equal. I am not.' The same rapturous note was struck in a letter to his cousin and most intimate friend Countess Alexandra Tolstoy. : 'While I write I hear the voice of my wife whom I love more than all the world. I have lived thirty-four years without knowing it was possible to love and be so happy. Why does such a being as she love me?'

The bride's happy letter to her sister, written a week after the wedding, ended:

'Leovochka wants to write a line to you, Tanya. So I must leave room for him. I sign myself importantly for the first time

Your sister
Countess Sonya Tolstoy.'

The reason she signed herself Sonya instead of Sofya was that her husband always called her by that name, as henceforth, for convenience' sake, this book will do. Sonya called him Lev, Leova, Leovochka, and various other pet names, using his formal name with the patronymic, Leo Nikolayevich, only when their relations were strained.

Tolstoy wrote a postscript to Sonya's letter:

'Today she is wearing a cap with crimson ribbons and playing at being grown up and mistress of this house, and she

38

does it brilliantly, very much like the real thing. . . . I love you
very much, Tanya, I know that you, like Sonya, love to be
loved. That is why I write.'

Consciously 'playing at being grown up', the new Countess
Leo Tolstoy enjoyed presiding over the ancient, pot-bellied
samovar, but Yasnaya Polyana was a curious sphere in which to
learn to keep house. Its odd collection of feudal retainers did not
make at all the kind of staff to which Sonya was accustomed in her
parents' home, where twelve more or less conventional servants
were kept. There was the witty old woman called Gasha, who, as
his grandmother's personal maid, had been the best-loved servant,
or, as domestics were then called, 'household serf', of Tolstoy's
childhood. Sonya may well have wondered why Gasha should
have come to be housekeeper, a post for which her most salient
characteristics scarcely seemed to qualify her. An unbridled
passion for animals—she was too fond of sheep ever to touch
mutton—was not limited to domestic pets, but embraced
creatures usually abhorrent to housekeepers. Mice were fed, and
she would allow no insect, not even a blackbeetle, to be killed.
In her unforgettably dirty bedroom, netted with cobwebs, cock-
roaches scuttled up and down the walls, and traces of mice lay
thick upon the floor. Whenever one of Tolstoy's many sporting
dogs was lost, Gasha, who was nicknamed the 'Kennel Governess',
would burn a wax candle before the icon of her favourite saint,
St. Nicholas; and each time puppies were born her bedroom was
converted into a nursery kennel, her own garments used as
swaddling clothes. A beautiful jacket Sonya gave her was put to
the same honourable use. Gasha, an inveterate knitter, walked to
and from the house to her lodging; her steel needles clicketing
every inch of the way. This unusual housekeeper, reputed to have
been very beautiful in youth and still an entertaining talker, had
already been immortalized by Tolstoy in *Childhood* and *Boyhood*.
Scarcely more conventional than Gasha was the old cook,
originally a serf in the household of Tolstoy's maternal grandfather, Count Volkonsky (in *War and Peace*, Count Bolkonsky),
where his job had been to play the flute in that nobleman's house
orchestra. Asked by Sonya why he had become a cook, he tersely
replied: 'Because I lost my mouthpiece.' Quite often this musician-
cook would be much too drunk to cook; but at that time Tolstoy

was more than tolerant of drunkenness; 'I'm terribly fond of the
drunks,' he declared, 'so much good nature and simplicity.'

The freak staff was not the only feature at Yasnaya Polyana
that most brides would have found trying. Never for one day
did husband and wife have their home to themselves. Tatyana
Ergolsky ('Auntie Tatyana'), the beloved foster-mother of
Tolstoy's orphaned childhood, was a permanent inmate. This
charming, deeply religious woman had played a larger part than
anyone else in his upbringing, and he never ceased to love her.
The most tender passages in his book *Reminiscences* are about her
and her loving kindness, a quality of which he declared her to
have had more than anyone he knew. Her devoted selfless love
for him had warmed his youth as well as his childhood, and,
incidentally, she had been the first person to advise him to write
novels. She and her companion, Natalya Petrovna, also a connection of Tolstoy's, shared a bedroom in which a lamp perpetually burned in front of a large statue of Christ.

Although Tolstoy's principles had not yet made him condemn
luxury on moral grounds, his tastes were extremely simple. In the
white-painted dwelling into which he had moved after the loss of
his old home the walls were roughly whitewashed, the wooden
floors unpainted, and most of the chairs and tables the work of
the estate carpenter. The house was, however, substantially built,
and double windows and Dutch stoves kept it reasonably warm.
But nearly all the rooms were uncarpeted; no silver appeared
on the dinner-table; only tallow candles were used; and until
Sonya succeeded in breaking him of this Spartan habit, Tolstoy
slept on a hard leather cushion without a pillow-case.

The garden had for years been so much neglected that to the
young bride's astonishment she found that none of the ground
immediately surrounding the house had been cleared. No foot-
paths; no flower-beds; weeds everywhere; and the coarse grass,
out into which the servants flung the garbage, growing right up
to the very walls. At first it did not occur to Sonya that Yasnaya
Polyana could be altered. She did not suggest, still less make, any
improvements. But before long her innate energy asserted itself
and drastic reforms were put in hand. Weeds were banished,
paths sanded, flower-beds planted. Tolstoy, like so many re-
formers, averse to the slightest change in his own home, could
see no need for any improvements, but for love of Sonya he at

once tolerated them, and soon began strenuously to help to clear and trim the paths, and to paint the benches. Before long a tennis court and a croquet ground appeared, and later a two-storeyed addition was made to the house.

Accustomed to living in a large city, Sonya at first found it difficult to imagine herself spending the whole year in the country. At the time of her marriage the weather was still fine and fairly warm, and it was delightful to be shown all over Yasnaya Polyana by its owner, who wanted his bride to love, as much as he did himself, the home of his childhood. He was especially fond of the lime trees for which his park was famed, and told Sonya that each year, after the fragrance of fruit blossom died away, the air would be laden with the scent of the lime flowers blowing everywhere. He showed her the four much-prized fishing-ponds, introduced her to their choruses of frogs, dilated on his boyhood's triumphs over carp and tench. Leading her into the dense forest he told her that in a few months its glades would be bright with wild flowers, and the nightingales would sing. Through the estate flowed the little river Veronka, in whose capricious waters he had learned, and intended to teach all his children, to swim. He drove her to the old highroad to Kiev, along which, half fascinated, half repelled, she watched the almost continuous stream of pilgrims from all parts of Russia. Mystics, professional beggars, prosperous-looking merchants, hideously deformed cripples, women, and children, they all pressed on towards the sacred city where, aflame with faith and hoping for miracles, they would light candles in front of icons, and pray by the relics of saints.

Before Sonya had been long in her new home, darkness fell and the interminable Russian winter set in. A time of violent blizzards; deep drifts of snow, and the whole visible world shrouded in whiteness and silence. No one to be seen but the swaddled peasants blowing on their horny hands and stamping their felted feet, and an occasional wayfarer in a sheepskin coat passing by on his sleigh. The snow fell until in the village the level of the road rose above the windows of the huts, and peasants would often have to be dug out.

In the cold silence and darkness Sonya missed her lively loving family and her young Moscow friends. Except for her husband, who was too often occupied with the management of his estate, she had no one to talk to but the old aunts, the freakish servants, and the rugged peasants.

On still, glittering nights, Tolstoy would wrap her up in furs and a sheepskin rug, and take her for long drives in his sleigh. She delighted in the swift exhilarating motion and the jingling of the bells, and he loved to watch her moonlit face under the sealskin hat, her dark eyes alight with love for him and pride in his love for her.

At last, with violent suddenness, came the thaw. Foaming streams overflowed their banks; wooden bridges were swept away by the torrents of spring; for weeks the country was cut off from the towns. The sun grew warm; the last shreds of snow disappeared, sheepskin coats and felt boots were put away; mooing and bleating broke the silence as the animals were released from their long internment. All at once, as though a wand had been waved over the white world, the buds on the gnarled oaks swelled, the fields yellowed with wild flowers, the woods became fragrant with lilies of the valley, the wild cherry trees blossomed, and the birds began to flute and twitter. Tolstoy took Sonya to the favourite grove of his boyhood, where trees were for ever being cut down and young ones growing up to take their place. Spring never failed to intoxicate him, and, as all around them nature quickened into life, Sonya caught his delight, and her heart glowed because she was to bring a child into this lovely world.

By this time, too, she had grown accustomed to the peasants who at first had struck her as almost repellently uncouth. She had been more embarrassed than gratified by the well-meant bucolic rites with which they had greeted her arrival. The first morning, while she was still scarcely awake, she had heard the sound of approaching singing. It drew nearer and nearer, as, clapping their hands to the rhythm of their song, the women of the village, in their gala dress of sleeveless velveteen jackets and gaudy blouses trimmed with multicoloured ribbons, gathered round the house to do honour to their master's choice. Tolstoy drew Sonya out of doors to meet them. 'Isn't our Count a knowing fellow! Just look what a beautiful young bride he has brought us from Moscow!' jubilantly shouted the singers. Stepping out of the ranks, two of them advanced towards Sonya, carrying a cock and hen, beribboned like themselves, and pressed them into the disconcerted bride's thin arms. She had no idea what to do with the flapping, pecking birds, nor how to respond to the robust ribaldry that made her cheeks flame.

The emancipation edict had been passed only in the preceding year, and many of those now called peasants instead of serfs were bewildered by their new 'freedom'; some even very highly suspicious of it. The easiest to liberate had been the 'household serfs', generations of whom had all over Russia belonged to generations of the same landowners. The post of coachman, or head cook, would often be passed on from father to son, and then again on to his son and grandson. At Yasnaya Polyana the serfs had grown so much a part of the family that they could grumble at their masters, and scold their children. Sharing the same interests as the landowner, they would be just as distressed over failures of the crops or ailments of the cattle, and take even more pride in the beautiful horses and sporting dogs.

Sonya, who, like Kitty in *Anna Karenina*, wanted entirely to engross her husband's thoughts, was jealous of the amount of time he gave to the concerns of the peasants. 'What swine and sluts they are!' he might exclaim, but nevertheless he felt a strong kinship with them. Many of them had been playfellows of his boyhood, and he had taught their children in his school. The large part they played in his life made Sonya realize in what wholly different worlds he and she had been brought up:

'I suddenly felt that he and I were on opposite sides. His peasants can't completely absorb me any more than I can completely absorb him. If I can't absorb him, if I'm a doll, a mere wife, and not a human being, then I can't live this life! . . . One day he will again centre all his love on the peasants and I shall be lost. And there is always Auntie, and once more Auntie. He does not *belong* to me.'

Yet at much the same date her husband was writing:

'I have broken with all my past as never before. Whenever I compare myself with Sonya I feel all my own vileness. But I cannot blot out the grievous past. It is terrifying to live as I live now, feeling that every second is for perpetuity, not as it used to be—just for the moment.'

Bridegroom and bride both had quick tempers. Neither could tell even the whitest of lies, and repression was not among their troubles. Quarrels were therefore inevitable. Within a week of their marriage Tolstoy wrote: 'There was a scene today. I'm sad to think that we are like others. I told her that she had hurt me in my feelings for her, and she wept.'

But far more often than not, they were both very happy. Entranced, Tolstoy wrote:

> 'I love her when I wake up at night or in the morning and see her looking at me, loving me. . . . I love it when she sits close beside me and we know that we love one another. Then she will say "Lyovochka", then hesitate: "Why do the pipes in the chimney run straight?" or "Horses don't die for a long time, do they?" and so it goes. Oh I love it when we have been alone for a long time and I say: "What shall we do? Sonya, what shall we do?" She laughs. I love it when she is angry with me, and instantly her eyes, her thoughts, her words are sometimes quite sharp. . . . In another moment she will be smiling shyly at me. I love it when she does not see me, is not aware of me, and I love her in my own way. I love it when she is a little girl in a yellow dress and pushes out her lower jaw, sticks out her tongue. I love it when I see her head thrown back, her face, sometimes serious, sometimes frightened, sometimes childlike, sometimes passionate. . . .'

Despite inevitable ebbs and flows and occasional friction, Tolstoy's diary of these early days continued to express passionate love and gratitude. Indeed, until the publication, long after his death, of Sonya's early diary, it was generally believed that the first sixteen or so years of their marriage had been wholly happy —that is to say up to the time that Tolstoy's biographers call 'The Crisis'; and he himself called his 'spiritual rebirth'. Nor is there even now any real reason why that reputed happiness should be denied, for much as the publication of Sonya's uninhibited diary revealed, it was also extremely misleading. The very first entry after her marriage declares that she writes in her diary only when especially depressed, and not long afterwards comes the admission: 'When I don't write in my diary for a long time I always feel sorry that I've not said anything about how happy I've been in the meantime.'

It can surely therefore reasonably be assumed that most of the days of which she left no record were happy; and it is noticeable that in this early phase there were often not more than two or three entries in a whole year.

The continual fluctuations of her spirits make her diary read as variably as a weather report. 'I wish my husband influenced me more,' she declared, soon after her marriage, a wish that showed discernment, for had she been intellectually as well as domestically a squaw, her lot would have been far easier. Soon, however, after this flash of perception, she fears he is influencing her too much. Beginning to 'see things through *his* eyes', she is afraid of 'losing herself'. To go out without him, she confesses, gives her a sense of freedom—escape. But whenever she does this, she imagines him worried about her absence, and feels impelled to run home. Now, she complains, he has begun to notice all her bad points. Now, she is happily sure that 'this angel of charm and strength, constantly striving after good, whose face expresses everything so beautifully', loves her with a constant love. Life therefore has become 'easy and simple'. 'Yes,' she declares, 'I could tolerate anything from him—were there anything to tolerate! One desperately homesick day she complains that Tolstoy resents her missing her own family; 'My dear mother and Tanya,' she bewails, 'why did I leave them!' Her husband, she declares, is 'wonderful'. Yet she knows that passion dies, and in a fit of self-distrust blames herself for having married him while he was 'trapped by his passions'. 'Why,' she asks, 'have I ruined him whom everyone loves?'

A sudden access of melancholy seized her immediately after her nineteenth birthday. She bewails the sadness of being 'old', trembles because she is so entirely dependent on a husband who 'either takes her love for granted or else doesn't need it'. The next day, her lost youth happily regained, she 'loves him madly'. All seems well, and the weather Set Fair for the married lovers. Nevertheless, before they have been married a year she has begun to hanker after an earlier phase in their relationship: 'What a wonderful time that was for me, thrilled by the vague suggestion of his love.'

One engagingly childish outburst, instead of mourning her vanished youth, blames precisely that youth for all her shortcomings as a wife. Her husband, she complains, is too old and solemn for her. She longs to do something crazy—would 'like to flirt with someone', or 'lose her temper with a chair'. 'Instead of going to bed, I should love to turn somersaults,' she writes, and then pathetically adds: 'But with *whom*?' Evidently Tolstoy, ardent gymnast though he was, would not oblige his bride by joining in this exercise. No great matter, for only a few days after this craving for somersaults, once again the diarist is overcome by old age!

Each quarrel was followed by a passionate reconciliation. After one she wrote: 'I could die of happiness and humility in the presence of such a man. . . . I love him to the uttermost limit with all my soul.' Two days later she complains that she feels like 'a devil in the presence of saints'.

The most astounding fact about this extraordinary couple was that by common consent each had free access to the other's diary. As a safety-valve, an introspective diary may well have its uses, but for a husband and wife to read one another's outpourings seems almost tantamount to a suicide-pact of mutual love. The wonder surely is not that the Tolstoys often quarrelled, but that two such moody people, both dangerously endowed with the gift for spilling themselves in ink, could read one another's diaries and yet stay under the same roof. That they could do this proves the strong tether of their love.

Nevertheless it was probably fortunate that in 1867 Tolstoy practically discontinued his diary for the next thirteen years. Before doing so he wrote: 'Relations between me and Sonya have been strengthened. We are dearer to each other than all other people in the world, and we see each other clearly. We have no secrets; nothing on our consciences.'

4

Sonya's Early Diary

SKIMMED through without attention to dates, Sonya's early diary might well give an impression of unhappiness; but not if readers remember how wide are the gaps (sometimes years) between the entries, and that it was avowedly a safety-valve:

> 'It *is* funny to read my own diary. What contradictions. What an unfortunate woman I seem to be! Yet is there really any one more fortunate than I? Do any happier and more harmonious marriages exist? Sometimes alone in my room I laugh with joy and cross myself. . . . It is always when we quarrel that I write my diary.'

Carefully considered, Sonya's disarmingly spontaneous diary cannot possibly be taken as evidence of an unhappy marriage. It does, however, flash with danger signals. Now consciously, now unconsciously, the over-emotional young writer reveals latent characteristics almost bound as they develop to make both herself and others unhappy. Nervous instability, in ailing old age to become hysteria, is already discernible, and a tendency to self-pity. Indeed for all the vivacity and merriment that captivated those who met her in her youth, she seems even before her marriage to have shown a streak of morbidity that at times made her gloomily introspective. 'Sonya was never really happy,' declared her fond father; and at sixteen she had written: 'Life is a hard thing. I'm no good at guiding myself. I've got such a queer silly temperament.'

To be very happy one day, very unhappy the next, is no uncommon thing in a temperamental young woman, but the see-saw of Sonya's spirits was alarmingly steep. She was also a prey

47

to nervous anxiety. Tormented by every kind of foreboding she had a persistent dread that her husband would die. 'This feeling grows stronger every day,' she wrote.

The readiness with which in youth Sonya admitted her own failings was as endearing as, in old age, her desperate attempts at self-justification became tiresome. Her early diary abounds in such disarming self-indictments as 'I'm very like my mother, and it grieves me to see in myself the traits which I've always disliked in her. Especially the conviction that I am a good woman, and that therefore all my weaknesses ought to be forgiven me.'

Perhaps not the least grave symptom in Sonya's diary is that her laughter—and she could be as merry as Natasha—springs much more from sheer high spirits than from sense of humour. She could be derisive, even caustic, but there are few signs of that gentle reconciling brand of humour that would have enabled her at times to see her giant of a husband as laughable. Loving banter —for Tolstoy could laugh at himself—might have helped where protest failed. 'Let the baby have his way, so long as he doesn't cry,' time was at length to teach Sonya wearily to quote from an old Russian proverb. A livelier sense of humour might have staved off the need for this wry shrugging of her shoulders. 'Unlike my mother,' wrote her son Ilya in his book *Leo Tolstoy By His Son*, 'Aunt Tanya could always understand a joke and answer back in the same way.' Perhaps, indeed, in her sister's place, the blithe mercurial Tanya might have smiled Tolstoy out of some of the violent extremes that were to make him so difficult to live with. Possibly. But how easy for a sister-in-law to laugh at what can be no laughing matter for a wife!

There is no reason why Sonya should be held mainly responsible for whatever squalls blew up in the essentially happy first years of their marriage. Devoted as they were to him, even Tolstoy's brother officers had pronounced him to be 'as difficult to handle as a powder magazine'.

One touchingly naïve entry in Sonya's diary shows how little she as yet realized the magnitude of what she had taken on in marrying a Titan. Seized with sudden misgiving she wrote in wild surmise: 'He isn't *eccentric*, is he?'

The most frequent cause of the Tolstoys' quarrels was that lifelong shared trouble, their unfounded mutual jealousy, and Sonya's diary reveals her early recognition of this threat to their happiness. Only three months after her wedding she wrote: 'My greatest misfortune is my jealousy. We must both watch this most carefully.' How clearly—for she never lacked self-perception—she saw the rocks ahead; how powerless she was to steer clear of them! She was even tormented by retrospective jealousy, and for this her husband's diary was largely responsible, for in that confession book she had, horrified, learned of his affair with the peasant girl, Aksenya, and she could not endure the idea that this discarded mistress, who had borne him a son, was still in the village. 'Never so much in love as now' Tolstoy had written of his passion for Aksenya, and this maddened Sonya. One day Aksenya came to the manor house to do some scrubbing, and was pointed out to the new mistress of the house. She had lost her youthful bloom and with it whatever beauty she may ever have possessed. 'She is just a plain peasant woman,' wrote Sonya, disgusted, 'fat, pasty, horrible!' Nevertheless, jealousy prompted the first of her many threats of suicide, made when she was going to have her first baby and the condition was upsetting her nerves. 'I shall kill myself with jealousy!' she wrote, a threat obviously intended for her husband's diary-reading eyes, and she went on to describe her satisfaction at the sight of his rifles: 'One jerk. It's so easy!' Disquieting reading for the expectant father. It is to be hoped that he was touched if not wholly reassured by the last line of Sonya's entry: 'If I could kill him, and then make another man exactly like him, I should do it.'

Retrospective jealousy was bad enough, but before long Sonya began to harbour preposterous suspicions. Despite Aksenya's 'fat pastiness', the thought of her only a few minutes away made her afraid that, put off by her own condition, Tolstoy might now return to his mistress. Driven frantic by this fear, she more than once dressed up as a peasant, and thus disguised, followed her husband when he set off with his gun, peering at him from behind trees with her short-sighted eyes to satisfy herself that he had really gone out to shoot game; not to meet Aksenya.

Tolstoy's jealousy was no less unreasonable. If any man so much as gave his wife an appreciative glance he would visibly and audibly grind his teeth; and once, with no plausible excuse whatever, he evicted a guest from Yasnaya Polyana merely because the unfortunate young man had been only one degree more cordial to his hostess than common civility dictated. This painful ludicrous incident, remembered by Tolstoy, was put into *Anna Karenina* in the scene where Levin's outrageous behaviour to his wife puts no slight strain on the reader's credulity.

Sonya's instinctive jealousy was aggravated by her experience of the violence of her husband's physical passions, her fears that she was not able to satisfy them and that he was disappointed. Her misgivings can scarcely have been allayed when he wrote *The Porcelain Doll*, a story describing how a man's bride turns into a doll. Ostensibly written as a mere pleasantry and sent in a letter to Tanya, this disquieting fable none the less betrays dissatisfaction:

> 'I opened my eyes . . . and saw not the Sonya you and I have known—but a porcelain Sonya. . . . I said: "Are you porcelain?" And without opening her mouth (which remained as it was with carved lips painted bright red) she replied: "Yes, I am porcelain." A shiver ran down my spine.'

To begin with Sonya had been more frightened than responsive. The thought of the many other women who had preceded her in her husband's arms made her feel polluted; and though her love for Tolstoy, at first romantic rather than passionate, never wavered, it did undergo a considerable shock, and a difficult phase of adjustment had to be passed through before her own passions were kindled.

'All physical manifestations are so repugnant to me,' she wrote two weeks after marriage, and her diary kept returning to that theme. Unfortunately, too, the violence of her husband's 'physical manifestations', as she called them, imbued in her the misgiving that he had been 'only physically attracted' to her, without really loving her. For those suspicions Tolstoy's diary was again to blame. Horror-stricken, she had read his self-accusation of 'terrible lust amounting to a disease'. Unfortunately, too, she had also read, not only of his expressed disbelief in 'romantic love', but of the agonizing remorse that followed his every act of immorality. She may well have asked herself whether his chief incentive to marriage had been not love, but caution—caution instilled by that prudent axiom of St. Paul's: 'It is better to marry than to burn.' Sonya's fear that Tolstoy loved her only physically, not spiritually or mentally, made her jealous even of women with whom he liked just to talk. She was distressed by the intimacy of his letters from his cousin Countess Alexandra Tolstoy, Lady-in-Waiting at the Court of St. Petersburg. This extremely clever as well as charming woman was eleven years older than Tolstoy (he had nicknamed her 'Granny') but she was his closest friend, and their mutual devotion probably had been tinged with romance:

'It wouldn't annoy me' (wrote Sonya) 'if they resumed their correspondence, but it would hurt me to have to think that Leova's wife was fit for nothing except the nursery and commonplace everyday relations. But I am well aware that no matter how jealous I may be about his spirit, Alexandra cannot and must not be cut out of his life; she has played a part for which I should be quite useless.'

One day even Sonya's adored sister Tanya aroused a twinge of jealousy:

'I'm angry with Tanya for poking her nose too much into Leo's life. . . . My jealousy broke out for the first time yesterday, and it makes me sad. . . . Now that I come to think of it, the real cause of all my troubles and bad moods is egoism, my idea that his whole life, his thoughts, must belong to me.'

In happy reassured moods, Sonya would feel confident that her husband was fully hers—mind, body, and soul; but the deeply imbued fear that he had been only physically attracted to her was always to lurk at the back of her mind, ready to spring out on her whenever she was overwrought, disinclined for amorousness, or afraid of starting yet another baby. This repugnance repeatedly comes out in her later diary; for instance: 'I so often long for spiritual intimacy with Leo, not just this disgusting bodily intimacy,' and the recurrent misgiving that her husband loved her only physically was never outgrown; witness that bitter complaint, made when she was fifty-three and Tolstoy sixty-nine: 'He needs me only in the *night*, not during the daytime.'

One immediate ill consequence of this obsession was that it made her especially suspicious whenever, as for many years was nearly always, she was going to have a baby. Before the birth of the first of her thirteen children, she wrote: 'I can bring him no joy of any kind so long as I am pregnant. How sad to discover that a wife learns only during her pregnancy whether or not her husband loves her . . .' And again: 'Leo deserts me more and more. . . . The physical side of love plays a great part with him. And that is awful. For me, on the contrary, it means nothing.'

Yet quite as many passages in this erratic diary exultantly refute the allegation that Tolstoy loved her 'only physically'; for instance, this, written as many as sixteen years after marriage: 'I don't believe two people could be *spiritually* more intimate than we are.'

Even if Sonya had been prone neither to morbid jealousy nor to self-pity, the first phase of her marriage could scarcely have been lived through without friction. Sex was far from being the only difficulty. Tolstoy's ideas of what a wife ought to be were so inflexible. In his opinion, once a woman was married she should give up what he called 'light-minded social life' and devote herself exclusively to her family. Thus, precisely those very qualities that had won his heart in his bride—her girlish gaiety, instinctive coquetry, delight in pretty clothes and dancing—warred with his preconceived ideal of a married woman. Even the most natural, indeed only proper, interest in her appearance was condemned as 'dangerous frivolity'. A pitiful incident occurred when at last, after months in the depths of the country, Tolstoy took his bride on a short visit to Moscow. Sonya, her bright eyes shining with glee at her reflection in the tilted mirror, was trying on a new hat, when, suddenly, Tolstoy upbraided her for 'light-mindedness' and love of flummery. What young bride would not have been hurt? Sonya burst into tears and stamped her foot, whereupon her horrified husband, shocked by his own harshness, wept with her. Tears flowed again over his disapproval of a married woman's displaying herself at a ball in a décolleté dress—'going naked', he called it. Evidently the Natasha of the epilogue to *War and Peace*, dowdified to disfigurement point by domesticity, was his ideal of a wife. A truly happily married woman could have no wish to attract anyone except her husband.

Delighted as Sonya had been to go with her husband to Moscow, their mutual jealousy made their stay there no easy time, and she was glad to be home again. Back at Yasnaya Polyana, she wrote to her sister: 'We are very happy. Leo is constantly avowing that he could never love me as much in

Moscow as he does here. What is the reason for this, Tatyana? And really he loves me so; it's *frightening*.'

Much as Sonya loved her new home, there were inevitably times when, accustomed to what she nostalgically called 'a boisterous family life', she felt chilled by what she complained of as the 'deadly stillness' of Yasnaya Polyana. How vividly in a fit of melancholy she described this stillness: 'The clock strikes mournfully; the dog is sad. The two old women are both so miserable and everything is dead.'

Tolstoy, however passionately in love, could not always be at home, and even when with Sonya he must often have been perceptibly preoccupied. Years later he was to write in *Confession*: 'The new conditions of happy family life completely diverted me from all search for the general meaning of life,' and it is true that the married happiness of which he had always dreamed did distract him from his search for 'Truth', but the crisis was only staved off. Perpetually seeking God, he could never have been wholly, or even nearly, free from spiritual growing pains.

If just at first the young wife could not find enough to do in the country, this, a never more than minor trouble, was very short-lived, and one of which in all the toiling years ahead she never again had cause to complain. Long before her first baby was born, her efficiency and immense energy had begun to find outlet. Instigating and supervising improvements in the house, she busied herself with every kind of domestic ploy. Soon, too, she found plenty to do out of doors as well as inside the house, and not in the neglected garden only, for, anchored to his home by domestic happiness, and anxious to make the utmost of his property, Tolstoy had now become an enthusiastic farmer. He planted a birch wood and orchards, restocked the farm with pedigree cattle; installed a dairy, a distillery and beehives; bred pigs with 'gorgeous snouts'; and soon, to his great joy, his admiring bride began to take an active part in all his new undertakings. With a huge bunch of keys jingling from her leather belt, she darted about the estate, doling out stores, keeping accounts, supervising the milking of the cows—helping in every way; and all this work was done, wrote her delighted husband, 'with the spontaneous joyfulness of a bird building its nest and singing as it builds'.

It began to look as though Tolstoy had really found the

happiness he had so long sought. All his life he had yearned to love and be loved. Now, he did love; was loved; and the woman he loved was his wife. And yet . . .

Sonya had no cause to be jealous of any contemporary women; but one great rival she did have—an unknown one. Her husband could not really remember his mother—she had died before he was two years old—but fancied memories and all that he had been told of her had created in his mind an imaginary woman whose influence over him never faded. Endowing this legendary being with every possible good quality, he had grown up hoping to find them all in the woman who was to be the mother of his own children.

'For me my mother was such a high, pure spirit,' he wrote, 'that often, even in middle age as well as in youth, I used, while struggling to overcome temptations, actually to pray to her, imploring help, and this prayer did often help me.'

Tolstoy's mother being safely dead, her supposed perfection was unchallengeable. She could never, as did other women, disillusion him; and his romantic idea of womanhood, derived, as it thus was, from one imagined and virtually impossible woman, had filled him with illusory hopes. No actual woman—certainly no woman who would ever have charmed *him*—could possibly come up to his preconception of the perfect wife, wholly dedicated, as he believed she should be, to the sacred vocation of marriage and motherhood. Some measure of disappointment was therefore inevitable. Shortly before his courtship of Sonya he had described, in a letter to his Auntie Tatyana, his dream of married happiness: 'My wife,' he had written, 'will be quiet, kindly, and loving.'

Sonya was very loving. She was also kindly. But she was *not* quiet. As a matter of fact her liveliness was precisely what had attracted Tolstoy.

On June 28th, 1863, less than ten months after the Tolstoys' marriage, their first child, a son, was born. The mother's sufferings were severe, and the father (as in *Anna Karenina*, he was unforgettably to tell the world) found the vicarious ordeal terrible. 'His face was pale, his eyes red with weeping,' wrote his sister-in-law, Tanya. 'It was obvious how distraught he was. Sonya's face was weary, but proud and happy.'

Once Tolstoy's terror was over, he felt and expressed immense happiness, and rhapsodized over Sonya's face with its charged initiated expression in which 'the very core of her soul was shining'. But alas, almost at once, this new joy was the cause of violent dissension. Tolstoy, needless to say, cherished the unshakable theory that every woman must nurse her own baby; and this, though for well-to-do women it was not then the usual practice, Sonya was passionately eager to do. Unfortunately, to Tolstoy's fury, some temporary physical trouble made the doctor forbid it. Sonya's parents supported the doctor, and a prolonged dispute ensued between them and their intractable son-in-law. Dr Behrs and his wife were devoted to Tolstoy—'We could not have wished for greater happiness for our duaghter,' they declared; but Tolstoy's attitude in this crisis infuriated them. Outraged in his dual capacity as father and doctor, Dr. Behrs wrote to Tanya Behrs, who was then staying at Yasnaya Polyana:

'As for Leo, just wallop him with the first thing that comes to your hand. He is a great master of words, but when it comes to deeds, it is a different matter. Let him write a story about a husband who tortures his sick wife by making her nurse her baby; all the women will stone him. Give him no quarter and see that he comforts his wife to the utmost.'

It is unlikely that Tanya was obedient enough to lay hands on her loved and revered brother-in-law. Besides, whatever sisterly resentment she may have felt was wholly disarmed when she found him alone with the squalling baby in the nursery, pathetically trying to stop wails that were disturbing the mother. With one large trembling hand he was poking a metal funnel into his grimacing son's tiny mouth; with the other cascading milk into the funnel. 'I shall never forget the sight,' credibly wrote Tanya, who fortunately came in just in time to save her nephew from being choked.

The battle over the sustenance of the baby and Tolstoy's unconcealed horror of the wet-nurse greatly upset the disappointed young mother, and her nerves were not soothed when in her husband's diary she read: 'It is revolting not to nurse one's own child.'

'Who says it isn't?' she wrote in her diary. 'But what can be done against a physical defect? This is another aspect of a husband's cruelty. At this moment I feel I don't love him at all. One can't love a fly that keeps stinging one all the time.'

Sorely hurt as Sonya was by her husband's injustice, she could not bear to end her record even of so unhappy a day on a hostile note, and added: 'It has begun to rain. I'm so afraid he'll catch cold. I'm no longer angry—I love him. May God bless him.'

Stricken with shame and remorse by his wife's laudably forgiving words, the 'stinging fly' wrote beneath them an admission that he had been 'cruel and unkind'—'and to *whom*? To the one being who has given me the greatest happiness in life, and the only one who loves me . . . Sonya, my darling, I was unkind and revolting. But,' he ended disarmingly, if a little irresponsibly, 'there is a good man within me who sometimes sleeps. Love *him*, Sonya, and don't blame him.'

Alas, this touching incident had a ludicrous sequel. Before the ink had had time to dry, tempers flared again and Tolstoy scratched out his own plea for forgiveness!

Soon after the birth of the baby, Sergei, there came into the young mother's life a second new absorption that was for years to keep her busy and fill her days with interest, joy, and pride. After a long interval of literary inactivity or of false starts, Tolstoy, at the age of thirty-five, became engrossed in his great epic novel, *War and Peace*. The gestation of this book had been agony. His mind was so overcrowded with ideas that he could not begin 'You can't imagine,' he wrote, 'how difficult is for me the preliminary work of deeply ploughing the field in which I must sow.' But after long deliberation he at last took up his pen and launched himself on to this immense work. 'Leo is writing all the time,' jubilantly announced Sonya's diary, 'writing with emotion with passion and with tears in his eyes.'

Tolstoy's handwriting was all but impossible to read. It often baffled himself. Determination, however, enabled Sonya to master it, and thus equipped, to become his invaluable, indeed inspired, secretary.

5
Sister Tanya

AFTER the Tolstoys' marriage various members of both their families often came to stay with them. There was Tolstoy's much loved eldest brother, the inscrutable Sergei, whom all through boyhood he had envied, for his good looks, charm, high spirits, and, most of all, for his indifference to what anyone thought of him. 'There is nothing good in the world,' Sergei had early in life declared, 'except love, and music and the nightingales.' Another frequent visitor was Tolstoy's only sister, Marya, and she would often leave her two children in Sonya's charge for months at a time. Tolstoy's beloved 'Auntie Tatyana' and Natalya Petrovna were permanent fixtures. Sonya was fond of these two old ladies and, on the whole, very good to them, but outbursts of petulance in her diary betray that their perpetual presence did at times irk her: 'There is no end of Auntie Tatyana and Auntie Pelagea.' 'Leo and Auntie Tatyana laying out perpetual games of Patience!' 'Auntie is in a peaceful friendly state of mind, yet I find her wearisome. She is *old*!' Equally characteristic flashes of self-discernment express contrition:

'I have a real affection for Auntie Tanya but I'm afraid her old age irritates me more than it makes me sorry for her. . . . Auntie has just been here and kissed my hand. Why did she do it? I was deeply touched. She is a dear old soul, and I am young and ought to be able to put up with her.'

It was probably just as well that Sonya had no mother-in-law to 'put up with'. To that relation, loving, lenient Auntie Tatyana was her nearest approach, but her own parents often came to stay, and it must have been odd for Tolstoy to remember that at nine years old he had been so much in love with his now rather stately mother-in-law that, furiously jealous because she talked to another little boy, he had once pushed her off a balcony with the result, as she was fond of reminding him, that she had limped for months afterwards. Tolstoy was on excellent terms with the charming if irascible Dr. Behrs (Sonya said that when her father was in one of his rages the whole house shook)—and he was immensely proud of his son-in-law's writing, and very fond of him. But they did at times fall out, notably, as has been told, in the battle that raged over Sonya's first baby. He fumed furiously too when his youngest daughter, Tanya, was admittedly as well as recognizably made the heroine of *War and Peace*, a distinction that he seemed to think might spoil her chances in life.

Further grist to Tolstoy's literary mill was Sonya's maternal grandfather, Alexander Islenev, famous both as a huntsman and as a gambler, reputed to have staked and lost one disastrous night, not only all his money, his wife's jewellery, his servants, and his horses, but, like Tolstoy, even the very roof over his head. This picturesque example of the hardy, intensely vital, old Russian provincial nobility fascinated Tolstoy, who, changing only two letters of his name, had immortalized him as Irtenev, the 'Papa' in *Childhood* and *Boyhood*. 'Cards and women,' he had written, 'were Irtenev's passion. He won several millions and had affairs with countless women of all classes. Everybody loved him. He was a subtle admixture of chivalry, enterprise, kindness and debauchery.'

Sonya's schoolboy brother, S. A. Behrs, aged eleven, spent the summer holiday of 1863 with her, and came back over ten years in succession. Long afterwards, in a book called *Recollections of Count Tolstoy*, he gave a wonderfully happy picture of those early years at Yasnaya Polyana and of the charm and vitality of his sister and brother-in-law, who seemed to him the most wonderful example imaginable of married happiness.

But of Sonya's family far the most frequent as well as most welcome visitor was her sister, Tanya. From all that can be read about her, this gifted, vital woman was one of the most entranc- ing beings who ever brightened existence. Born to 'haunt, to startle and waylay', she was as likeable as she was alluring. Aspen slender, exquisitely graceful, she had dark wavy hair, a delicate complexion, a large generous mouth and brilliant, expressive eyes. Her speaking voice was gay as a bird's after rain, and she sang so beautifully that Tolstoy called her Madame de Viardot after the great Spanish singer to whom Turgenev was nearly all his life enslaved. In Tanya's elfin, high-spirited childhood, Tolstoy had nicknamed her 'The Imp'. Prone to spurts of exuberance, she used then often to hop wildly round and round the room or turn chains of somersaults. A letter, written when she was sixteen, told how she often felt 'that kind of overflow of love for everyone and everything that gives the highest kind of happiness'. In such moods her joy might be expressed in loud exultant shouts. 'I'm in a whirl—a whirl!' she would cry; then sing one of her favourite songs or jubilantly exclaim: 'I feel I'm soaring up into the heavens!'

Tanya's excessive sensibility, her very joyousness, alarmed those who loved her. How could such a girl fail to be vulnerable? 'I'm afraid you are snatching at life too eagerly for your age,' warned her mother. On the other hand, Tolstoy in a letter implored her 'always to keep that dear, mad, energetic temperament in happiness, and never never to change or lose heart even in misfortune or sorrow'.

In Tanya's favour all Tolstoy's Yasnaya Polyana rules were suspended. 'Let her be, Auntie,' he would say to his Aunt Tatyana, 'laws were not made for her.'

Apart from the radiance and charm that enchanted everyone this quicksilver girl had a depth that Tolstoy valued even more. He loved what he described in a letter as the 'wonderfully sweet nature which, for all its laughter, had so much poetic seriousness.'

So responsive a heart was unlikely to remain long immune. Before Tanya was seventeen she became engaged to a man twenty-two years older than herself, Tolstoy's elder brother, Sergei. This was not her first love affair. At fourteen she, like Sonya, had had a childhood's sweetheart, her cousin Alexander Kuzminsky. Her love for him was followed by a brief, but violent, infatuation for a handsome, dashing philanderer called Anatole Shostak, who, thanks to Tolstoy's strange habit of using the actual names of his models, figures in *War and Peace* as Natasha's would-be abductor, Anatole Kuragin. But Kuzminsky, Anatole, and all other former admirers were forgotten when Tanya fell desperately in love with Sergei, a passion which, she

said, lasted all her life. They became engaged; but their romance
was doomed. Tanya had no idea that for the last fifteen years
Sergei had been living domestically—just as though she were his
wife—with his gipsy mistress, Maria Mikhailovna, who had
borne him several children. Told of her lover's engagement,
Maria Mikhailovna was heart-broken, and Sergei could not bear
to see her suffer. Deeply in love as he was with Tanya, he realized
that his conscience would give him no peace if he deserted the
mother of his children. He confided in Sonya, and she told
Tolstoy, who, furiously condemning his brother for having
drifted into an engagement with a young girl, undertook the
terrible mission of enlightening Tanya. He felt as though he were
shooting down a young bird. Desperately unhappy but resolute,
Tanya at once wrote to Sergei to tell him she could not marry
him. He must not desert his family.

'You gave a beggar a million and now take it back,' answered
Sergei. Nevertheless he accepted the fact that the marriage could
not be, and later legitimatized his children by marrying their
mother.

'It cost Tanya terribly much,' wrote Tolstoy, 'but she has the
greatest consolation in life—that of knowing she has acted well.
From being a child she has turned into a woman—a splendid
woman.'

For all this reputed consolation, the poor 'splendid woman'
was unable to conceal a capacity for grief equal to her capacity for
joy. She was like a skylark that has been winged. 'It breaks my
heart to look at Tanya,' wrote her sorrowing sister. Like the
heroine of a Victorian novel Tanya now 'fell into a decline'.
Symptoms appeared, alarming as those of Natasha Rostov's in
War and Peace, and Kitty Scherbatsky's in *Anna Karenina*. Consumption was even diagnosed. In the hope that a complete change
might help, Tolstoy took her to stay with him and his family at
Nikolskoye, a neighbouring estate to which he had succeeded on
the death of his brother Nicholas. From there he wrote to Dr.
Behrs, telling him that his daughter was sweet, gentle and submissive, but that there seemed no way to help her. Even her perpetual fountain of music was stilled. Never now, unless greatly
pressed, would she so much as take up her guitar, and if she could
be persuaded to sing, it would be only in a tiny subdued voice
that very soon died away

'Three doctors are still attending me,' wrote Tanya, several months after her engagement had been broken off, 'but no capsules or drops can help. Oh God! How is it possible not to understand this? Leo alone understands.'

In every phase of her life Tanya was devoted to Tolstoy, called him her best friend and second father—told him all her loves, joys, and sorrows. 'When he looks at me with those penetrating eyes,' she declared, 'I can keep nothing back.' At this juncture he probably saved her reason.

In time Tanya's natural resilience triumphed. Gradually her health recovered, and once again her beautiful contralto voice filled the house, repeatedly singing to Tolstoy's accompaniment his favourite song with Lermontov's words: 'And when I hear thy voice ringing so tenderly.'

All through this ill-fated love-affair, Sonya had agonized over her sister, and she was deeply grateful to Tolstoy for his love and care of Tanya. Not even in its most carping moods could her diary deny that he had handled the situation with wonderful delicacy and patience.

More than ever Tanya now clung to her sister and brother-in-law and loved to be with them. 'You shall come back to us with the swallows,' Tolstoy would say to her each autumn when she had to return to her parents in Moscow. One day she suggested that perhaps she came too often to Yasnaya Polyana and stayed too long.

'What nonsense you do talk!' he exclaimed. 'You don't suppose, do you, that you are living with us free of charge? You are sitting for your portrait. I'm putting down everything about you in black and white.'

'Leo!' she vainly pleaded. 'All I beg is that you won't describe my romance with Anatole Shostak!'

But she was not spared. As has been told, her youthful infatuation was described in *War and Peace*, Anatole Shostak becoming Anatole Kuragin. Her romance with Sergei was also immortalized, their ill-starred love for one another being transmuted into that between Natasha and Prince Andrey.

Tolstoy made no secret of the fact that the enchanting heroine of *War and Peace*, Natasha, had been drawn from Tanya. With deliberate intent he had carefully studied her spontaneity, fleeting moods, eager passionate heart. Everything had been set down, even that incident of her childhood when, compelling her future husband solemnly to kiss her favourite doll, she had made him kiss herself instead.

Sonya used often to say, 'Leo took me and Tanya, ground us together and out came Natasha.' Her detractors declare that Tolstoy said this only to please her. As a matter of fact both sisters are blended in *War and Peace*. The young Natasha is as unmistakably, as she was avowedly, a portrait of Tanya. The matronly domesticated Natasha of the epilogue to the book closely resembles Sonya after marriage. So, too, does the later Kitty Scherbatsky in *Anna Karenina*.

Sonya must at times have envied her sister's capacity to catch thoughts on the wing and to go through life on the tips of her toes, crying with one side of her face and laughing with the other; but except for that one outburst of jealousy quoted from her diary, there seems no evidence of her resenting her husband's devotion to Tanya. She was not jealous even when the privilege of having part of *War and Peace* dictated to her fell to Tanya. This happened when Tolstoy had to be in Moscow, for an operation, and Sonya, unable to leave the children, could not go with him. As Tolstoy was leaving, Sonya thrust into one of his pockets a letter to Tanya confiding him to her charge:

'Take care of him. Don't let him catch cold. See that he doesn't over-eat. Please, sister darling, don't leave him long alone. Sing for him. Give him jam (he loves it) and don't let Styopia' (her nine-year-old brother) 'disturb him when he's writing.'

'Tanya darling,' wrote Sonya on Tolstoy's return from Moscow. 'You have become a hundredfold dearer to me because of all your care of Leovochka. He told me how you were both his scribe and his friend, how you waited on him, how you exchanged confidences. I'm so glad that you are so close and friendly together. I love both of you so much that I can well believe that you were depressed after he left. His presence reminded you of our world which you love, and he does understand you better than anyone. You can imagine how happy I am now he is back. Now, everything here is so well, happy and gay.'

To this letter Tolstoy scribbled the postscript: 'Sonya has the knack of loving so warmly and simply, *and* of saying it better than *I* ever could.'

In 1867 Tanya, perhaps to her own, as well as to everyone else's, surprise, became the wife of Count Alexander Kuzminsky, the good-looking but rather dull cousin she had been in love with at the age of fourteen. Marriage, however, did nothing to sever her from the Tolstoys. For the next twenty-three years in succession she, her husband and their rapidly increasing family spent every summer in the white, green-roofed building in the garden of Yasnaya Polyana which, formerly used by Tolstoy as a school, was now called the Kuzminsky House.

Much as Tanya loved and revered her brother-in-law, she had too much independence and sense of humour to become a 'Tolstoyan'. No new dogmas could fetter her buoyancy. She revered the spirit of Tolstoy's teaching, but saw its impracticability and did not hesitate to tell him so. He never resented this, and would laughingly complain that he had not even been able to convert her to vegetarianism. Her liking for what he called 'eating corpses' was incurable. One day he dragged a protesting hen into the dining-room, tied the loudly clucking creature to Tanya's chair, and placed a great butcher's knife by her napkin. When Tanya asked why this had been done, he replied: 'But didn't you want chicken? All right, there's one—a very fine one, for you. Only we haven't anyone who will assassinate the bird; so I've provided everything you need to do it yourself.'

For Tanya, egotistic, but intensely loving, existence remained an eternal springtime. She was one of those blessed beings full of laughter who cannot enter a room without lifting the air, and each time she 'came back with the swallows' she vivified everyone else into enjoyment. To believe that such a wellspring of life could ever age or die was not possible.

'Tanya,' said Tolstoy to her once, 'do you know that some day you will die?'

'I die?' she exclaimed. *'Never!'*

6

Family and Friends

FOR some time after Sonya's marriage, except for relations and Tanya's 'followers', guests were a rarity at Yasnaya Polyana. Railways did not yet exist, the roads were atrocious, and most of the neighbouring landowners bored Tolstoy. A little hut had been built in the woods to which he could escape to write, and if unexpected callers came he would often whisper to Sonya 'My address is the forest' and hurriedly exit. He was, however, invariably friendly to a sometime landowner, virtually turned tramp and become a hopeless drunkard. Every now and again this long-haired, bloodshot-eyed man would turn up in the tattered monk's cassock that was his habitual wear, and wheedle out of the servants the special concoction made at Yasnaya Polyana of vodka infused with herbs. Uplifted —at times he became alarmingly drunk—he would then talk to Tolstoy for hours, or sing songs. His host always found him funny and touching, but Sonya was bored by his too frequent visits. 'What *do* you find so entertaining about Voyeskov?' she asked.

'I love picturesque buffoonery, and I insist on encouraging it,' firmly answered Tolstoy.

Disinclination apart, neither husband nor wife had spare time for unexpected callers. The nursery speedily filled. The first daughter, christened Tatyana (called 'Tanya') was born the year after Sergei, and then came two more sons, Ilya and Leo. Looking after this rapidly increasing brood, copying out her husband's mammoth book, and helping him in his ambitious farming schemes, Sonya had very much more than a full-time job. There was also her Lady-of-the-Manor rôle. Peasants who felt ill or had hurt themselves flocked to consult her and they thought her treatment and advice so good that if she told them to go to the hospital they felt aggrieved.

Both parents gave the children lessons. Until special teachers were engaged for French, German, music, and Russian literature, Sonya taught all these subjects and dancing as well; Tolstoy arithmetic and, later, Greek. When at last the children had been put to bed, and the manuscript on which Sonya was working laid aside, husband and wife would sit down to the piano and play duets far into the night, or read aloud some favourite book. Tolstoy gave Sonya her early lessons in English. He wanted her to be able to read Dickens, for many years his favourite writer, but the first book they read together was *The Woman in White* by Wilkie Collins. Later she learned the language from the children's governess, at Tolstoy's choice an English woman. 'If I hadn't been born Russian, I would like to be English,' he used to say.

One of Sonya's early complaints was that Tolstoy did not show enough interest in the new-born baby. 'I cannot,' he said in self-defence, 'hold a little bird in my hands without visibly trembling, and I am just as much afraid to hold a small baby.' But by the time his son had reached the age of two Sonya was forced to admit that Lyova had 'grown very tender towards Sergei' and constantly played with him. Her next grievance was that, fascinated by the dowager baby, Tolstoy was now neglecting his new-born daughter. But before long she wrote to her sister, 'Lyovochka has now simply gone out of his mind about baby Tanya.'

Not many mothers would have wanted the father to play a more active part in their nursery. They would have thought their own sphere of authority invaded, not only on that early occasion when Tolstoy all but choked his first-born by over-filling him with milk, but also when he forbade shop toys on the grounds that they atrophied the imagination. Determined, too, that his children should have only 'common-sense' clothes, he tried to insist on their wearing over the expensive imported underwear he had himself ordered for them peculiarly hideous shirts made of specially coarse flannel. Mercifully, he soon forgot these 'philosophical garments', as he called the atrocities.

Despite this and further meddling, Sonya's diary continued to deplore her husband's insufficient interest in the children. He used laughingly to say that she was always accusing him of not realizing that one or other of them was on the point of death!

But these charges of neglect were made only when she was confessedly out of humour, and other passages in her own diary flatly contradict them. Tolstoy certainly gave others the impression of being a devoted, as well as a delightful, father. When his brother-in-law, Stepan Behrs, grew up he declared that the fact in his life he would always most regret was that he had not been born Tolstoy's son.

Here is Tolstoy's own description of himself in early fatherhood: 'I try very hard,' he wrote to his cousin, Countess Alexandra Tolstoy, 'but I never succeed in not being proud of my children.' Later, aged forty-two, he wrote: 'I have a fat fund of silly joys, and the great joy of an extremely happy family; all the children lively, healthy, and, I'm almost convinced, clever, and unspoiled.'

Directly the Tolstoy children could toddle, their allegedly 'neglectful' father would lead them out into the woods to show them where the best mushrooms grew, and as soon—or rather sooner—than they were old enough, he taught them gymnastics, riding, swimming, and skating, at all of which he excelled, and took them out hunting and shooting. The most enlivening playfellow, the most understanding companion, he seemed able still to share in all the wonder, thrills, and jokes of childhood; and, never embarrassingly demonstrative, knew how to win and keep the confidence of any little boy or girl. Not that there was any need to tell him their thoughts. He could always guess them. Snuggling close up to him, a small son or daughter would wetly whisper into his ear that it had a great secret to tell. But before words could be found, he would whisper back what the secret was. 'Ah! what a wizard Father is!' the child would cry. 'How *did* he know!' Ingenuity, as well as divining power, made his children suppose him to be a magician. Who else, out of mere paper, could make birds that flapped their wings, boxes that opened and shut; illustrate whatever book was being read, improvise on the piano, coin words, disguise himself as a performing bear?

With characteristic, almost violent, energy, Tolstoy invented every kind of unusual pastime, some so over-exciting that they would nearly send his family into convulsions. For small children there was the almost unbearably thrilling game in which a little boy or girl would be folded up and packed into a laundry basket.

Tolstoy would then carry the heavy, quivering basket upstairs, downstairs—all over the house. At last it was lowered on to the floor, and the enclosed child, who could see nothing, had to guess which room he was now in. 'Are you in the dining-room?' Tolstoy would ask as dramatically as if the child's life depended on its giving the right answer. 'Or is it the hall? The nursery? Or my study?' Another game, a glorified edition of 'Follow My Leader', was called 'The Charge of the Numidian Cavalry'. All of a sudden, perhaps in the middle of a meal, Tolstoy would spring to his feet and, with one uplifted hand grasping an imaginary bridle, career at a wild hopping gallop from room to room all over the house; and shrieking with laughter, the whole company, old and young, hopping as best they could, and imitating all his antics, would follow at his Pied Piper's heels until at last—exhausted, panting—they collapsed back into their chairs. 'The Charge of the Numidian Cavalry' was often indulged in to celebrate the departure of some pompous visitor, whose presence had too long oppressed the atmosphere. Sonya joined in all the tomfoolery her husband inspired and no one enjoyed it more. She did, however, protest when he used her best rugs as sleighs on which to drag the children along the floor; and she was not always sorry when at last the time came for her overwrought family to be settled down to play Tolstoy's inspired 'cooling-off' game. This was very subtle. He would make the children stand in a corner, and then very solemnly tell them that they must *not* think about a white bear.

In the winter there were theatricals. Tolstoy would write and produce the plays, Sonya distinguish herself as an actress. 'How wonderfully well Sonya acts!' wrote her sister Tanya. 'She makes me cry.'

The children saw much more of their father in the summer months, for though never moving without the pocket-book in which he was for ever jotting down notes, he did not then, as in the winter—the season when, as he put it, his 'sap flowed'—shut himself up for hours at a time to write, but took part in all the walking and riding parties, picnics, bathing, and the dramatic games of croquet, often play.d out to their thrilling finish by the light of guttering candles.

A scene of endless family fun was the Bath House, a thatched, timbered cabin especially built for steam baths. Every Saturday its floor was spread with fresh straw, the cauldrons filled, and when the iron stove had been made red-hot, pails of hot water were poured upon it to sizzle until clouds of steam arose, in which, blissfully relaxed, the assembled family would lie and sweat for hours. Sometimes, overcome by dripping heat, the children would dart out of the cabin to roll in the snow, and then scuttle back to cook themselves up again. Sonya regarded the Bath House as a hygienic necessity as well as a pleasure, for though in time she did install a bath in the house, no running water was ever laid on indoors, and whenever anyone wanted a bath the porter had to drive half a mile to fetch the water in tubs.

Sonya thought Tolstoy's interdiction of bought toys over-austere; but, apart from that, in the early years they mostly agreed about the bringing up of the children. Their original intention had been to do without a nurse; but with all the other things on Sonya's hands this at once proved impossible. Responsibility was, however, never delegated. No one but the father or mother was allowed to punish a child, and their punishment seldom went beyond treating the culprit coldly, and ceased the moment contrition was shown. Telling a lie was considered a serious offence; but even for this no child was ever forced to say it was sorry or made to promise never to tell another. The children, strictly forbidden ever to give an order to a servant, were taught to ask very civilly as a favour for anything they wanted, and in this, as in other ways, visitors were expected to set a good example.

Plenty of liberty was allowed, and except when at lessons, the children could always be with their parents. Visitors had to make the best of their presence at meals, and were expected to refrain from unsuitable talk. 'Now we are freer!' Tolstoy would say when at last bedtime left the grown-up people to themselves.

In 1866, after the birth of the second son, Ilya, Hannah Tracey, the English nursery governess chosen by Tolstoy, joined the family at Yasnaya Polyana. Her nationality was at first inconvenient to Sonya, who had to follow her about, dictionary in hand. But she soon became very fond of this pretty young girl, who, bright and determined, promptly insisted on introducing her own ideas on cleanliness and hygiene. To the horror of the old Russian nurse, she washed the children—the house boasted one bath-tub—in completely cold water, and took them out in all weathers. Liking her charges to look their best, she firmly eliminated from their wardrobe Tolstoy's 'philosophical garments'. The children loved her, especially little Tanya, who when homesick for her beloved England, Hannah used tearfully to warble 'Home Sweet Home', would pick up the tune and sing and weep with her. Hannah stayed six years, and other English governesses succeeded her, teaching all the children from the age of three to nine.

In the early stages of fatherhood, Tolstoy, not yet either—according to the point of view—the full-blown inspired saint or impracticable crank he was to become, spared no money to equip his elder children for what he then thought befitted their station. Many of the new educational theories tried out in his own school were abandoned. For example, unlike his school pupils, his own children were not allowed to choose which subjects they would study. At one time no fewer than five foreign tutors lived in the house; the elder boys were taught six languages, the girls only one fewer. Other masters came to teach divinity, mathematics, music and drawing. If life at Yasnaya Polyana was never luxurious, it was undoubtedly what would now be envied—or stigmatized—as privileged, and not without a considerable dignity of its own.

All who came in those early years to Yasnaya Polyana found Sonya a charming hostess. One of Tolstoy's greatest friends, the famous lyric poet, A. A. Fet, was enchanted by her from the first moment he saw her before the first baby was born, come running down the hill in a white dress, with a huge bunch of keys hanging from her waist, and lightly leap over the fence to greet him.

'That evening,' wrote the poet, 'was one truly filled with hope. It was a sight to see with what pride Tatyana Ergolsky, the kindest of aunts, gazed at the two young people she so much loved. As for the Countess, life to one, who for all her exceedingly interesting condition, so lightly leapt over fences, could not but be lit with the brightest expectations. Tolstoy himself, who had passed his whole life in ardent search, had evidently entered into a world unknown, in the mighty future of which he believed with all the enthusiasm of a young artist. I myself was carried away by the general atmosphere of happiness.'

Fet used to say that into the rather austere house had 'come flying a beautiful bird who brightened everything by her presence'. After nearly each one of his very frequent visits to Yasnaya Polyana, he sent his hostess a 'Collins' in verse, and several of his most famous poems were dedicated to her. Here is a translation of a verse that pleased her:

And, behold, here enchanted
By thee here, remote,
I understand, bright creature,
All the purity of thy soul.

Another great friend of Tolstoy's from earliest youth was Dimitri Dyakov, portrayed by him in *Childhood* as Nekludov. He delighted Sonya by his charm, sense of humour, and unfailing good nature, and after his wife's early death became one of Tanya's many adorers. A more recent friend, N. E. Strakhov, famous critic, future biographer of Dostoevsky, and one of the earliest devotees of Tolstoy's writing, came so often that the children called his favourite garden path 'Strakhov's Walk', and until his death in 1896 he seldom failed to spend several months of the summer at Yasnaya Polyana. Another visitor, Count Sollugob, a well-known writer who often showed Sonya his work and took her advice, delighted her by declaring her to be the ideal wife for a writer, 'the skilled nurse of her husband's genius', a tribute which in the long lonely bewildered twilight of her life she was often to show to others as a testimonial to herself as a wife. Another great friend of Tolstoy's, of whom she made an immediate conquest, was Prince L. D. Ursusov. This charming man used to tell people that it had been at Yasnaya Polyana where his young hostess gave him so much 'friendship, kindness, sympathy, and care, that he had first known and shared in real family happiness'. Indeed, he conceived and cherished a romantic love for Sonya of which his widow was to tell her only after his death in 1895: 'How he spoiled me,' wrote Sonya, 'with his unending sympathy and his belief that I was worthy of everything good—that I could do whatever I wanted, and that everything I did was right.'

To feel herself being anxiously inspected and appraised by her husband's greatest friends and admirers can have been no slight ordeal for Sonya; but evidently she came triumphantly through it. Visitors found an active however much occupied host as well as hostess. In these early days Tolstoy, an inspired impresario of balls and masquerades, accompanying himself on the piano, would often hold everyone enthralled by his singing, in fancy dress, of passionate gipsy songs.

Later Yasnaya Polyana, now become the Mecca of the whole reading world, was to be positively infested with famous guests, but by that time Sonya had become a hardened hostess. In that rôle her trepidation probably reached its peak on the eve of Turgenev's first visit. Besides her awe-inspiring veneration of him as a writer, she knew too much about the chequered nature of the friendship between him and her husband. At their first meeting in 1856 Turgenev had acclaimed the ten years junior Tolstoy, then straight from Sebastopol, as 'The Coming Greatest Writer'. 'When this young wine ripens it will be a drink fit for the gods,' he declared, and he loved to call himself Tolstoy's 'literary midwife'. 'I have grown to love Leo Tolstoy with a feeling that is almost parental,' he wrote in a letter, 'you can have no idea what a lovable and remarkable man he is.' At the same time, because of a certain uncouthness, and at times almost savage obstinacy, in the young Tolstoy, he nicknamed him 'The Troglodyte'.

Tolstoy was pleased by the homage of the famous Turgenev; but though fond of him in theory, he never found his company really congenial. It was not long before they had their first quarrel; and after that the relationship between the two writers grew increasingly stormy. Tolstoy complained that Turgenev was too 'ineffably reasonable'. Worse, he lacked spirituality. Besides, whenever they met, a certain quality in Turgenev— 'spiritual flabbiness', Tolstoy called it—almost invariably got on his nerves. Added to all this, he had a lifelong contempt for Liberalism. It exasperated him. 'Look at Turgenev,' he once barked out, 'strutting up and down wagging his democratic haunches at me!' Nor could he ever like the literary society of which in Russia Turgenev was then the king. 'The contributors to *The Contemporary Review* repel me,' he snarled. 'A meeting of *littérateurs* is revolting!' Quarrel after quarrel broke out between the two great writers, but however much annoyed Turgenev might be, he remained irresistibly attracted to the ever contradictory Tolstoy, and invariably wanted to make it up again. One reconciliation meeting in Turgenev's country house was memorably, comically unsuccessful. After the sumptuous peace-offering dinner had been enjoyed, the host manœuvred his 'troglodyte' on to a sofa, arranged the pillows for him, lit several candles, provided him with cigarettes and drink, and, giving him the newly finished manuscript of *Fathers and Children*, left him alone to read this masterpiece. Alas, Turgenev prided himself on his cook. Tolstoy had dined well. The sofa was comfortable. The novel did not strike him as 'important'. He fell fast asleep. Aroused by a surreptitious sound, he awoke just in time to see the broad back of the chagrined author—his host—disappearing through the doorway. Impatient for praise, Turgenev, to whom it had not occurred that his novel would act as a soporific, had stolen back to peep at the enthralled reader. Deeply offended, he was now tiptoeing out of the room.

The day after this luckless evening the two writers drove together to stay with the Fets. Again the champagne flowed to celebrate their reunion, and that evening all went well. Unfortunately, at breakfast the following morning, Turgenev pokered Tolstoy's smouldering irritation into blaze. He was telling the company—smugly, thought Tolstoy—about the upbringing of his natural daughter. Her education, he explained, included mending the clothes of the poor.

'And you think that good?' asked Tolstoy truculently.

'Certainly,' answered Turgenev, 'it puts her in touch with reality.'

'And *I* think,' broke out Tolstoy, 'that a well-dressed girl who sits with stinking rags on her lap is acting an insincere theatrical part—a farce!'

Fet tried to intervene, but the quarrel flamed until, white with rage, Turgenev shouted at Tolstoy: 'If you speak to me like that I'll punch your nose!' and, clapping his hands to his head, rushed from the room. A moment later he reappeared to apologize to his appalled hostess for his 'hideous behaviour' and rushed out again. This ludicrous affair actually led to Tolstoy challenging Turgenev to a duel. Fortunately this was never fought, but it was many years before these two mutually explosive geniuses met again. They agreed to differ at a distance.

Sonya had read the letter Turgenev, then thirty-eight, had written to the twenty-eight-year-old Tolstoy:

'I shall never cease to love you and to value your friendship, though—probably through my fault—each of us, in the
presence of the other, will be bound for a long time yet to
feel a certain embarrassment. . . . You are the only person in
the world with whom I have misunderstandings, and this
comes precisely from the fact that I have wanted not to limit
myself to simple friendly relations. I've wanted to go further
and deeper, but I've been doing this in an indiscreet way: I
hooked on to you, made demands on you, and then, becoming aware that I had made a mistake, relinquished you,
it may be too hastily. That is what has caused the gulf between
us.'

At length, however, in 1878, Tolstoy, hating not to be on
good terms with any former friend, asked Turgenev, whom he
had not seen for seventeen years, to come to Yasnaya Polyana,
and somewhat to Sonya's dismay the invitation was joyfully
accepted. But she was immensely struck and charmed by the
magnificent brow and wide-apart greenish-brown eyes of the
'giant with a silver head', as Maupassant called Turgenev. The
children were half impressed, half tickled by the gentle giant's
mane of white hair, his large flabby legs and wide-toed (he
suffered from gout) soft leather boots, womanish voice, and
falsetto laugh. His clothes, too, were so remarkably unlike their
father's; velvet jacket and waistcoat, in one pocket of which re-
sided a superb chiming watch, in another an exquisite snuffbox.
To their eyes he seemed, at sixty, immensely old, and they were
delightedly amused to find him and their father playing see-saw
together.
Since the last meeting of the two writers, Tolstoy had become
an ardent practical Christian. Contentious subjects were avoided,
and there were no disputes, but the guest said he felt apprehensive
when he beat his host at chess, for it did not seem to him that, as
yet, the 'new saint' found it easy to practise the meekness he now
preached. He admitted, however, that in allowing his guest to do
some of the talking, Tolstoy did show some progress in Christian
humility.
Despite this seemingly successful burying of a very old
hatchet, the essential incompatibility of the two great writers
persisted. In a letter Turgenev referred to his host as 'The Great

Crank'; and Tolstoy could never really respect a man, in his own words, fated to 'cling precariously to the edge of a stranger's nest', which was how Turgenev's letters described his *ménage à trois* with the prima donna, Madame de Viardot, and her husband. 'From the first moment I saw her,' he confessed, 'I was entirely hers. I belonged to her just as a dog belongs to its master.'

Turgenev was delighted with Sonya. 'I was very glad to make it up with Tolstoy again,' he wrote to Fet. 'His whole family is very sympathetic and his wife is a *darling*'; and at Sonya's request he wrote for her brother's magazine his only story for children. When he came to stay a second time Sonya asked him why he no longer wrote. 'In order to write,' he said, 'I have always to be a little in love. Now I am old, I can't fall in love any more. That is why I have stopped writing.'

The young Sonya was as much appreciated by her own family as by Tolstoy's friends. 'We all loved Sonya so much that we felt we *had* to see her every day without fail,' declared her sister Tanya in her book *Tolstoy As I Knew Him*; and Dr. Behrs wrote: 'Your letter is as sweet as yourself. Come to Moscow to cheer up your father, who loves you more than anything in the world. . . . How much peace and happiness is in store for me when I see you again!' This is surely a good testimonial from a father to a daughter, and whatever, even in the early years of their marriage, the quarrels between Tolstoy and Sonya, wives with far easier husbands might well have been reassured by his letters to her. For instance, this, written five years after marriage: 'I can't describe the tenderness even to tears that I feel for you every minute of the day. My soul, my darling, the best in the world! For God's sake don't fail to write to me every day.'

Detractors of Sonya are too fond of triumphantly quoting as evidence against her the allegedly autobiographical dialogue in *War and Peace*, in which Pierre, supposedly a self-portrait, advises Prince Andrey not to marry 'or all that is good in him will be wasted on trivialities'. It would be easy to quote plenty of passages in direct refutation of this misogamy.

7

'War and Peace'

IT TOOK Tolstoy over six years, 1863-9, to finish *War and Peace*
—no wonder with so vast a canvas to cover and 500 speaking
characters to bring to life—and all through these years of
excitement and strain, during which three more children, Tanya,
Ilya, and Leo, were born, Sonya worked with him. Enthralled
interest in her husband's book gave the young mother strength to
work—leaving off only to nurse the latest baby—often for eight
hours at a stretch, copying out in her clear round handwriting all
that had been scrabbled the day before. Webs of corrections in
between the lines, and filling up all the margins, were so minutely
written that a microscope had to be used. Night after night Sonya
sat up to all hours, her back aching, her eyes bleared, but feeling,
declared her diary, 'too much uplifted, exalted—carried away into
a world of poetry to know that she was tired'.

According to her son Ilya's book, *Leo Tolstoy By His Son*, she
copied out the manuscript of *War and Peace* no fewer than seven
times. Besides her skill at deciphering what no one else could, she
was able telepathically to guess at the meaning of unfinished
sentences, notes and marginal jottings. Even after the book was
well under way there were often times when things went hard
with the writer—days on which he would find he couldn't write
at all. Then he would go off on an immensely long ride or a ten-
mile walk. There were worse days when the pangs of creation
became agonizing, and stifling oppression would pervade the
whole house. Sonya—wife, mother, housekeeper, and scribe—
would feel she couldn't breathe, while obsessed, tormented,
Tolstoy became unapproachable. 'My only excuse,' he once explained, 'is that to write at the high tension necessary for creation
one has to forget everything else,' and in a letter to Fet he wrote:
'The writer takes out of his life the best that is in it, and puts it
into his work. His work is therefore beautiful and his life—bad.'

At times Tolstoy wrote so long, so frenziedly that he gave himself spells of dizziness, and his head became racked with pain. Occasionally—very seldom—intense nervous overstrain was betrayed by alarming bursts of unexplained anger. One day, to Sonya's astonished terror, he suddenly yelled at her to get out of the room, and then—his only recorded act of physical violence—in uncontrollable rage snatched up a tray laden with tea-things and hurled it to the floor.

But on good days, and they were many, when ideas swarmed and words raced them, after hours of writing he would fling down his pen and jubilantly declare that he had 'left a piece of his flesh in the inkpot'. Then he would be so alive, so full of joy that no one could fail to share his exhilaration.

Sonya's secretarial work is all the more astonishing when it is remembered that in the mornings she gave her children lessons, and somehow also found time to make their clothes. Besides this ceaseless mothering, she shouldered all her husband's business affairs; and, a vigilant effective watchdog, kept off every possible disturbance: 'No hen must cackle, no dog bark near his window.'

In the evening, after the long day's work, he would read to her what he had written, and as he read, her listening face with its widening, delighted eyes gave him confidence. He encouraged her to make comments, and her criticisms, often subtle as well as shrewd, pleased and not seldom influenced him. Inspiration flared and flickered. Some nights Tolstoy would again be deeply depressed. Convinced that the work of a whole week must be scrapped, instead of reading aloud, he would groan over his dissatisfaction with what he had written, and his dread of the dauntingly difficult corners yet to be turned. Then Sonya's sympathy would soothe him, her eager interest stimulate him, revive his flagging confidence and energy—make him eager to be back at his writing table.

War and Peace first came out in instalments in *The Russian Messenger*, and then one by one in four volumes. When Tolstoy had gone to Moscow to see about the serialization of his book, Sonya had to post him some manuscript. 'Sending it off,' she wrote, 'I felt as though I were sending off a child, and now I am so afraid that some harm may come to it.' He wrote to tell her that his extremely high terms had been accepted: 'I felt grieved,' he said, 'by what will probably gladden you. I can no longer correct it and make it still better.' Far from being gladdened, Sonya suffered acute sentimental pangs. 'It pains me that you have sold it,' she wrote. 'Terrible! To think of your thoughts, emotions, genius, nay your very soul—sold!'

The most difficult phase was while the proofs of the book were being corrected. At first just their margins would be spattered with hieroglyphics; then whole sentences changed until the galley sheets would be all chequered with black patches, and no one but Sonya could make anything of the tangle of alterations, transpositions, erasures, and additions. Again she would sit up half the night to copy out the whole thing afresh. In the morning the proofs would be laid out in perfect order on Tolstoy's writing-table, all ready to be sent off by post. But 'just to have one last look' he would carry them back to his study, and by the evening everything was in a worse mess than ever. 'Sonya, my dear,' he would sheepishly say, 'I'm sorry but I've spoilt all your work again. I promise I won't do it any more. We'll send them off to-morrow without fail.' Day after day that 'tomorrow' would be put off for weeks, sometimes months. 'God knows what you are doing!' wailed his publisher. 'Most of your besmearing is un-necessary, and meanwhile the printing bill soars! For heaven's sake stop picking away at it.'

'I can't help messing it up,' replied Tolstoy. 'But say what you will, the parts you like would be far worse if they had not been scribbled over at least six times.' Not until the exasperated pub-lisher had sent him the fifth set of revised proofs would Tolstoy pass them for press, and even after that he often telegraphed to have one single word substituted for another.

Not even the most determined detractors of Sonya can deny her immense usefulness to Tolstoy through his long travail over War and Peace, and he himself fully and gratefully realized what an admirable helpmate, in the most literal sense of that word, she proved herself. Indeed, at one time when circumstances kept him in Moscow and she had to stay with the children, he found it all but impossible to work without her. Every single day, all through this long separation, he wrote most lovingly to her. Here is an example:

'Thank the Lord that all our memories and our dreams of the future are both so good! . . . What happiness is ours: and

yet, when I came back we shall probably quarrel at times. . . .
I love you so all the time, with every manner of loves, my
sweet friend. And the more I love, the more I fear.'

Four years later Sonya, gratefully conscious of her continuing
happiness, wrote in her diary:

'Sometimes when I'm alone in the room I just laugh with
joy, and making the sign of the cross, say to myself: "May
God let this last many, many years. . . ." I shall soon have been
married six years, and I love him more in the same restless,
passionate and poetic way.'

After this paean it was two whole years before Sonya again
had recourse to that bad weather record, her diary. Can it not
therefore reasonably be hoped that during that long silence the
married lovers enjoyed a halcyon spell? This hope is strengthened
by a letter from Tolstoy to his cousin Alexandra ('Granny'), who
had written to complain of his silence. 'Les peuples heureux n'ont
pas d'histoire. That is the case with us.'

If Sonya's work on War and Peace had been extremely hard,
it had also been very rewarding. Probably, indeed, it had made
the years of its creation the happiest in her life. Her children were
still small and not yet too many. She was enjoying the sense of
being indispensably useful to the man she loved; and he cannot
have failed to know that he—and the world—were indebted to
her for far more than her clerical labours, however skilled.
'Certain features in the characters of the women in War and
Peace could have been known only to a woman,' declared Maxim
Gorky, 'and it must have been Sonya who prompted Tolstoy. I
think too,' he added to this tribute, 'that there would have been
even more theorizing and less harmony in Tolstoy's great novel
had the feminine influence upon it not been so strong. And it was
most likely at Sonya's request that the moralizing part of the book
was postponed to the end where it interfered with nothing and
nobody.'
It was not until Tolstoy's immense book was finished that
Sonya's difficulties as the wife of a literary genius really began.
A second masterpiece would soon be embarked upon. This she
confidently expected. In the meantime she looked forward to an

interlude in which, released from toil, her 'Leovochka' would be free to become the close companion that, like Kitty in *Anna Karenina*, she always longed to find in her husband. His mind at rest, his time disengaged, what should now prevent him from sharing her own continuous absorption in the daily details of domestic life, talking over with her the body, mind and soul of each child? In optimistic flights of fancy she even expected her husband to take her own hourly interest in all the vagaries of the latest baby's digestion!

But once Tolstoy's great work was done, he, like lesser writers, suffered from reaction. Nervous exhaustion set in, and that sense of aimlessness that often follows achievement. The sustained absorption of his book had for years taken up nearly all his time and energy. Combined with the, at least intermittent, great happiness of his marriage, this had distracted him from the questionings that had always troubled his mind and his conscience. But as soon as he was left without any urgently compelling purpose, all the old problems assailed him.

For a while, realizing that his mind was much too restless to lie fallow, Sonya patiently watched him seeking distraction in a succession of newly adopted, feverishly pursued interests. One whole winter he concentrated on reading philosophy; but the conjectures and conclusions of other people could never long check the questings of his own creative mind, nor stave off attacks of melancholy so acute that at times he feared he was going mad. Philosophy abandoned, he plunged into an intensive study of Greek, mastering it with a speed that astounded the Moscow Professor of Classics. Elated by his own progress, Tolstoy wrote to Fet that he was now 'living in Athens and talking Greek in his sleep'.

Sonya, by this time longing for another book to be started, had little sympathy with this preoccupation with a dead language; she thought it waste of time for a man who could write masterpieces in a living one. 'Not to no purpose is Greek dead,' she warningly wrote to Tolstoy, 'for it brings a man to a dead state of mind.'

On this score her fears were unnecessary. It soon became evident that Greek had ceased to act as dope. Tolstoy now turned his attention to drama, and read the works of every playwright he had ever heard of. But no self-imposed task could long fend off the anguish that overwhelmed him the instant the latest interest failed to distract him from the spiritual and moral problems obsessing his mind.

Before long this ceaseless intellectual and emotional turmoil began to make him physically ill—visibly so; and in the summer of 1871 Sonya, long bewildered and now seriously alarmed, urged him to go to Samara to try the 'Kümiss' Cure, a treatment that consisted of drinking beakers of the fermented milk of mares, eating quantities of mutton and being made to sweat.

Sonya could scarcely bear his absence. 'Without you Yasnaya Polyana is without its soul,' she wrote. 'You alone are able to infuse poetry and charm into everything.' 'Are you drinking your Kümiss? Are you putting on weight?' she anxiously asked. In reply to a letter imploring him to give up that 'hateful Greek', Tolstoy wrote:

'Your letters are more harmful to me than Greek because of the agitation into which they throw me. I can't read them without tears, and I tremble all over and my heart thumps. Though you write anything that comes into your head, every word is significant to me, and I read them over and over again. . . . At this moment I love you so much that I want to weep.'

For a time the Kümiss Cure seemed to do Tolstoy's rheumatism and general health good, but probably what benefited him was not so much the treatment as the quiet routine, and the fact that the six weeks spent at Samara, bracketed off both from the past and the future, were no more than a parenthesis in his life. Besides, while there he spent most of his time with the local peasants, and their kindliness and simplicity had a temporarily healing effect on his strained nerves. But as soon as he came home it was painfully clear to Sonya's anxiously searching eyes that whatever superficial good the cure had done was not to last. Physically he looked well, but that disquieting look at the back of his eyes was still there.

'The two months' cure has done Leo no real good,' sadly stated her diary. 'The disease is still with him. I can't *see* it, but I can *feel* it as I watch that strange apathy towards life and his

surroundings which began to show itself last winter. A shadow
seems to have passed between us and divided us!'

Her diagnosis was right. After years of trying to believe that
he had found complete companionship, Tolstoy could no longer
hoodwink himself. As sooner or later nearly everyone must, he
was now finally accepting the fact that, spiritually and intellectually, he would always be alone.

After his return from Samara he reverted for a time to educational work and concentrated on writing an admirable reading
primer called *The ABC Book*. In 1872 he even remounted a
favourite old hobby horse by opening a school for the children
on his estate. Strenuously riding pillion on this hobby horse,
Sonya helped to teach the thirty-five little boys and girls in sheepskin coats who assembled every afternoon, and enlisted her own
eldest son and daughter, now aged eight and seven, as pupil
teachers. Throwing all her energy into this school, she made the
delighted children's lessons very lively and stimulating. Discipline
was not oppressive. 'Schools based on compulsion,' declared
Tolstoy, 'provide not a shepherd for the flock, but a flock for the
shepherd.'

Filled with the joyful zest of a born teacher, Tolstoy wrote:

'When I see these dirty tattered thin lads with bright eyes
and—how often!—angelic faces, I am seized with fear and
anxiety, as though I were seeing drowning people. Lord! how
to save them and whom to save first. What is drowning is
that which is most valuable—it is that spiritual element, so
evident in children.'

But Tolstoy's immersion in this kind of work could not long
satisfy the consciously ambitious wife of a literary genius. 'Schools
occupy him from morning to night,' she lamented in a letter
written in 1874. 'I look on astonished and deplore the energy spent
upon this instead of on writing. And I am sceptical as to its being
of any real use. After all, his efforts benefit only one tiny corner
of Russia.'

The school became a cause of disagreement. But Sonya need not
have worried. Like so many others, this phase soon passed. Despite
the 'drowning look' in those 'angelic faces', the school was given up.

8

The Crisis

THE over-simplified story of Tolstoy's life divides it into two separate parts, so distinct one from the other that the first might almost be called the B.C., the second the A.D. phase of his existence. It is true that it was not until some time after *War and Peace* was finished that what his biographers call 'The Crisis', and he himself called his 'spiritual regeneration', became apparent to others. But to suppose that there had ever been a time when he had not been deeply troubled by thought is a fallacy. All his life he had searched for some satisfying explanation of the universe; now doggedly, now desperately, groped after the God for whom his soul yearned. Intertwined with all the mundane matter in his early diaries writhes through its pages the kind of questioning expressed in the entry: 'My God! My God! What am I? Whither going, and where am I?'

Now that question had to be answered. Lifelong hunger had risen to starvation point, his quest for God become frantic.

Even if, as is possible, Tolstoy had not spoken much to Sonya of his spiritual yearnings while they were still only quiescent, she could not have read his diaries without realizing that his mind could never really be at peace until he found it possible either to return to the beliefs of his childhood, or was able to carry out his idea, conceived many years ago at Sebastopol, of founding a religion of Christ 'purged', as he put it, 'of dogmatism, and not promising future bliss, but giving bliss on earth'.

The failure of his health after the prolonged strain of *War and Peace* had predisposed him for a long deferred crisis; and the first chilling inroads made by death upon his own home precipitated it. In November 1873, after only a few days of sudden illness, the youngest child, Petya, a bright little boy, died, a tragedy of which his heart-broken mother with characteristic poignancy wrote: 'I believe he did not suffer much, and I thank God for that. . . . But ten days have gone by and still I am lost, still I am waiting to hear his steps, his tiny voice calling to me.'

Very soon after this searing grief came the death of eighty-year-old 'Auntie Tatyana'. Her loss was quickly followed by the death after a week of agony from water on the brain of yet another child, a little boy, only ten months old. The next year, 1874, Sonya caught whooping-cough nursing the elder children and developed peritonitis. While still critically ill she gave birth to a baby girl, and it did not live. Then, yet another inmate of Yasnaya Polyana died, Tolstoy's only surviving aunt, Pelagaya Yushkova. Thus in rapid succession the Tolstoys saw, under their own roof, five deaths, two of them however sad, the sufferers being old—natural; three unnatural. It is difficult to say which most affected the imagination of Tolstoy, who had an almost obsessive horror of death, and could never think of dying without a shudder. 'Soon an eternal night!' That thought was seldom long out of his mind, and the physical facts of death presented themselves as vividly to his imagination as they did to Shakespeare's Claudio in the condemned cell. If, sooner or later, the end of everything was to 'lie in cold obstruction and to rot', what then did anything really matter?

'If a man must die, what even is truth?' he asked.

'And so,' he lamented, 'one passes one's whole life seeking distraction in hunting or in work merely not to think of death, for if one should think deeply and picture death vividly, one can't live!' And how vividly Tolstoy could picture death, one has only to read his story *The Death of Ivan Ilyich* to know. In early youth, like most vigorous young men, he had felt immortal. But as the years passed and the hope of an after-life faded, the inevitability of death became more and more deeply impressed upon his nervous imagination, and his unhappiness grew fiercer and fiercer. 'In this meaningless and sad life,' he wrote, 'nothing awaits one but suffering, sickness, old age and annihilation. . . .' 'I can't help seeing day and night going round and round and bringing me to death. The two drops of honey which had diverted my eyes from the cruel truth, my love of family and of writing, are no longer sweet to me.'

A letter to his cousin, Countess Alexandra, told of Tolstoy's growing fear of death for others as well as for himself: 'There are times when one forgets about it. But there are others when one sits with those one loves as though in *hiding*. One fears even to think of their fate.' This was after Sonya, usually so well, had been desperately ill.

Tolstoy's growing horror of death made him find it no longer possible to bear existence unless behind it all he could discover some great purpose. For years he had been searching after some Principle which he could call God. Now that Principle *must* be found. Brought up in the orthodox faith, he had in childhood dutifully said his prayers, and then lapsed into a perfunctory acceptance of revealed religion as 'a kind of family tradition the true explanation of which had long been lost'. Looking about him now in his new desperation, he was struck afresh by the fact that the only human beings who, despite the hardness of their lives, appeared to be happy—happy even in the face of death—were the peasants. The reason was plain. To their childlike faith, orthodox Christianity was as literally true as is a fairy story to a child. Evidently, then, religion, and religion alone, gave meaning and purpose to life. Without it, all was darkness. But how could he regain his childhood's faith? The Orthodox Church seemed to 'insult his reason'. Could he yet somehow contrive to reconcile Christianity with the Church that professed to preach it, and in so doing find an acceptable reason for living? Forcing himself back into apparent orthodoxy, deliberately trying to repress his own scepticism, in 1877 he again became a regular church-goer, and for nearly two years observed all the rites of the Church and kept its fasts—for him no easy matter.

His sudden abstinence worried Sonya. Tolstoy was a man of amazing physical strength. Lying outstretched on the floor he could, it is stated, lift up two heavy men, one standing on the palm of each hand. His health, however, had never been good. All his life he was afflicted by digestive troubles, and whether these were more aggravated by eating too much or too little it was difficult for Sonya to judge. According to her doctor father, Tolstoy was a lifelong sufferer from that great source of physical and mental misery—liver.

Tolstoy's phase of religious observance could not last long. It was like trying to compel himself literally to believe in a fable just because it was beautiful and held valuable symbolic meaning. Once again, to him, professed orthodoxy appeared a 'loathsome deceit'. Nor, as Sonya well knew, was it by any means only its dogmas that raised an insuperable barrier between him and the Church. Temporal as well as spiritual standpoints alienated him. He could forgive neither the sanction of war, nor the sanction of capital punishment, both of which horrors—to his mind each premeditated murder—illustrated the hopeless divergence between the Church and Christianity.

Sadly disappointed by her husband's failure to return to the Church, Sonya, terrified, had next to watch him through a phase of almost utter despair. Suffering that dreadful sense of orphanhood he was later to describe in *Confession*, Tolstoy felt alone in the dark. 'It was then,' he wrote, 'that I, supposedly a happy man, had to remove a rope from the crossbeam in my room for fear that I should hang myself.'

Less fortunate in this respect than Dostoevsky, whom Turgenev described as the 'most evil Christian' he knew, Tolstoy could not sin his way to God. Painfully, laboriously, he had to reason his way to Him. Gradually, agonizingly, with 'how many dyings down and revivings', he did at last succeed in battling out his own sense of God, defined by himself as 'Love, the Spirit, Truth, The Principle of all Things'. 'Christ's Christianity' he called his new religion. Turgenev curtly dismissed it as 'a new sort of Nihilism'.

↘ Unhappily for their relationship, Tolstoy was not able to transmit to Sonya his newly realized sense of God. Relieved as she was to see that he had again come to terms with life, his new 'faith' seemed to her no better than 'christian anarchism', and she never ceased to yearn for him to return to the Orthodox Church. This, he insisted, he could no more do than a flying bird could re-enter the shell from which it had broken.

The transitional phase was an agonizing time for Sonya. 'Leo was not only sad,' she wrote, 'he was absolutely broken. He did not sleep, he did not eat. He even wept. I thought I should go mad. His eyes were strangely fixed. He scarcely spoke. He did not seem to belong to this world.'

How much, it may be wondered, did Tolstoy try to take Sonya step by step with him on his long and agonizing spiritual pilgrimage? Probably not much. Very far from a feminist, he had both in speech and in writing repeatedly expressed contempt for the minds of women. In the early 'sixties he had written in his diary: 'Had a discussion with "Auntie" about religion! Futile!

Must remember this with my future wife.' 'With women reasoning leads nowhere,' he declared to his sister-in-law, Tanya. 'It is useless. Their intellect doesn't work properly. And I'll say more. However reasonably a woman may judge, she will nevertheless always act by her emotions.'

Nor did Tolstoy really wish women to have ideas of their own: 'The only true woman is the woman who has the gift of imbibing and assimilating ideas, and who accordingly looks at everything through the eyes of her husband.' . . . 'No woman can stand to me in the place of a friend.'

Sonya was understanding enough to realize that Tolstoy attacked the Church only to save Christianity from what he thought its misrepresentations. But was he not, she wondered, substituting dogma for dogma? At all events, his new religion without rites, sacraments or mysticism seemed to her terribly bleak: 'religion without a sky' Dostoevsky called it.

Thanks to Sonya's own, now sweet, now bitter, personal experience as well as to her husband's early diary, she fully recognized his bewildering many-sidedness. Life with so complex and self-contradictory a man was like being married to not one but several different and seemingly irreconcilable husbands. It must indeed often have felt like psychological polygamy. But from the onset of the 'Crisis' Sonya became progressively widowed, as one by one various members of the large cast of characters bound up in a single man gradually ceased to play their parts in the drama. All through the years in which *War and Peace* was being created, so many diverse Leo Tolstoys, simultaneously taking the Yasnaya Polyana stage, had flourished; while other characters in the *dramatis personae*, quite as inherent, and far more difficult to live with, had been, or had at least seemed to be, in almost total abeyance.

'Some aspects of Tolstoy,' wrote Derrick Leon in his book *Tolstoy, His Life and Work*, 'had died a natural death because of the want of conditions necessary to sustain them, while others were merely waiting like actors in the wings, ready to reappear as soon as they received their cues. The man of fashion, the gambler and the promiscuous lover of women were never to reappear; the libertine, the glutton and the aristocrat, though now under control, were still for many

years from time to time to raise their heads, while the moralist, the philosopher and the lover of God, for the time wholly
subordinate to the poet, were later to reassert themselves with
a vigour all the more powerful for their long suppression.'

The 'man of fashion' died early. In youth, Tolstoy's recorded
obsessive ambition had been to be 'conventional and *comme il faut*
to the marrow of his bones', and scantily endowed as Sonya may
have been with that sense of humour of which few wives
have ever stood more in need, she could not have failed to laugh
over the self-confessed absurdities of his gilded youth. One diary
entry explained that his method of classifying people was into
those who were '*comme il faut*' and '*comme il ne faut pas*'. Among
numerous rules drawn up for his own conduct was: 'Ask for
dances only of the most important persons'; and he had once
proclaimed a man to be a 'scoundrel' simply because he did not
wear gloves! Unworthy as Sonya thought such values, and
strange as it seemed that a man, who had devoted hours to 'trying
to even the ends' of his own moustaches, should rebuke his
eighteen-year-old bride for enjoying a new hat, she was none
the less, in the course of time, driven to wish her husband more
capable of compromise in clothes as well as in more important
matters. As sensitive as most women to opinion, she was to
suffer agonies of self-consciousness when straight from what he
called 'bread work' in the fields, Tolstoy would stride into her
drawing-room, smelling of manure, his hair dishevelled, his
sleeves rolled up, his unbuttoned peasant's blouse showing his
bare chest. The man she had fallen in love with had been a well-
groomed soldier, whose military uniform had probably played
no small part in his romantic appeal. In her girlhood's love-sick
dreams at all events, she had always visualized him as a soldier,
and it was not easy to learn to readjust herself to this new husband
who, besides looking more like a peasant than an officer, declared
himself violently against everything military. Inconsistent as this
seemed to Sonya, it was not really as fickle as might appear to
Tolstoy's young self. Despite his enjoyment (of which later he
became so much ashamed) of battle, even the early pages of his
diary reveal the germ of the pacifism that, gradually developing
into his creed of total non-violence, was to land so many of his
disciples in gaol.

The gambler, the 'man of fashion' and the soldier, all died young and easily. The 'glutton' and the 'sportsman' died very hard.

Once dropped from the cast, the 'promiscuous lover' played no part in the Yasnaya Polyana tragi-comedy. In practice, as in theory, the libertine became an unshakable monogamist. This does not mean that other women than his wife could not at times still greatly tempt Tolstoy. Finding himself one day seized by a sudden desire for the cook, he implored the flabbergasted tutor to accompany him on his walks so that he could have no opportunity to succumb to temptation until, which fortunately was soon, this inconvenient desire had passed off. But against whatever temptations he had to contend, his struggles were not in vain. No other life has been subjected to sharper scrutiny, yet all biographers agree that throughout the forty-eight years of his married life he remained, in act, an absolutely faithful husband.

This commendable self-control did not, however, have its full reward, for as Sonya was constitutionally jealous, it did not prevent her from harbouring suspicions. Furthermore, in a man so violently passionate, physical fidelity brought its own drawbacks. Sonya had grown ardently to love her husband, and her maternal instinct was intensely strong—a family saying declared that 'her ideal would be to have one hundred and fifty babies who never grew up'. Nevertheless, she did find the incessant bearing and nursing of babies too much. For the first fifteen years of her married life she was nearly always either still nursing the latest or about to have the next, and Tolstoy did not show sufficient sympathy for this protracted plight. After the birth in 1871 of Sonya's fifth baby, Masha, had all but killed her, she was understandably reluctant at once to start another, and told Tolstoy so. This offended and shocked him, and his uncompromising attitude led to a violent quarrel.

Despite these matrimonial difficulties with all the suffering and strain involved for Sonya—and even her constitution did eventually suffer from the effects of thirteen births and three miscarriages—she endured the conditions of non-stop motherhood less complainingly than would most women. If only Tolstoy had been expressedly grateful, she would even have derived a certain pleasure from conscious self-sacrifice. But as time went on Tolstoy's expanding moral code was to demand the renouncement

of all 'service to self', as he called any physical indulgence.
Monogamy ceasing to seem sufficient restraint, total abstention
had next to become his goal. He, who had believed, and taught
his wife to believe, marriage to be so holy a thing, began to call
it 'domesticated prostitution'. 'The family is flesh,' he declared.
What could be more hurting to Sonya, whom he had so carefully
moulded to believe wifehood and motherhood the sole and
sacred purpose of her existence? But this is to anticipate. In the
'seventies, this, their thorniest trouble, still lay far ahead.

The most disruptive immediate result of Tolstoy's 'spiritual
rebirth' was his new attitude towards private property. Whatever
certain economists might say to the contrary, he was now convinced that, supported by violence, wealth inevitably became the
direct means of exploitation. This conviction, and his wish to act
upon it, inevitably clashed with a wife who, like ninety-nine
women out of a hundred, was far more concerned with the
future of her own children than with humanity in general. Agreeing with Ruskin's dictum that the 'only way to get rid of the East
End was to get rid of the West End first', Tolstoy began to suffer
acutely from the conviction that he ought himself to live in
poverty. But much as he longed to put his theories into practice,
he was not ruthless enough to impose upon other people ideals
they did not share. Thus, inevitably, husband and fatherhood
forced upon him a compromise between his declared principles
and his way of living. This not only made him very unhappy, it
exposed him to ceaseless criticism. Worse, it inevitably gave him
a grudge against Sonya, who could scarcely be blamed for being
unwilling to sacrifice her family to his urge for renunciation.
How many mothers would have consented to consign their
children to poverty? Nor was she ever even fleetingly convinced
that such a sacrifice would do any good whatsoever. Who
would benefit? Who, because the Tolstoys had less, would have
more?

At times she was sympathetic, at others derisive, as when she
called Tolstoy's struggles to live in artificial poverty 'playing at
Robinson Crusoe'. The defects of her virtues grew more pronounced with the years. The spontaneous candour of her girl-
hood had been one of her principal attractions to Tolstoy, who
thought sincerity the most valuable of all qualities; but as she
grew older she tended to express her opinions too vehemently,

or bitterly, as in the written complaint: 'When Leo turned to Christianity, the martyrdom was *mine*, not his.'

The autobiography she was to write in widowhood ably summarizes the difficulty of her position at the time of her husband's 'regeneration':

> 'I didn't know how to live with such views. With all those children I couldn't like a weathercock turn in the ever-changing directions of my husband's spiritual going away. With him it was a passionate sincere seeking. With me it would have been a silly imitation harmful to the family. Besides, in my innermost being I didn't want to leave the Church to which from childhood I had turned in prayer. . . . Leo began to suffer through our apparently luxurious mode of life which I couldn't alter. Nor could I alter conditions not created by ourselves. If I had given all our fortune at my husband's desire (I don't know to *whom*), if I'd been left in poverty with the children, I should have had to work for the whole family—to feed, do the sewing for, wash, bring up children without education. Leo, by vocation and inclination, would have done nothing else but write.'

To do justice to Sonya's sense of values, what she minded most about her husband's 'spiritual regeneration' was its effect upon his art. His expressed contempt for writing that did not preach a religion or inculcate a code, made her fear that the new preacher she did not trust would destroy the writer she revered. And, indeed, he did begin scornfully to dismiss his own novels as 'artistic'—from his lips a derogatory term.

Unprecedented sums were paid for *Anna Karenina*, which came out in instalments 1885-7. Waving his arms, Dostoevsky ran about the streets, crying out that Tolstoy was the God of Art! 'This novel,' he wrote, 'is incomparable.' Millions reading this book forgot, and still forget, their own troubles. But despite its effect on others, its creation had never, as had that of *War and Peace*, engrossed Tolstoy. Too many urgent moral questions were now tearing at his mind and heart. 'I can't drag myself away from living creatures, to think about imaginary ones,' he declared while writing it, and later he definitely despised his own book and would have liked to repudiate it. 'I have depicted an officer in love. So what?' he virtually asked. 'There is no difficulty in telling how an officer falls in love with a married woman. No difficulty and no good in it!' He even spoke of 'the wearisome and vulgar Anna Karenina'.

Disillusioned, Tolstoy wrote in a letter to Fet: 'Art is a beautiful lie and I can no longer lie.' From time to time, irresistibly allured, he would to the end of his days relapse into telling that 'beautiful lie'; but from now on his writing could give him no real satisfaction unless it conveyed some moral truth. Calling *War and Peace* 'verbose trash', he preferred to use only words simple enough for the uneducated to understand, as in his beautiful moral fables written for the peasants, which for a long time sold three or four million copies a year. But Sonya was never to cease to mourn for all the other great un-didactic novels he might have written. In vain she would remind him of his own memorable words of self-defence against the critics when they attacked his fiction for its avoidance of the social problems of the day:

'The aims of art are not to resolve a question irrefutably, but to compel one to love life in all its manifestations. And these are inexhaustible. If I were told that I could write a novel in which I could indisputably establish as true my point of view on all social questions, I would not dedicate two hours to such a work; but if I were told that what I wrote would be read twenty years from now by those who are children today, and that they would weep and laugh over it and fall in love with the life in it, then I would dedicate all my existence and all my powers to it.'

With all her heart and all her mind Sonya approved this literary creed, and she could not bear its public repudiation, nor the mood in which her 'regenerated' husband wrote: 'What if my fame *should* be greater than the fame of Gogol, of Pushkin, even of Shakespeare, or of all the writers on earth? What does it matter?'

Sonya had gloried in her rôle as the wife of a great writer— the 'skilled nurse of his genius'! 'It is not the money I regret,' she assured her sister in a letter about Tolstoy's 'artistic suicide'. 'There is something lacking in my life, something that I loved, and that is Leo's literary work which had always given me such joy and inspired me with such reverence. You see, Tanya, I'm a true writer's wife, so greatly do I take his writing to heart.'

Again and again, both in the near and in the distant future, Sonya was to implore her husband to remember the touching letter written to him by the dying Turgenev, who, for all his wrangles with Tolstoy, still acclaimed him 'the kindliest man on earth and an artist the latchet of whose shoes he was not himself worthy to stoop down and unloose'.

'Dear Leo Nikolaevich,' wrote Turgenev, 'I have not written to you for a long time, for to be frank I have been, and still am, on my death-bed. I am writing to tell you how happy I was to have been your contemporary, and to make you one last request. *My friend, go back to literature.* It is your gift, which comes whence all else comes. Ah! how happy I should be if I could believe that my words would influence you!'

9

The Move to Moscow

Tolstoy's slow painful evolution as he turned from
agnosticism towards orthodoxy, and thence through a
phase of total disbelief, to his own interpretation of
Christ's teaching, had been an immense strain on Sonya. It was
like nursing him through a long illness, and all the while her
hands were far too full of other things. The elder children were
growing up; the schoolroom and nursery still overcrowded. Her
life was an endless round of nursing; copying out Tolstoy's
chaotic manuscripts, collecting the rents on the estate, superintending governesses, tutors, servants; looking after guests, fuss-
ing over bills of fare and housekeeping accounts; not to mention
—though surely this cannot have been necessary—the constant
making and mending of clothes. In December 1877, after the
birth of her ninth child, Andrey, she wrote to her sister: 'I teach
and nurse like a machine from morn to night, from night to
morn.' And meanwhile she was ceaselessly worried and distressed by the change in Tolstoy, in whom she missed the 'unregenerated' man she had married, and the way his bright grey
eyes, now veiled in sadness, used so quickly to light up with love,
gaiety or humour.

Each summer Tanya came to stay for months, bringing with
her her own large brood of children. This meant a whirligig of
every kind of fun—picnics, games, sports, music and dancing;
and for Sonya, ceaseless anxiety as well; so afraid was she that,
among the hurly-burly of boys and girls (in all about a dozen),
some would quarrel, have riding accidents, get drowned, or in
one way or another come to grief. With so many children of all
ages there was indeed every peril from teething troubles to falling
in love. Whatever happened, Sonya, an indefatigable housewife,
saw to it that the children were lavishly and delectably fed. Their

favourite confections were castles and cottages, fabricated by the chef out of waffles, and served with sour cream.

The attempt to summarize Tolstoy's 'Crisis' may have given the impression that it was much more rapid and consecutive than was really so. But towards the end of the 'seventies, Sonya noticed with concern that the elder children had become distressedly aware of the change in their father, which to them appeared a sudden instead of a gradual process. 'What *has* happened to Papa?' they asked. 'Before our eyes,' his second son Ilya was to write in his book, *Leo Tolstoy*, 'our former enlivening companion changed into a stern and censorious moralist; and to relieve the unbearable tension of the thoughts that troubled him, he poured them out to us boys. Frightened, we slunk away.'

Sonya resented this disturbance of her children's hitherto carefree happiness.

Relatively grave and subdued though Tolstoy had become, he was still subject to bursts of exuberance. Flinging back his great head, he could, and to the end of his life often did, laugh louder than anyone else—laugh until his whole body rocked, and often the laughter would be at his own expense. His absorption in religious and sociological questions did not prevent him from contributing to the popular family institution known as the 'Letter Box', a receptacle nailed to the wall by the great chiming clock on the landing into which everyone was encouraged to post what he or she cared to write—stories, verses, jokes, or personal remarks about one another; and each Sunday the box would be ceremoniously opened and the unsigned contents read aloud by Tolstoy, Sonya or Tanya. Here, headed *Case Book of the Yasnaya Polyana Asylum*, is one of Tolstoy's contributions:

> '*Case No.* 1. L. N. Tolstoy. One of the harmless sort. The patient is subject to the mania known to doctors as "World Reform Delusion". His hallucination consists in thinking that you can change other people's lives by words.
>
> *General Symptoms:* Busying himself with unsuitable occupations such as cleaning and making boots, mowing hay, and so forth.
>
> *Treatment:* Complete indifference to whatever the patient may say, and occupations calculated to use up all his energies.'

Tolstoy's not untender diagnosis of his wife is revealing:

> '*Case No. 2.* Countess S. A. Tolstoy. Belongs also to the harm-
> less sort, but sometimes has to be suppressed. The patient
> is subject to the "Hurry Scurry Mania". Her hallucination
> consists in thinking that everyone demands so much of her
> and that she cannot manage to get everything done.
>
> *Symptoms:* Straining to solve problems which don't exist;
> answering questions before they've been put; refuting
> accusations which have never been brought; satisfying
> demands that haven't been made.
>
> *Treatment:* Hard work; diet; avoidance of frivolous worldly
> people.'

To amuse the horde of sons, daughters, nephews, and nieces
gathered under his roof, Tolstoy drew a comparison between his
wife and her sister:

> 'In a difficult situation Aunt Sonya thinks: "Who needs
> me? To whom can I be of use?"
>
> Aunt Tanya thinks: "Who can be of use to me? Whom
> can I send where?"
>
> When Aunt Sonya plays croquet, she invariably finds
> things for herself and others to do, such as flattening down the
> turf or mending mallets. She says she is too active only to
> play, or watch other people playing a game. Aunt Tanya,
> on the other hand, plays the game with fury, hating her
> opponents and forgetting all else.
>
> When a child is ill Aunt Sonya pores gloomily over
> medical books and prescribes opiates. Aunt Tanya gives them
> a scolding and castor oil.
>
> Whenever Aunt Sonya is enjoying herself she has to feel
> a little sad. Aunt Tanya flings herself whole-heartedly into
> enjoyment.'

The radiant Tanya was never to lose her power to make
Tolstoy laugh at himself as well as at her. She too, however, at
this time became oppressedly aware, not only of the change in
him, but of the fearful strain that it was putting upon her sister.
Tolstoy had always enjoyed agricultural work. Ploughing and

scything intensified his sense of oneness with the earth which he
loved. This practice now rapidly grew upon him. 'Bread Work',
as he called it, became to him a religious duty as well as a pleasure
—'In the sweat of thy brow shalt thou work.' At first the elder
children, as well as their mother, deplored his growing habit of
'busying himself with unsuitable occupations'. 'The Master works
for his soul,' tolerantly declared the peasants. But what possible
point was there, asked his family, in exhausting himself by getting
up in the cold and the dark to pump water and lug it home? Why
should a writer of genius squander time on mindless, menial
work—saw and stack wood, cart manure, stand for hours at a
time felling timber or mowing in the fields, dust his rooms, clean
his shoes? Besides, his 'Bread Work', seeming to reproach their
own idleness, made them feel uncomfortable—ashamed of their
trivial amusements. Little by little, however, his continued
example, and his evident *enjoyment* of manual labour, influenced
his family. First Ilya, the second son, asked to have some outdoor
jobs assigned to him, and his elder and younger brothers, Sergei
and Leo, were not long behind. Later on, work in the Yasnaya
Polyana fields became so much the fashion that in the middle
1880s for hours at a time visitors would blithely swelter in the
sun, blistering their hands mowing or turning the hay. At last
even Sonya capitulated, and wearing a becoming adaptation of
a peasant's dress, joined in the field work, bringing with her the
younger children and their governesses, and ultimately all three
daughters became enthusiastic converts to their father's belief in
the sanctity of 'Bread Work'.

Despite the great alteration in her husband and consequently
in the atmosphere of her home, the outward course of Sonya's
life continued unchanged throughout the 'seventies. Except for
occasional visits to Moscow and to Samara where Tolstoy had
bought a small estate, she spent the whole of every year at Yasnaya Polyana, ceaselessly running a house surging with family
and guests, and perpetually at the beck and call of children, either
turbulently well or plaintively ill. For the most part she was
sufficiently content with a life that gave such scope to her energy
and practical ability. Passionately loving her children, she agreed
with Tolstoy's views about the vocation of women, and most of
the time continued thankfully to count her blessings: 'Roses and

mignonettes stand on my table. Good, dear children are around
me, and in a minute the tender Leovochka will join us. This is my
life.' Nevertheless, now and again, when over-tired, she became
depressed by always living in the country:

'Oct. 12th, 1875. God knows how this year I have had to
wrestle with a shameful sense of boredom; how I have tried
to remind myself of all that is good in my life, fortifying
myself with the thought that country life is much the best
thing for both the moral and physical well-being of the
children.'

Complaining of a sense of apathy, she wrote: 'What will en-
liven me? In the evenings it's the same old darning of holes, with
Auntie Pelagea and Leo laying out their eternal hateful games of
Patience. Reading gives me pleasure—but how many good books
are there?'

Another day, suddenly reminded of the swift flight of the
years, she complained of the 'monstrous drudgery' of domestic
life; and as early as 1873, when only twenty-nine, she ingenuously
wrote: 'I would like to have a good time in frivolous company
and new clothes. I want, before it is too late, to be admired, and
to hear my beauty praised,' and later: 'I hate those people who
tell me I'm beautiful . . . I never thought this, and now it is too
late. Leovochka would grow used to the ugliest face, if only his
wife were quiet, worshipping, and lived the kind of life he has
chosen for her.'

In 1881, thanks largely to Sonya's decision, a departure was
at last made. In the middle of September the whole family moved
to Moscow for the winter. Sonya was determined that her eldest
daughter, Tanya, should soon be properly launched into Society.
Meanwhile she was to work in an Art School. Sergei, the eldest
son, aged eighteen, was to go to the University, Ilya and Leo to
private schools. A house was taken in—distasteful address for
Tolstoy—Money Lane.

Seven children still survived. Sonya's first-born had brought
her ecstasies of joy and pride, but, unusually soon, Sergei had
changed from a baby into a grave, clumsy, bluntly truthful,
rather aloof boy; and now he seemed able to unlock his heart

only at the piano. Pretty Tanya, the first daughter, had at once shown the charm and companionability she was never to lose for her mother. Fraught with maternal instinct, she had always protectively ordered about her elder brother and looked after the younger children, who still clung to her. When she was eight her father wrote: 'Everyone says Tanya is very much like Sonya, and though it is almost too good to be true, I believe it.' The second son, blue-eyed, handsome, robust Ilya, now fourteen, had given Sonya very little worry in babyhood. Scarcely ever ill, he enjoyed life as much as he enjoyed food, but, become a passionately keen rider and huntsman, he now sometimes alarmed his mother by disappearing for days at a time into the woods. In contrast to him, Leo, two years his junior, had been a delicate, nervous child, and Sonya had passed innumerable sleepless nights watching by his cot. This, perhaps, as well as his immense love for herself, made her specially devoted to him. Of all the Tolstoy children this son, called after his father Leo Lyovich (Lion—Son of a Lion) was the most unlike him. In looks, tastes and mind he was, and always remained, very much his mother's child. Masha, the second daughter, was now ten years old. Tiny, thin, pale without Tanya's prettiness or sparkle, she never enchanted her mother as did her sister. Perhaps, too, unconsciously, Sonya associated this child with three very painful memories; her own agonizing illness at the time of her birth; the clouds of disagreement then gathering between herself and her husband; and the onset of her first almost claustrophobic resentment against the ceaseless cares of an overful nursery. Sonya still often dreamt of healthy, happy little Peter whose death, her first great sorrow, had torn her heart. The sixth son, Andrey, was now four. Like Leo, an ailing child in his nursery days, he too was a great favourite. Andrey was now the dowager baby; happy, healthy, much-loved little Michael, having been born at the very end of 1879.

The move to Moscow was not conducive to domestic happiness. Grown to hate city life himself, Tolstoy could not help rather despising those who enjoyed it. On the other hand, Sonya, still under forty and looking less, arrived in high hopes of enjoying some harmless social gaiety. Unfortunately for this prospect, Tolstoy, determined to see the very worst of Moscow, soon made his way to the most poverty-stricken quarter of the town. The horror of the doss-houses, the degradation of their lodgers, the general filth, stench, and squalor, had the most terrible effect on him. To Sonya's horror he came home violently sobbing with distress. Much as he despised 'the vomit disgorged by the rich', as he called piecemeal or perfunctory charity, the desperate urgency of the need had compelled him to dole out hot drinks and dispense small sums of money. What virtue was there in that? Conscience-stricken, he felt he ought at least to have parted with his overcoat. Appalled that such abject poverty could exist side by side with the blatant luxury of Society; convinced, indeed, that one extreme was the cause of the other, he now felt that, as long as he himself still possessed anything superfluous, he was conniving at a crime against humanity. The glaring contrast between the slums and the thickly carpeted house in which on his return he found his family enjoying a five-course dinner served by 'lackeys in white gloves', was more than he could bear. 'One *can't* live like this!' he cried. 'It's impossible!'

Matters were not improved when he volunteered to help with the three days' census of the town. This again took him into the worst slums. His state of mind became alarming. He couldn't sleep; he wouldn't eat. Sonya did not know what to do. For a whole fortnight the sight of his suffering made her cry every single day. She began to feel she would go mad.

Misery could not, of course, continue at so high a pitch. Tolstoy quietened down. But the modest luxury of his home life continued to give him an almost unbearable sense of guilt; and from now on, until the end of his life, the white gloves worn by his footmen—no great extravagance (they were knitted and cost only about twopence a pair)—were detested by him as offensive symbols of plutocracy. The hapless Sonya felt that this state of mind, intentionally or unintentionally a reproach to everyone else, threatened to make life in Moscow impossible.

'Why is Leo set on making me feel guilty?' she wrote. 'He seems determined to make me miserable by forcing me to think of nothing but poverty, illness and misery—actually to *look* at it; and he expects the same of the wretched children. Is there any need for healthy human beings deliberately to dwell on suffering—to *seek* it out? Must one keep on going to hospitals to listen to the groans of the dying? If you come

across a sick fellow creature, by all means take pity on him—do
all you possibly can to help him. But need you *search* him out?'

Tolstoy's present obsession with suffering may well have
made Sonya regret that lost Leo Tolstoy of the past, who, insu-
lated in his own happiness, had, a year after marriage, written:

'It is absolutely immaterial to me that Poles are being
thrashed, that someone is taking Schleswig-Holstein, that
other people make speeches at congresses. . . . Butchers are
killing bulls too, and we are eating their meat; but I feel no
moral obligation to give any thought to it all.'

Sonya did not herself ignore or even underrate the appalling
problem of poverty, but she believed that Tolstoy over-simplified all the complexities of life; and she would have been more
sympathetic towards his reaction to the slums had she not, both
from observation and from his diary, known how disproportion-
ately he was affected by what he actually saw. If imagination lay
in the power to get inside the skins of other people, then, as a
writer, he had as much, if not more, imagination than any other
writer—living or dead. But as a man he seemed less able than
others to conceive of anything of which he had not been an eye-
witness. Not until he was shocked by the actual sight of some
horror did the thought of it ever greatly concern him. Then his
imagination would be so fired that all sense of proportion
vanished. Had he, for instance, ever greatly objected to war
until, taking part in it, he himself saw the mutilated and the dead?
Again, like everyone else, he must always have known about
capital punishment, but its existence did not greatly trouble him
until in Paris he saw a man beheaded. This made such an impression on him that until his dying day, he said, he would still
hear the sound of the head rolling into the wooden basket.
Appalled, from that hour he began to think any violence, hence
all punishment, indeed any compulsion, wrong. Thence, gradually, inevitably, followed the belief that government must be
wrong. But how, without government, could civilization survive?
wondered Sonya, who had no more hope than Turgenev of what
he called 'Christian Nihilism'. And now it seemed to her that
precisely the same thing was happening over again. Tolstoy must
always have known that there were appalling slums in Moscow,

but because for the first time he had been to look at them, he was
so much shocked by social injustice that all of a sudden he
couldn't even bear to see his family enjoying their meals—the
kind of meals at which he himself habitually ate far more than
anyone else. And his personality was so strong that in his presence
no one could be so little sensitive as not to suffer from his disapproval, even if it remained unvoiced. Everyone developed a
sense of guilt and became miserable. Why, indignantly asked
Sonya, should innocent children suddenly be made to feel in dis-
grace for living in the way in which their father had himself
brought them up? Did Leo assume that people who behaved
normally were necessarily indifferent—that no one but himself
was capable of compassion?

Social injustice was no new preoccupation to Tolstoy. The
truce with his conscience had never been complete, not even
during the respite afforded by those 'two drops of honey, love of
family and love of writing'. Only two years after marriage he
had betrayed his uneasiness by crying out while coming round
from an anaesthetic: 'No, my friend, it is impossible to live in
this way! I think I've decided . . .' Now the last vestige of the
flimsy 'truce' with his conscience was destroyed.

Even in Moscow Tolstoy was of course not always devas-
tatingly unhappy. Brighter moods intervened. Some days, while
Sonya, a charming hostess, presided over the samovar, he would
stride into the drawing-room and, radiating charm, behave with
the utmost courtesy to the company. On these occasions his
behaviour was everything either hostess or guests could wish, and
so many admirers now flocked to see him that often the room
would be as crowded as a busy railway station. On other days, to
Sonya's acute embarrassment, his growing contempt for convention would be expressed by refusal to put on a coat; or,
pointedly absenting himself, he would withdraw into his own
room to write if the ferment of his mind permitted, if not to do
some manual work. Or, striding out of the house, he would cross
the river to the Sparrow Hills,[1] and saw and split wood with some
peasants with whom he had made friends.

In the autumn of 1882 Tolstoy, gloomily resigned to the fact
that the education of his sons demanded years of term-time

[1] Now the Lenin Hills.

residence in a large town, bought, for the then equivalent of £3,600, a permanent house in Moscow. This new house, needless to say not in the fashionable part of the town, was in its south-west outskirts. Screened by a high wall from the street, the property included a large garden and every kind of outhouse—a porter's lodge, a carriage house, stables, three barns, and even cowsheds. The harassed housewife would rather have had an in-door supply of water, but in this respect Sonya was no better off in Moscow than in the country. Pumped up from a distant well, the water was carried, often by Tolstoy himself, to the house in buckets on a yoke, or when snow lay deep, on a sleigh. The house, a two-storeyed wooden structure, was shabby inside, but Sonya soon furbished it up, repainting the dingy brown walls of the reception rooms rose-red, and their shutters pistachio green. The dining-room and most of the family's small bedrooms were on the ground floor; the two drawing-rooms upstairs and in a remote corner of the house, separated from all the rest, the holy of holies, Tolstoy's study.

The great charm of this new home was the garden, round which, while his saddle-horse grazed, Tolstoy would stride, his beloved Eskimo dog Belka at his heels. For Sonya it was a wonderful and comparatively safe place for the children to play in; and to them it seemed an illimitable paradise. Endless alleys and impenetrable thickets. Apple and pear trees; a high green mound to clamber up and an enchanted summer-house lined with a frieze of galloping horses. In the winters quite a large skating rink was made by pouring hundreds of barrels of water on to a space in the courtyard.

From this new setting the slender graceful Tanya was launched on to the social world by her lively, engaging mother, who had by no means lost those good looks she had hankered to hear praised. Both enjoyed a great success. Tanya was not strictly beautiful, but her wavy chestnut hair, dazzling complexion, brilliant dark eyes and well-chiselled, uptilted nose made her extremely attractive, and she must have been an ideal daughter to take out. She so much enjoyed things and old and young were enchanted by her manners, vivacity, and wit.

Tolstoy thought his wife and daughter were leading a de-plorably empty, frivolous existence. 'You are probably just getting ready to go to a ball,' he wrote one day when, to take refuge in a 'bath of country life' at Yasnaya Polyana, he had fled from Moscow. 'How I pity you and Tanya!' Neither mother nor daughter had any need of pity. They enjoyed that ball so much that they stayed until six o'clock in the morning. Revelling in the gaiety, Sonya wrote rapturous letters to her sister Tanya telling of her young namesake's success, and of all the fun they were enjoying together. Descriptions of the dresses worn by herself and her daughter made a pleasant change from the wearisome lists of groceries and medicaments that usually employed her pen:

'It was a wonderful ball last night. Tanya wore a shell-pink dress with plush roses. My velvet dress was lilac with pansies of every possible shade of yellow. Tomorrow we go to another ball, for which Tanya has a wonderful dress—tulle—"Illusion", pale greenish blue with pinkish lilies of the valley. Next night another big ball at the Obolenskys. They are all simply running me and Tanya off our feet!'

At much the same time she wrote to Tolstoy, who had sent her his article on 'Moral Perfection', asking for her opinion:

'Of course it's impossible to dispute your theory that it would be fine if people could be perfect; and of course you are right to remind them of this and to point out the path of perfection. Yet I can't refrain from saying that it is hard to give up all the *toys* of life. Perhaps I grasp these toys more eagerly than others. I do so love the way they glitter, tinkle—delight.'

Sonya may well have snatched at 'the toys of life', but awareness of the growing disharmony between herself and her husband made only their very brief enjoyment possible. She was too conscious that the weather, always unsettled, of their relationship was becoming consistently stormy. 'God sees,' she wrote, 'but no one will know what went on in my heart.' It seemed that her beloved 'Leovochka' had turned against everything he had always taught her to think right and to hold dear; and on the principle of 'he who is not with me is against me' she began to fear that he would never be able to forgive her for not being his whole-hearted disciple. Strong mutual affection still bound them together. Passion still frequently flung them into one another's arms; but from now on they no longer wanted to live the same kind of life.

Sonya respected her husband's ideals. Theoretically she even sympathized with many of his opinions. 'He is quite right,' she once said, 'but we can't do what he demands. Five hundred years hence people will tread the path he points out.' Regarding him as an idealist immeasurably in advance of his time, she, a realist, could not believe it any more practicable for one man to attempt to put such Utopian ideals into practice than for one nation to adopt pacifism before there was General Disarmament. She saw him as a great signpost pointing in the right direction, but did not believe him capable of making a road that others could tread. She felt sure that it would be wrong to impose upon children ideals which they could not even understand, and yet—and this made her very sad—she was painfully conscious that by the mere fact of her existence she was barring her husband's way—making it impossible for him to live according to his own interpretation of Christianity.

Had he and she been mutually indifferent, arrival at a peaceful compromise would have been comparatively easy. As it was, awareness of the widening gulf between them set up a chronic state of tension, bound at intervals to explode into quarrel. Possession of a second home only aggravated their difficulties. When they were together in Moscow, where Tolstoy was so unhappy, Sonya was inevitably oppressed by his all-pervading presence. 'Our life would be fine,' she wrote, 'if only Leo were not so miserable here. He is much too sensitive for city life.' On the other hand, she was hurt when Tolstoy, as he often did, fled from 'the empty sumptuous deceitful Moscow life' to the solitude of Yasnaya Polyana. Her letters—tangles of love, reproach and self-commiseration—strike at this time a new, or at all events a more sustained, note of bitterness. Contrasting herself with a re-markable new friend of her husband, a peasant called Syatev, she wrote: 'You and Syatev may not feel any special love for your own children; but we other simple mortals are neither able, nor anxious, to stifle our natural instincts and to justify our want of love for mankind in general.' Her letter ended on an hysterical note: 'I'm vile, I'm sick! I cry all day, and if there were poison at hand I think I might do away with myself!'

At much the same date Tolstoy wrote of his family:

'I am sad because of the triumphant self-assured insanity of the life going on round me. Often I don't understand why it has been granted to me to perceive this insanity, while they are quite unable to understand their own madness; and so we stand face to face, not comprehending each other, and wondering at and condemning one another. But they are legion and I am alone.'

Whenever Tolstoy was away from Sonya he still wrote to her almost daily. One letter apologized for his absence from home on the pleas that he must have quiet to write in, that it was 'good for him to escape from the hurly-burly of Moscow and by getting back into himself be free to think, not about people, but about God'. 'Here there are grass, birds, and honey-bees, no policemen, no pavements, no cabmen, no smells.' It was so pleasant, too, he added, to listen to the 'chattering' of the 'kennel maid'. Gasha had loved Tolstoy ever since the days when, because of his extreme sensibility, he was nicknamed 'Cry Baby', but she had come to be a great supporter of Sonya's and always took her side: 'Now you leave her alone in a great city with eight children to look after and sit in the country and stroke your beard!' she indignantly complained to the master, of whose 'regeneration' she could never learn to approve.

Sonya, at that time still easily mollified, answered Tolstoy's letter with the assurance that in all the world there was only one thing she really wanted, *his* 'peace of mind and happiness'.

In another letter, written with irrefutable good sense if insufficient tact, she implored him to take care of his health which, rightly, no doubt, she believed to be to blame for much of his unhappiness:

'I begin to think that if a happy man can suddenly see in life only everything that is terrible and shuts his eyes to all that is good, then this must be the result of some illness. I am convinced that you should take a cure. Long ago you were as unhappy as you declare yourself to be now. Then you said you wanted to hang yourself because you lacked faith. Why then are you so unhappy now? You must have known before that hungry, sick, evil people existed. Surely you would do

better to look around you. There are, I assure you, plenty of
happy, healthy and good people.'

To this Tolstoy, trying to reconcile himself to the scarcely
surprising fact that his wife felt her proper concern lay, not with
humanity in general, but with her own family, wrote a gentle
reasonable answer. He even admitted that there might be truth
in her diagnosis that his present horror of civilization had some
connection with his physical health. 'One's liver,' he wrote, 'does
no doubt count for something, nevertheless one's spiritual life *is*
independent.' 'Sonya,' his letter ended, 'you write "I love you,
but you no longer want my love". But it is the one thing I *do*
want. Only you can cheer me, and your letter has gladdened me
more than could anything else in the world.'

10

The Sky Darkens

OR several years in succession now each winter was spent
in Moscow, and Yasnaya returned to for the summer. The
annual move was no light matter. It involved transporting
horses, carriages, a cow, wagons of hay, huge stores of preserves,
barrels of salted cucumber, and sauerkraut. Through the winter
Tolstoy frequently bolted back to the country. He found it very
difficult to write in a town: 'In Moscow, my nerves are out of
order, the hours turn to minutes, and the people I don't want
turn up as though on purpose and prevent my seeing those I do
want.' It had, however, been in Moscow that a delightful new
friend, described by himself as 'a charming talented, ancient
child', had first come into his and Sonya's lives. This was the
famous painter N. N. Gay, later known as the 'painter of Tolstoyism'. Recently become a whole-hearted disciple, he one day
presented himself, and fervently embraced Tolstoy. 'Leo
Nikolaevich,' he said, 'I've come to do anything you wish.
Shall I paint your daughter?'

'Much better paint my wife,' replied Tolstoy.

Thus began a devotion to husband and wife that was to last
until the death in 1894 of the painter, who, loved by all its sons
and daughters, had virtually become a member of the family.

Sonya enjoyed posing for Gay in an elegant black velvet dress
trimmed with Alençon lace, and liked the result; but Gay himself
did not approve of his picture, he condemned it as 'too like an
aristocrat, seated idle in a velvet gown with at least forty thousand
rubles in her pocket', and that was not in the least how he saw
his 'Mamenka', as he fondly called Sonya. No, he must paint a
'real woman—a mother'. To the regret of the family he destroyed
his canvas, but some years later he again painted Sonya, this
time with her youngest daughter in her arms, and the portrait
still hangs in the museum at Yasnaya Polyana.

The first part of 1882 appears to have been peaceful but, after a gap of six months, Sonya's diary of August 26th tells of a terrible storm:

'Twenty years ago, happy and young, I began writing this book, the story of my love for Lyóva. There is hardly anything else in it. And now, after all these years, I am sitting up in the night weeping over the loss of my love. For the first time he has run away from me and is spending the night in his study. We quarrelled over mere trifles. I blamed him for not troubling himself about the children, for not helping me to nurse Ilya, who is ill, or to make jackets for the children.'

The wife of a towering literary genius could scarcely bring against him a more absurd charge than that he did not help her to 'make jackets' for the children. With some return to rationality, Sonya continued:

'It isn't a question of jackets. The fact is that he is growing cold towards me and our children. Today he cried out that his most passionate desire was to get away from the family! To my last breath I shall hear that cry. It seemed to tear out my heart. Now I am imploring God to let me die, for without Leo's love I cannot live. I can't tell him again how much I love him. It would humiliate me and annoy him. He is full of Christianity and the idea of self-perfection. . . . God help me! I want to kill myself. My thoughts are all confused. . . . The clock is striking four. If he doesn't come back, it will mean that he loves another woman. . . . He hasn't come back. Duty? I used to know so surely *what* my duty was. But what is it now? . . . He did come back, but we did not make it up until twenty-four hours later. Then we both wept, and with joy I saw that the old love, the loss of which I had mourned all through that dreadful night, was still very much alive in him. Never shall I forget that lovely clear cold morning with the silver dew sparkling on every leaf, in which, after a sleepless night, I walked alone through the woods to the Bath House. Seldom have I seen nature in such triumphant beauty. For a long time I sat in the ice-cold water with the idea of getting a bad chill and dying. But I did not. Instead I went home and nursed my fat little Alyosha who was glad to see me and smiled.'

The suicidal impulse related here is clearly not to be taken seriously. Probably, indeed, it had been written on purpose for her husband to read. After this entry Sonya left her diary practically blank until March of the next year (1883) when she wrote rejoicing in the spring sunshine, but characteristically bemoaning the necessity to wean her beloved Aloysius, a sorrow in which, as the child was already sixteen months old, she could scarcely expect much sympathy. 'Once again I am feeling the pain of the same old grief over the first separation—a grief from which there can be no escape.'

Her husband, she declared, was 'calm and contented'; and at this time there did appear to be a check in the deterioration in their relationship. Tolstoy's disapproval of the costly life of frivolity his family led in Moscow had not diminished, but in a phase of humility he was making an effort not to voice his feelings. Too easily reassured, Sonya wrote to tell sister Tanya of her relief. Leo, she said, was in fine spirits, and so much gentler that in several months they had had only one quarrel. 'It is delightful. May God grant that it lasts.'

Husband and wife were evidently now both making an effort. Aware of the depth of the change in her husband, Sonya was trying to be more tolerant of its inevitable repercussions upon herself:

'Every now and again there are diatribes against the social life and the idle rich, but I know that he can't help it. He is a leader, one who walks ahead of the crowd pointing out the way that others should tread. But I am of the crowd. I see the light of the lantern which Leovochka carries, and I recognize it to be the light, but I can't keep up with him. Environment and habit hold me back.'

Meanwhile Tolstoy, now hard at work on *What I Believe*, was taking more trouble to explain and to propitiate: 'Don't be angry,' he disarmingly wrote to Sonya, 'when I mention God. I can't help it, for He is the very basis of all my thoughts.'

Buoyed up by her own diagnosis, Sonya tried to persuade herself that her husband's moral and spiritual crisis would pass

like an illness, taking with it, among other symptoms, one she
found particularly tiresome—his new craze for learning Hebrew.
This not only seemed to her a futile waste of time, but distressingly
reminded her of that obsession with learning Greek that years
ago had coincided with his physical breakdown.

In the autumn of this year, 1883, a new crisis perturbed
Sonya. Summoned to serve on a jury, Tolstoy refused to obey.
This was more than a protest against the brutalities of the prisons
or the whole system of public injustice; it was a deliberate expression of his complete and lasting conversion to the principle
of non-resistance by force even to evil, which he now believed
to be the most essential doctrine in all Christ's teaching. 'But I
say unto you, resist not him that is evil' must, he felt, be taken
quite literally, acted upon, and applied to governments as well
as to individuals. This his first public repudiation of established
authority, refusal to serve on a jury, was an important milestone
in his evolution as a Christian Nihilist, and as such gave Sonya
great concern.

Another matter soon maddened her. A public celebration was
to be held in honour of Turgenev, who had lately died, and, as
Russia's foremost writer, Tolstoy had been asked to give the
address. He re-read the works of his former 'literary midwife',
thereby discovering that Turgenev was, a fact which he had
denied, a 'great artist', and also that he had loved him 'terribly'.
He spent much time and trouble over his address, and Sonya
exultantly looked forward to a public triumph. Suddenly, largely
because of Tolstoy's recent refusal to serve on a jury, the Minister
of the Interior forbade the meeting. Bitterly disappointed, Sonya
exploded in a letter to her sister:

> 'Leo's address in honour of Turgenev has been forbidden
> by your disgusting St. Petersburg! It was to have been utterly
> harmless and perfectly peaceable—no firing-off of contro-
> versial squibs. How could there be any danger to the Govern-
> ment? Everyone is furious about it except Leovochka, who
> seems delighted to escape a public appearance!'

Before long there was yet another turning-point. Tolstoy's
important book *Confession*, which he had been writing since 1878,
was banned. From now on collision with the censorship became

a recurrent trouble. In reality, the more Tolstoy's books were banned the more they were read, for lithographed copies were widely circulated in Russia and, printed both in England and in Germany, they were translated into every known language. Sonya's indignation over their intended suppression was none the less voluble. Her delight whenever her husband relapsed into what, with a genuflexion in her voice, she described as 'pure art' was one of her most endearing traits. On one of his many retreats from Moscow he wrote to tell her that an idea for a 'poetical work' had just occurred to him:

> 'What joy I felt,' she answered, 'when I read that you again feel an impulse to write in a poetical vein. That is what I have so long hoped and waited for. In that lies your salvation and happiness. . . . This is the kind of work for which you were created. Without it there can never be any real peace for your soul.'

She had so often told him that, try as he might, he would never be able to kill the 'artist' in himself. She longed for him to embark on another great novel, and this year her hopes were raised: 'I know that whenever Leova begins to read English novels he is sure to start writing again, himself.'

In March 1883 Sonya rejoiced that 'Leo, growing gentler every day, was calm and contented', and after that happy entry there was a gap of nearly two years in her diary. But alas, this silence did not denote a long spell of fine weather. Far from it. Apart from the growing disunity between herself and her husband, other worries had beset Sonya who, like Martha, 'long cumbered with too much service', was now visibly exhausted by the many overdrafts on her time and her strength. Tolstoy's absorption in moral and spiritual matters had made him so much neglect his land that farming at Yasnaya had long since become a costly failure; and as he was no longer writing fiction, there had at the same time been a great drop in his literary royalties. Housekeeping and educational expenses were extremely high. Eleven indoor servants were kept; five teachers lived in the house; five others came daily. Tolstoy refused to concern himself with the family budget; but Sonya, a vigilant as well as clever housewife, worried so much over the impossibility of keeping expenses down to income that, over-driven as she was as wife, mother, housekeeper, and hostess, she now cast herself for yet another rôle. Borrowing money from her mother, she became a publisher, and ably shouldering this new burden, brought out at a moderate price a very carefully edited and well-produced complete edition of all her husband's uncensored works. Reading the proofs of his first book, *Childhood*, evoked one of the most wistfully tender of her letters, in which she entreated Tolstoy to reinstate the literary god of her childhood, and drive out of himself the interloper, squandering genius in futile attempts to establish a kingdom of heaven on earth:

> 'As I went through the chapters of *Childhood* all the emotions I had felt at twelve revived in me. Once again my eyes grew dim, and instead of correcting the misprints, I took to weeping. I love the same things in you today. But certain other things which have been added to them and are crystallizing I do not love. They are excrescences. Oh! scrape them away, and what will be left will be pure gold.'

Publishing concerns now frequently took Sonya to St. Petersburg, and one day while she was visiting a relative who happened to be in Court circles, the Empress was unexpectedly announced, and Sonya enjoyed some minutes' conversation with her. On her elated return to Yasnaya Polyana she told her disappointingly unimpressed husband how cordially the Empress had enquired after his health, and what great regret she had expressed when told that he did not intend to write any more fiction.

At about this time Tolstoy's growing aversion to money and his longing to renounce it made him attempt to reach a compromise with his conscience. He decided legally to hand over to his wife all his property, including the copyrights in his books. Calling her into his study one morning he told her of this decision. She was flabbergasted. Were they not on good terms? Did they not share the same children? What possible need, she asked, could there be for so extraordinary an arrangement?

Tolstoy explained that he had come to think property an evil, and could no longer bear to possess it. 'So you want to hand that evil over to me!' she exclaimed, bursting into tears. 'I don't want it, and I won't accept it!'

A quarrel broke out, but like so many before and after was patched up with what Tolstoy scathingly called 'the sham cement of kisses'.

Later in the same year Sonya compromised by consenting to administer Tolstoy's affairs under power of attorney, and at the same time accepted the copyrights in all his books written before 1881, which included *Anna Karenina* as well as *War and Peace*.

The spring of 1884 ushered in a very long spell of bad weather. Sonya, now nearly forty, was again pregnant, a condition in which she always tended to become unbalanced, self-pitying and, latterly, resentful. Before the birth of her fifth baby she had written: 'I am now nothing but a miserable crushed worm whom nobody wants and no one loves; a useless creature with morning sickness, a battered sense of dignity, and a love that no one needs, and which is driving me insane!'

That complaint had been made no fewer than ten years earlier, and shortly after the birth of her last baby in 1881 she had, in a frantic letter to her sister, Tanya, declared her unwillingness to have any more children: 'At times I would like to escape to you and Mamma to Moscow—or to anywhere away from my half-dark bedroom, where bending over the flushed face of my new baby fourteen times a day, I almost faint from the pain in my breasts.'

Why, it may be asked, did she need to nurse her baby fourteen times a day, and why did her bedroom have to be half dark?

She had often lamented, too, the solitary life forced upon her by this incessant child-bearing. Her protests had, however, been ignored by her husband. But now, after twenty-four years of married life, in which she had had eleven babies, and thrice been through the anguish of watching a child of her own die, she felt she could not face either the ordeal of yet another birth or any further addition to her overwhelming load of care. Suddenly, it had all become too much for her. So many children of all ages to look after, the unending succession of illnesses through which she had to nurse them; the immense cost of their upbringing! Her nervous system was exhausted. She felt like screaming. Meanwhile, dusting his room, hammering nails into boots, reading Confucius, her husband, so her diary alleges, watched her with 'silent, critical eyes'.

It has been complained that Sonya's behaviour at this time greatly heightened Tolstoy's own unhappiness. Of course it did. But who was responsible for her condition? Tolstoy's diary contritely admits: 'She is seriously mentally ill, and the cause is this pregnancy. It is a sin and a *shame*.'

But concern for his wife's bodily sufferings could never long take Tolstoy's mind off the after-pains of his own spiritual rebirth. Tenderly expressed solicitude would have heartened Sonya to bear almost anything. As it was, her will as well as her constitution rebelled. She longed to escape from having this twelfth baby. Nothing illegal was resorted to, but various bungling attempts were made to bring about a miscarriage. She lay in baths so hot that she nearly fainted; sat with her feet turning crimson in all but boiling water; and to the terror of the old Russian nurse, repeatedly clambered on to the top of a high chest of drawers and jumped off it. As her time drew near the atmosphere of the house became more and more overcharged, and for hours on end Tolstoy would shut himself up in his study to escape the sight and sounds of her misery. 'I'm trying to keep cheerful,' he wrote in a letter to a friend, 'but it is very hard. Whatever I do seems wrong. It is as if I, alone, were not mad in a house run by lunatics!'

Despite this seeming self-centredness, he did acutely suffer from the consciousness that he had failed—indeed, not even tried —to find the right way to make his wife share his convictions.

> 'I often speak coldly to her,' he wrote in a letter, 'even in a hostile manner. Never have I entreated her with tears to believe in the truth, or told her everything simply, lovingly, softly. Yet here she lies beside me, and I say nothing to her . . . but what ought to be said to *her*, I say to God.'

Several times in the course of this year (1884) Tolstoy had seriously thought of leaving home. Acutely sensitive to criticism, he could not bear being criticized for preaching renouncement and living in luxury. Hitherto, however, love for his wife and family had prevented him from going away: 'We do not become Christians until late in life and then there are ties' he would say with a sigh.

Unhappily on the very evening of the night in which the

unwanted baby was born, an absurdly unnecessary wrangle with Sonya made him lose his temper. Shouting out that he was going away at once and would never come back, he did in fact set out and walked several miles before the recollection that his wife was on the verge of bearing him a child made him think better of it and turn back. Compunction had brought him home, but without sufficient impetus to make him comfort Sonya as he alone could have done. He did not even go to see her, but hurrying straight to his study, fell asleep on the sofa. This unhappy incident has been the subject of endless altercation. Whatever provocation she had given, Tolstoy's apparent callousness in leaving his wife at that moment has troubled the loyallest of his partisans.

Sonya was not keeping her diary that nightmare summer; but, years later, reminded of its dreadful climax by her youngest daughter's birthday, she wrote:

'This is Sasha's birthday. She is thirteen. What a terrible memory I have of her birth! . . . We were talking about the horses. I told Lev Nikolaevich that he ran everything at a loss. He had had some wonderful stud horses in Samara, but had over-worked them all to death, so that neither horses nor money were left, and they had cost thousands! He was always disagreeable to me during my pregnancy—probably my appearance annoyed him—and all through the last months he had been especially irritable. This time one angry word followed another, until he quite lost his temper, and stuffing some things into a calico bag, shouted out that he was leaving home and would never come back! And in spite of my entreaties he went off. Just then my labour-pains began. I was suffering—and he wasn't there. I sat alone on a bench in the garden and the pangs grew worse and worse—and still he was not there. Young Leo and Ilya came and asked me to go in and lie down. But I was as though paralysed by sorrow. The midwife arrived and my sister and the girls, who were crying. They took me under the arms and led me upstairs to my bedroom. The pangs became more frequent and stronger. At last, after four in the morning, he returned.

I went downstairs to him and found him angry and gloomy. "Leovochka," I said, "my pains have begun. Why are you so angry? Forgive me, if I am to blame. I may not survive this birth." He remained silent. And suddenly it occurred to me that he might again be feeling jealous or suspicious. So I said: "Whether I live or die, I must tell you that I shall die true to you in body and mind; I have never loved anyone but you. . . ." He looked round suddenly and gazed fixedly at me, but did not say a single kind word to me. I left him, and an hour later Sasha was born. I gave her over to a wet nurse. I could not then nurse a baby. Lev Nikolaevich had recently handed all his affairs over to me, so that suddenly I had had to carry both the man's and the woman's burdens. What a hard time that was!'

Written at the time, Tolstoy's version expresses no contrition:

'June 1884. In the evening I cut some grass, and then I went to bathe. Came back in a buoyant mood and suddenly my wife began to nag me about some horses. I wouldn't answer back. I became very depressed. I went away, intending to leave for good, but when I had gone half way to Tula, her approaching confinement made me turn back. Tanya told me where Sonya was. "I don't want to see her," I said. I went to my study to sleep on the sofa. But I couldn't. I was so unhappy. Oh how hard it is; and yet I'm sorry for her. I had just fallen asleep when she came and woke me up. "Forgive me," she said, "the baby is coming. Perhaps I shall die." Then she went upstairs. The birth began. What should have been the most joyous event in a family went by like something unnecessary and hard.'

Thus, inauspiciously, began the life of the Tolstoys' third and last daughter, christened Alexandra, called Sasha, destined near the end of her father's life to become the closest to him of all his children, and consequently the most critical of her mother.

Her birth was followed by that former outrage to Tolstoy's sensibilities—a wet-nurse, in his view an insult to nature impossible to forgive. 'God gave the infant, and God will give the food,' was one of his glibbest over-simplifications. As before, the mother was blamed. But, poor woman, what could she do? After the shock and misery of that dreadful night she had nothing to give the baby.

II

'What Then Must We Do?'

FOR nine months after the birth of Alexandra, Sonya made no entry in her diary. Tolstoy's, however, records violent emotional disturbances. Precipitated, no doubt, by Sonya's highly nervous condition, there was even, as it were, another rehearsal for his ultimate flight from home. Again he went so far as to pack a few things into a bag, and woke Sonya to say goodbye, but after a talk with her finally agreed not to go. This was one of the rare occasions on which a storm did act proverbially. The air was cleared. Recovering her health, Sonya ceased to be hysterical, and the remainder of the summer, in which Tolstoy worked hard in the fields, passed tranquilly enough. In the autumn, Sonya took the family back to Moscow while Tolstoy for some time stayed by himself at Yasnaya Polyana, and the letters they then wrote to one another show how far their relationship, recently so near breaking-point, had recovered. By this time Sonya fully recognized that physical labour was very good for Tolstoy, and as a respite from intellectual toil she quite approved of it, but she still deplored its being taken over-seriously and using up too much time that might have been employed in writing another work of genius. In a letter, written in a rather uncharacteristic vein of humour and irony, she reproached Tolstoy for 'playing at Robinson Crusoe' in the country instead of dedicating himself to that creative work which was 'higher than anything else in life'. If that was the way in which he wished to spend his life, she could only wish him happy, but she could not help regretting that such a mind should be thrown away on digging, sawing wood, and making shoes. 'Enjoy yourself, however,' she wrote, amiably shrugging her shoulders and for the first, but by no means the last, time pacifying herself by quoting the old Russian proverb: 'What matter how the child amuses itself, so long as it doesn't cry?' Had she bottled up her feelings they would, she told him, have soured. But now she had become 'quite smilingly calm'. Afraid, however, that this slightly derisive note might jar on him in his solitude, she wrote the same day another remarkably understanding letter that ended with a burst of affection:

'Farewell, my dear. I kiss you. All of a sudden I am able vividly to visualize you, and a flood of tenderness bubbles up in my heart. There is something in you so wise, kind, naïve and stubborn, and it is all lit up by that tender solicitude for others—for everyone—natural to you alone, and by that look of yours penetrates straight into other people's souls.'

This tribute to her husband's solicitude for others is pleasantly inconsistent with earlier and later allegations. Tolstoy wrote a grateful reply, and during this salutary separation all bitterness seems to have evaporated from both their harassed hearts. So much so that Sonya wrote:

'You ask why I don't summon you home? Ach, Leo-vochka, if I were to write how much at this moment I long to see you, I would have to tell you everything I feel, and that would release such a pent-up flood of passionate, tender, but demanding words that you would not rest content with mere words. I *am* often irrepressibly sad without you, but I have accepted that I must fulfil my vocation as wife to a writer to whom freedom is the most important thing. So I make no demands upon you.'

At a distance, harmony is easily kept. When Tolstoy rejoined his family in Moscow the reconciliation proved too brittle to survive reunion and the effect of city life on Tolstoy's nerves. Once again the atmosphere became tense, and after less than a month Tolstoy, pleading that he needed quiet to write in, made yet another retreat from Moscow. Sonya was disappointed and hurt. Had he been engaged upon another great novel she would cheerfully have acquiesced; but she was well aware that it was not to write a book of the kind she approved that he secluded himself. Far from it. He was now engrossed in trying to finish his extremely didactic work, begun in 1882, called *What Then Must We Do?*—a book of great autobiographical interest, written with the skill of a literary artist, but decidedly not in the category extolled by Sonya as 'purely artistic' (she did, however, translate it into French). *What Then Must We Do?* is a one-sided indictment vehemently stating the case of the poor against the rich. Sonya did not quarrel with Tolstoy's diagnosis of the appalling problem of poverty, but she could not see that he had any practical cure to prescribe that could possibly work in any world not exclusively peopled by other Leo Tolstoys.

Written with a certain ethical arrogance, *What Then Must We Do?* betrayed Tolstoy's tendency to over-simplification, which in this case made him under-estimate the complexities of economics. Condemning the system of 'masked slavery' still prevailing in Russia, under which the 'idle and ever-feasting' held in virtual bondage the 'famished and ever-working', he summed up: 'Property today is the root of all evil. . . . The division and safeguarding of it occupies the whole world.'

If the problem of poverty were not soon solved, he was convinced that a workers' revolution must inevitably break out with every horror of destruction. Over thirty years before the revolution of 1917 he grimly warned his generation: 'The catastrophe draws nearer, and one hope only is left for those who do not wish to change their way of life; and that is that things will last their time. After that let happen what may!'

The import of *What Then Must We Do?* was 'Change your way of life or you will perish.' Sonya was alarmed. Might not the next text be 'Leave thy wife and follow me'? Nor was there anything to allay her personal fears for the future in the appeal to mothers with which the book ends: 'Oh women—mothers! In your hands lies the salvation of the world!' Stating Tolstoy's uncompromising views on the vocation of women, the book contains the much-quoted indictment: 'Every woman, however she may dress herself, and whatever she may call herself, who refrains from child-bearing without refraining from sexual relations is a whore.' Her husband's glorification of the fruitful wife who devotes herself to the bearing of children filled Sonya with apprehension. 'She performs the best and highest service of God, and no one ranks above her. If you are such a woman you will not either after two, or twenty children, say that you have borne

enough, any more than a workman of fifty will say that he has
worked enough while he still eats and sleeps and has muscles
demanding work.' *Twenty* children! Sonya quailed.

In the summer of 1886 Tolstoy's heart was gladdened, and
Sonya's troubled, by Tanya's and Masha's growing allegiance to
their father's ideals. Tolstoy had begun to regard Tanya—in her
childhood such a favourite of his—as a mere charming social
butterfly; turning serious, she now ardently took up work both
in the house and in the fields. Fifteen-year-old Masha outdid her
in zeal, and even, to her mother's concern, became an uncompromising vegetarian. Slight, sallow, retiring, Masha, with her
straw-coloured pigtail and high forehead, had never, like Tanya,
been a favourite of Sonya's, and, craving for love, she had always
been irresistibly drawn to Tolstoy. The small grey penetrating
eyes that glinted like his own would questioningly gaze at him,
and long before she was able really to understand his words, they
had sown seeds in her quick mind and tender heart. As soon as
she was old enough, she began to make herself useful to him, little
by little learning to carry out his wishes, voiced and unvoiced;
and in so far as she was allowed, putting all his precepts into
practice. 'That little creature is going to be an enigma,' predicted
Tolstoy, when Masha was only two: 'She will suffer, search, and
never find. She is always going to reach after the unattainable.'
No one has ever more ceaselessly reached after the 'unattainable'
than Masha, and few have come nearer to success, though her
sister Tanya's book *The Tolstoy Home* has revealed that the battle
was more hardly won than had been supposed. A 'practical
Christian' in the most literal sense of that term, she became a
whole-hearted disciple of her father, in time acquiring a saintly
quality that scarcely anyone could be too obtuse to perceive. She
studied medicine, qualified as a primary school teacher, and, thus
equipped, taught the village children, nursed the sick and in
every way devoted her life to carrying out her father's ideals. She
even wore shoes of his make, further than which her mother
thought devotion could not go. (Tolstoy had taken up cobbling
in 1884, and in time became quite skilled.) Become Tolstoy's
favourite daughter, Masha largely took over her mother's task of
copying out his writings. Highly cultivated, she had a lovely
singing voice and, though at first sight plain, was full of charm;
but to her mother's distress she refused ever to go into Society,

and until her marriage at the age of twenty-six, sacrificed everything to her passion for hard work, often visibly exhausting her
delicate frame by working for hours in the broiling sun beside
the robust peasant women.

Sonya, who had long dreaded the practical effects her husband's influence might have on their children, resented this reversal of everything in which, at *his* instigation, she had pains-
takingly trained her daughters. Their elaborate expensive education was being thrown away, and the sense of their 'station' in
life, formerly so carefully instilled by himself, destroyed. Why,
demanded Sonya, should her family not continue in the traditions
in which they had been brought up? 'Counts and Countesses you
were born, and Counts and Countesses you will remain!' she
tartly exclaimed when they wanted to drop their titles as, intermittently, their father tried to shed his. 'Why do you call me
Count?' he would ask visibly embarrassed peasants. 'I am plain
Leo.'

Despite Tolstoy's efforts to give up his title, the 'aristocrat'
still lurked in the wings of the Yasnaya Polyana stage, and was
never finally dropped from the cast. All of a sudden the rôle of
the self-deposed 'Count Tolstoy' might disconcertingly be revived. Maxim Gorky described one of these resuscitations:

'Tolstoy would come in looking rather small, and immediately everyone around him would grow smaller than he.
A peasant's beard, rough but remarkable hands, simple
clothes. All this external simple democratization deceived
many people, and I often saw Russians who judge people by
their clothes—an old Slavish habit—begin to pour out a
stream of their odious "frankness", which is more properly
called the "familiarity of the pigsty". .... And suddenly under
his peasant's beard, under his democratic peasant's blouse,
there would rise the old Russian Bärin, the grand aristocrat.
Then the noses of the simple-hearted visitors instantly became
blue with the intolerable cold. It was pleasant to see this
creature of the purest blood, to watch the noble grace of his
gestures, the reserve of his speech, to hear the exquisite·
pointedness of his murderous words. He showed just as much
of the Bärin as was needed for those serfs, and when they
called out the Bärin in Tolstoy, it appeared naturally and

easily and crushed them so that they shrivelled up and
whined.'

By the middle of the 'eighties Tolstoy had come far towards
winning his hard battle of self-denial. It would be difficult to
assess which was hardest for him to leave off—hunting, shooting
or tobacco. The practice of abstinence makes no man easy to live
with, and Tolstoy's struggles to give up so many enjoyments inevitably reacted on Sonya, who, in addition, had to suffer from
his remorse whenever, as was often, he broke his own rules.
Leaving off smoking was torture. If anyone else in the room
smoked, his nostrils would visibly dilate as deeply inhaling he
drew in the forbidden fragrance. Backslidings were frequent.
Finally to overcome the tobacco temptation took him several
years, and for the rest of his life Sonya missed the quietening
effect that smoking used to have on his nerves.

Sonya had never herself liked blood sports. She was, her
family complained, always unconcealedly delighted when the
hunted animal escaped. But squeamishness did not prevent her
from taking pride in her husband's prowess, or from preferring
him to behave as did his fellow-landowners. Besides, his new
scruples against killing animals induced extreme crankiness about
food which gave Sonya eternal housekeeping troubles. But what
worried her about her husband's vegetarianism far more than its
practical inconvenience was its effect on his health, to which she
thought it probably more harmful than his previous gluttony.
Now wine, too, had to be relegated to the past. Only jugs of
Kvass, a sour, non-alcoholic drink made of rye, were allowed on
the dinner-table, and this further aggravated Sonya's difficulties
as hostess. She had to tell guests who could not do without more
stimulating drink to bring it, and enjoy themselves somewhere
well out of sight.

Meanwhile Tolstoy, now nearing sixty, but still at the height
of his physical strength, and, unfortified by alcohol, was able to
enjoy any amount of strenuous outdoor work. Besides for his
own pleasure, like his creation Levin, scything in the fields, he did
every kind of job to help the peasants—carted manure, brought
in the hay; felled trees for those who needed timber. He was good,
too, at mending roofs, and with a handsaw hanging from his
waist and a chisel thrust into his great leather belt, was often to

be seen straddled across the top of a hut. Peering up at him through her tortoiseshell lorgnette as he cut a groove into which to fit the cross rafter, Sonya would, according to her mood, smilingly or frowningly, shrug her thin shoulders. In theory, too, Tolstoy liked to do everything for himself in the house as well as out-of-doors—to dust his room, make his bed, clean his boots: but on occasions he forgot his own orders, and finding his room not 'done', rebuked a servant for laziness.

His growing reluctance to spend money on himself, combined with his love of fresh air, walking, and of hobnobbing with the unsophisticated, often made him, rather than go by train, journey vast distances on foot—sometimes all the way, a hundred and thirty miles from Yasnaya Polyana to Moscow, carrying with him only a minute amount of food, a notebook with a pencil tied to it, two pairs of socks, some handkerchiefs, a change of linen, and a small vial of stomach-drops. At the end of this long tramp the once determined dandy, who had cut a man merely because he did not wear gloves, would turn up in Sonya's elegant crowded drawing-room looking exactly like a peasant: sheepskin coat, greased home-made boots, his hands in his pockets, his dog at his heels. Once or twice, to Sonya's intense embarrassment, he appeared precisely thus—dog and all—at a fashionable ball! This was not, as has ignorantly or ill-naturedly been alleged, a pose, but preoccupation with more important concerns. Naturally social, Sonya now gave balls, parties and concerts in the Moscow house, and every Saturday a reception attended by what Tolstoy scathingly called 'all the cream of Society'.

The number of Tolstoy's disciples was now rapidly increasing, and the fashionably dressed guests would often stare askance at various uncouth strangers who, determined to see the 'Master', shuffled through the crowded drawing-room to seek him out in one of the two small rooms he occupied at the back of the house.

In the autumn of 1885 Sonya's comparative peace of mind was shattered by yet another violent domestic storm. Precisely what precipitated this one is not ascertainable, but no doubt it had long been brewing. The difficulty of trying to reconcile his ideals and the claims of family life had become too heavy an accumulated strain upon Tolstoy. He was annoyed, too, by Sonya's extremely successful sale of his books; it outraged his conviction that everything he wrote ought to be given free to humanity. Besides, as he had publicly professed this opinion, it exposed him to being called a hypocrite. Tactlessly, Sonya reminded him that she was charging considerably less than he himself had for *Anna Karenina*. This did not have a soothing effect; it may indeed well have set the match to the powder magazine; but according to Sonya the storm broke over her head out of a perfectly clear sky.

'I was sitting at my table writing,' she wrote to her sister, 'when suddenly Leo, looking distraught—his face was terrible—strode into the room and said: "I've come to tell you that I want a divorce. I *can't* go on living in this way. I'm going to Paris or America!" Imagine, Tanya, if the whole house had toppled down on my head I could not have been more taken by surprise!'

Tolstoy had so carefully instilled in Sonya a reverence for marriage as the be-all and end-all of a woman's life. That he could even mention to her such a word as 'divorce' was unbelievable. 'What *has* happened?' she asked, shrivelled with shock. 'Nothing,' he answered, 'but if the cart is more and more overloaded the horse at last stands still and can't draw it.' Sonya declared she had no idea what was being 'loaded' on to Leo, but, supposing he must have gone off his head, she bore his outburst with patience (for this, admittedly, we have only her own word). More and more violently reproachful, Tolstoy finally shouted out: 'Wherever you are the air is poisoned!' This was too much for Sonya. Deciding to go for a few days to stay with her sister, she had her luggage fetched. Just at that moment the younger children came tumbling into the room, and at sight and sound of the disturbance broke into loud wails, upon which Tolstoy himself suddenly burst out sobbing. 'It was simply frightful,' wrote Sonya, credibly enough. 'Think of Leovitch all torn and twisting! At that point my heart melted for him.'

The outcome of this boiling-over was that not Sonya, but Tolstoy, went away for a few days to visit friends in the country. Before leaving he left a long letter, half appeal, half ultimatum, to Sonya. Summarizing the position, it explained how his 'spiritual awakening' and its complete conflict with the way in which she and most of her family lived, had inevitably raised a barrier between them. No agreement, he maintained, could possibly be reached unless, either through love of him or through spiritual conversion, she could come to share his beliefs. Her way of life was like a terrible nightmare that had all but driven him to suicide, but from which, by the mercy of God, he had been delivered. He could not possibly return to anything so soul-destroying as well as unhappy. Besides, he had publicly denounced it as evil. Could she not make a real effort to join him and lead with him a life, lived not for one's own ambition or satisfaction, but for God and for others? Surely she must see that he could not reject the faith he had found, or let it remain only theoretical? He accused her of having at first dismissed his great spiritual experience as merely a theme for literary work, instead of as the star by which he must steer his course. And when at last she was compelled to recognize the seriousness of his struggles to lead a new life, then she had diagnosed them as symptoms of insanity from which it was her duty to protect the children. Hitherto he had resisted the temptation of the simple, however sad, solution of leaving home. But now, unless his family tried to live as he thought right, he could no longer stay with them. The letter ended with the ominously uncompromising words: 'Between us there is a struggle to the death. Either God, or no God.'

There was really nothing new to Sonya in this communication; but it clarified the situation and closed loopholes. Her first reaction was anger. She knew Tolstoy's averred dislike of proselytizing was genuine. How then could he be so inconsistently and crudely didactic? None the less she condoned the letter as the agonized appeal of a man who, because of his love for her, yearned to stay at home, but felt he could not unless his family would live according to his beliefs. It was, indeed, the utterly sincere letter of one perplexed in the extreme, as she too was long before she reached its end.

Once safely at a distance, Tolstoy's ferment rapidly cooled into remorse, and he sent Sonya a written apology: 'Ah, my darling, how grieved I am that you torment yourself so much. . . . I rejoice that I am again in such a normal state that I shall not distress you as I have lately done.'

In answer to this, Sonya, not entirely placated but rapidly thawing, wrote reasonably enough: 'What I will never understand is why the truth must bring evil and dissension—dissension not among ruffians, but quiet *loving* people. For the first time in my life I was glad that you had gone away. How sad that is! But, of course, I shall be still more glad when you return.'

At the beginning of 1886 fate took a hand in the slow undermining of Sonya. She had grown passionately fond of the now four-year-old baby, Alexey, a charming, gay little boy. According to his governess, Anne Seuron, he had inherited the good qualities of both his parents, and strikingly possessed what she described as that 'electric fire of his mother's that matched her quick, lively talk'. One morning, radiant with health, Alexey darted out of the nursery, his large, heavily lashed grey eyes bright with their usual eagerly expectant expression. All at once he was seized by an infection of the throat. After thirty-six hours of raging fever throughout which Sonya never left his bedside, he suddenly sat bolt upright, his shining eyes open wide and in them a look of delighted astonishment. 'I see ... I see ...' he said, and fell back dead in his mother's arms.

Despite Tolstoy's denunciations of priests, he had the humanity to allow a funeral with full orthodox rites. Everyone had loved the little boy, and he was missed every moment; but sad as was his father, he had his new faith for solace and the book he was writing to distract him. Anguished, Sonya intensified her grief by persuading herself that this beloved child's death was a judgment on her for not having welcomed him into the world. She tried to numb herself by overwork on the production and sale of her husband's books and on household affairs. But no exhaustion could deaden her pain. Tolstoy sympathized with the inconsolable grief in which she turned to him, but kind as he was, she could not but know that, engrossed with his self-imposed task of reforming humanity, his mind was constantly slipping away from her back into the absorption of his book. Afraid to clutch, she felt alone in the darkness of grief. The other children? For the time being, no use. Bereft of loving little Alexey's gladdening presence, her home had gone cold. 'We have been more lovingly and more closely united by this death,' wrote the father. The mother pined alone.

12

The Tolstoyans

AFTER the death of little Alexey, Sonya, who usually turned to her diary in anger rather than in sorrow, wrote no word for over nine months. Then came an entry full of self-pity. Feeling herself the scapegoat as well as the Martha of the family, she complains that she bears all the brunt, and gets all the blame:

'Everyone, Lev Nikolaevitch as well as the older children who follow him like sheep, has come to think of me as a scourge. After throwing on me all responsibility for the little ones and their education, the management of the estate, and the complete control of the money (of which they all spend far more than I ever could) they keep coming to tell me with a superior pious look on their faces that I must give such and such a peasant a horse, or some flour, or some cash, or something or other. These perpetual demands, the worthiness of which I've neither time nor knowledge to judge, annoy and bewilder me. How often I long to drop it all and be done with this exhausting existence! God! I am so tired of the endless struggle and suffering! How deep is the unconscious hatred of even one's nearest people, and how great their selfishness. Why I go on with it all I don't know, and yet I believe it to be right. I shall never be able to do the things my husband wants (or says he wants) unless I can break some of these family and business fetters. To get away somehow or other from this house, or indeed right cut of the world, is the thought that obsesses me night and day. As it grows dark I begin to feel happier. Then my imagination can evoke all the things I used so much to love, and I sit here gazing at these phantoms of the past. Last night I caught myself talking aloud when I was alone. What if I am going mad? And nowadays I love darkness. Am I then to come to love death too?'

A woman who, because she catches herself thinking aloud, fears for her sanity, has a high standard of normality; but, hoping to harrow him into expressed sympathy, Sonya may well have written this passage on purpose for her husband to read.

As often becomes the way with the unhappy and overtired, Sonya was now in that condition to which any crisis, however distressing, brings relief. In the summer of 1886 Tolstoy hurt his leg while working in the fields and it became badly infected, but he refused to pay any attention to it or to see a doctor. Alarmed by the swelling, Sonya, feigning neuralgia, went to Moscow ostensibly to consult a doctor for herself, but really to bring one to Yasnaya Polyana. Meanwhile Tolstoy's temperature had flared and he had become dangerously ill with threatened general blood-poisoning. The necessary immediate insertion of a draining-tube was very painful, and for some days after this his life was almost despaired of. As a rule he was a grateful, gentle, uncomplaining patient, but when the pain of his leg became unbearable his shrieks were so terrible that everyone except Sonya fled from his room. He had to stay in bed for over nine weeks. For the first month he was not allowed to put pen to paper, but at the end of that time he became enthralled in writing the most famous of his six plays, *The Power of Darkness*. Based on a case recently tried in the Tula law courts, this stark drama, a crescendo of horrors which include incest and infanticide, was too much for Sonya's nerves, and she protested against its unrelieved sordidness. This had, however, been deliberate. 'When I write a novel,' explained Tolstoy, 'I paint and so to speak work with a brush. I can change it, add colour, or amplify. But a drama is so different. It is a sculptor's work. No shadows. No half-tones. Everything must be clear cut and in sharp relief.'

Thought likely to give Western Europe a bad impression of the Russian peasantry, *The Power of Darkness* was banned from the stage for nine years; but, translated into nearly all languages, it was read by millions, and when at length it appeared in the Russian bookshops, 250,000 copies were sold in three days.

After the acute anxiety subsided, Tolstoy's illness made a happy interlude for Sonya. Once again she had felt indispensable with a definite job and one at which she knew she was good, for plenty of practice as well as natural aptitude had made her a highly skilled nurse.

'I nursed him day and night,' she wrote, 'it was such a happy natural thing—the only thing I can do really well—to make a personal sacrifice for the man I love. The harder it was on me the happier I felt. But now that he is up again he is making it quite clear that he no longer needs me. I am cast aside as of no further use except that I am still expected to do the impossible—to go against my convictions and renounce our property, and consequently the education and welfare of my children, a thing that not only I, but practically all mothers, would be incapable of doing. . . . I shall have to go on keeping the family together, handling all the publishing and all the practical side of life, and scraping together all the necessary money which of course Leo Nikolaevich with an air of injured innocence will be the first to ask me for to distribute it among some of his favourites, who aren't really any poorer than others, but more brazen. . . . Oh to get away from all this! And one way or other I shall!'

After this outburst Sonya naïvely betrayed awareness of her habit of using her diary as a safety-valve: 'For the moment I shall write my diary. It may make me more kindly and self-controlled. Perhaps indeed all my irritation will get worked off on it.'

Another engaging flash of self-discernment made her write: 'I am reading philosophy. It is so difficult to keep balanced. I keep looking for all those things that tally with my own views and emotions. Consequently, though I do try to be less biassed, it isn't easy for me to learn anything.'

Before the end of 1886 Sonya's mother died, a grief, but as of late years they had seldom met, not of so absorbing a nature as to distract her from the multitudinous worries of home affairs. Her diary had lamented that the children were all following their father like a flock of sheep. This was not really so. The daughters, it is true, were now almost whole-hearted adherents of their father; and Sonya never ceased worrying about their destroying their health—let alone their looks and their futures—by what she regarded as futile self-sacrifice. In early boyhood the sons, too, had all worshipped their father, but now they disagreed about him. The eldest, Sergei, made no pretence whatever of sharing his views. Ilya, now twenty years old, was still trying hard to believe and to act upon them. Leo, a handsome temperamental

youth of only seventeen, had at first showed every sign of becoming an ardent Tolstoyan; but before long he became so
violently antagonistic to his father's doctrines as to oppose them
even in print, and adoring his mother, took up the cudgels in her
defence too violently to be just to his father. His book, *The Truth
About Tolstoy*, is therefore not the truth. The younger sons,
Andrey (Andrusha) and Mikhail (Misha) at this time still mere
boys, were distressing Sonya by their idleness at school. Not
having known their father in his unregenerate days, they had
never been so much under his spell as had their elder brothers and
sisters, and directly they were old enough, they both defied his
principles by volunteering to serve in the army.

In the summer of 1887, Sonya's brother, Stepan Behrs, returned to Yasnaya Polyana after an absence abroad of nearly
nine years. He was painfully struck by the change in Tolstoy,
whom he found so much aged, saddened, and subdued that his
personality as well as his countenance, ravaged by all the mental
anguish he had been through, seemed entirely different. Stepan
noticed, too, that his former habit of alternating bouts of violent
fun with hours of complete isolation when no one was allowed
to disturb his writing, had given place to general accessibility.
All who wanted to see him were admitted at any time of the day,
unless Sonya, thinking his health demanded rest, resumed her
old rôle of watchdog and kept everyone off.

Tolstoy told Stepan that, for fear some of his family might,
just to please him, follow his teaching without real conviction,
he had tried very hard not even to impress, still less to force, his
beliefs upon them; and Stepan saw that he had succeeded in
making his children feel quite free to believe and act as they
chose. On the other hand, he noticed with concern an appreciable
change in the relationship between husband and wife. Tolstoy's
manner to Sonya unmistakably betrayed dissatisfaction, even a
hint of reproach. It was obvious that he could not help blaming
her either for obstructing his desire to give away his property, or
for continuing to educate the younger children in the old way of
which he no longer approved. It seemed to Stepan that, pulled
like a cracker between her husband and her children, Sonya was
in a quite impossible position. Tolstoy's demands upon her were
not reconcilable with her duty as a mother. 'Conflict had therefore inevitably arisen,' wrote Stepan in his book, *Recollections of*

Tolstoy. Apart from this, he could see no other cause of disagreement. 'In all other respects,' he declared, 'they were still a model couple.'

Though Stepan missed Tolstoy's former high spirits he did not find him in the least morose. He still delighted in all the family turmoil—the excited discussions, the eternal singing and piano-playing, but no longer took an active part in the bear-fighting, until struck by Stepan Behrs' sadness at the change in himself, he one day disconcertingly reverted to his old playfulness, and ambushing himself behind a curtain, sprang out and leapt upon the startled young man's back!

Among various confidences, Tolstoy told Stepan that since, out of pity for animals, he had given up hunting and shooting, he could no longer imagine how he could ever have enjoyed such cruel sports. It struck Stepan that the sole personal pleasure Tolstoy now allowed himself was indulging his delight in flowers. He always had some by him; in a vase on his writing-table, stuck into his broad leather belt or just held in his hands. The children's governess, Anne Seuron, noticed this too. 'You should see,' she wrote, 'with what enjoyment the Count presses the flowers to his big nose as though thanking God for the gift of flowers.'

A new element had entered into the family life. For some time 'the Tolstoyans', as Tolstoy's disciples were called, had been a growing annoyance to Sonya. Both at Yasnaya and in the Moscow house, their invasion disturbed the atmosphere of her home. 'Who is with the Count?' she had one day asked a man-servant. 'I cannot say, Your Excellency,' he answered. 'Some dark person or other.' The epithet 'dark' clung, and 'The Dark Ones' became the generally accepted term for the Tolstoyans. The servants did not like them. They 'brought in dirt' and did not tip. They much preferred the mistress's smartly dressed visitors who usually drove up in carriages and gave lavish tips. The frequenters of the house accordingly now fell into two categories, the 'Dark' and the 'Bright'. Sonya's diary makes spirited attacks upon the 'Dark Ones', most of whom really were, as she complained, fanatics, cranks and freaks; some even frauds. A few shining exceptions, for instance the painter N. N. Gay and P. I. Birukov, became real friends of the family.

Sonya, who, like most intelligent women, loved to preside

over well-conducted conversation, felt that her home was losing
its hitherto agreeable social atmosphere. Tolstoy's desire to improve others as well as himself was certainly not conducive to
good company in any sense of that term. Asked one day by the
harassed hostess why he found it necessary to entertain a certain
man who, beside being the bore he so obviously was, seemed to
her also to be evil, Tolstoy answered: 'If he *is* an evil man, I can
be a greater help to him than to his betters.'

'This,' caustically comments Sonya's diary, 'explains my
husband's relationship with many of the *wicked* as well as insignificant characters nearly all these disciples of Leo's are!' Soon
after this infiltration of her home had begun, she wrote:

> 'Not a single sane person among them. Nearly all the
> women are hysterical. . . . I find it very trying not to be able
> to choose my own friends, but to have to entertain anybody
> and everybody. . . . Lyov has his dark people with him, a
> disagreeable lot of strangers in our family circle. And so many
> of them! It's a very heavy price to have to pay for Leo's fame
> and original ideas.'

Later on her diatribes gained in violence.

> '1890. The Dark Ones have arrived. That insane Asiatic
> Popov, and that fat fool of shop-keeper origin, Khoklov.
> And these are the followers of the great man! Miserable
> abortions of human society; aimless babblers, uneducated
> loafers!'

> '1891. They are gloomy and silent. They wear rough
> peasant clothes and won't eat like other people. Some of them
> are University men. These I can't understand. Surely *they*
> ought to realize that this loafing tramp's existence isn't the
> right kind of life. Leo says they work. I've never seen them
> do any serious work. They just sit about and mumble.'

The enforced hostess of the 'Dark Ones' was not unnaturally
vexed when her son Andrey told her that one of them had prevented him from doing any work that morning. 'Why do you
study?' he had asked the boy. 'You will destroy your soul. Surely
your father cannot wish you to do this.' Of all the 'Dark Ones',
probably the most unprepossessing was a Swede who was so

fanatical a vegetarian that he had forsworn milk as well as eggs. One day Sonya found this 'old monster', as she called him, asleep under a table with his head pillowed on a bottle. He was half naked, and the few tatters still clinging to him were filthy. 'He lies on the grass like a cow,' complained Sonya of this extreme case, 'rootles in the earth for potatoes, eats quantities of them raw, just rinses himself in the river, and then comes and sleeps on the floor.'

Many people shared Sonya's feelings about the Dark Ones. Maxim Gorky's impression: 'It is strange to see Tolstoy among the Tolstoyans. There stands a majestic belfry whose bell resounds ceaselessly all over the world; and around and around scurry cautious little curs who yap to the tune of the bell, stealthily, suspiciously eyeing one another to see which will yap the best. It always seems to me that these creatures pollute Yasnaya Polyana with an atmosphere of hypocrisy, pettiness, and mercenary expectations. Almost all of them like to sigh and embrace one another. They have boneless, perpetually sweating hands and false eyes.'

Not a pleasing description, and its writer was not, as was the unfortunate Sonya, obliged to house and feed 'the creatures' who polluted her home. As for Tolstoy himself, touched as he was by their allegiance, the lesser Tolstoyans often bored and irritated him almost more than he could bear; but, unfortunately, loyalty forbade him to gladden Sonya's heart by admitting this. Still, however hard he tried to be patient with the rabble of his followers, he could not always restrain himself. 'Tolstoyans,' he once burst out, 'are the most insupportable people. No one is more repugnant to me!'

Tolstoyan 'Colonies' rapidly sprang up in various parts of Russia, and later in England, Holland, and America. At first these had Tolstoy's approval. They became, however, the bane of his existence, for the axiom 'if you love God, you must unfailingly love your fellow-men' did not enable Tolstoyans to keep the peace without the policing of organized government. In theory they agreed that private property was wrong; in practice they could not bear to share a frying-pan; and invariably, before long, individuals took the law into their own hands, violence broke out, and by bitter experience the community learnt the indispensability of laws. In the absence of any impartial arbitration for the settlement of disputes, the principle of non-resistance, which forbade the use of force either to compel men to do what they did not want to do, or to desist from doing what they wanted to do, proved the downfall of the Tolstoy Colonies. Publicly demonstrating the unworkability of Christian Anarchy, they all ended in chaos and disillusion. Even before their failure Tolstoy had really agreed with Sonya's distrust of any organized attempt to create a moral oasis. He could not believe that to isolate oneself in artificial conditions was right. 'Live in the world,' he said, 'and be good.' Realizing that his so-called disciples parodied himself, travestied his teaching, and misinterpreted the gospels, Tolstoy came to agree with Ruskin, who declared: 'No true disciple of mine will ever be a Ruskinian.' Once he even went so far as to pronounce Tolstoyans the most incomprehensible beings and the most alien to himself.

'I shall soon be dead,' he lamented, 'and people will say that I taught men to plough and make boots, while the *one* thing I do believe in, they will forget—the eternal lesson of the Gospels, which bids Man to realize his sonship to God. Once a man has fully understood that, he enters into free communion with God and has nothing more to ask of anyone.'.

There were, of course, among the Tolstoyans, admirable exceptions, devoted, sincere, and brave men; but many even of these became sources of bitter, self-reproachful grief to their master, for, acting upon his pacifist principles and refusing to serve in the army, they were imprisoned and exiled.

Though undeniably a trial to a self-respecting housewife, the swarm of lesser Tolstoyans infesting Sonya's home were nothing more serious than an annoyance, a social encumbrance and an expense. They might impair the agreeableness of her house, but could be no real threat to whatever happiness it still held, or further undermine her relationship with her husband. Irritated by this small fry, Sonya did not for some time realize that the one really important Tolstoyan had entered the scene. As far back as 1883 her husband had made the acquaintance of Count Vladimir T. Chertkov, who as, according to some, his 'Guardian Angel', according to others his 'Evil Genius', was henceforth to play the leading part in his life, and to cast an ever-deepening shadow over Sonya's. She could not complain that this handsome Tolstoyan of fine physique, commanding presence and good, if rather wooden, manners, was an 'aimless babbler'; still less that he was of 'shopkeeper origin'. The son of a famous general and himself a personal friend of the Czar, Chertkov, unlike nearly all the other Tolstoyans, was a man of her husband's own class, tradition, and education. This was not only a recommendation to herself; it amused as well as pleased her to see that, try as he would, her husband had not succeeded in ridding himself of an instinctive sympathy for his own class.

Chertkov had been an officer in the Guards, a career that, to quote his own characteristically stilted words, 'exposed him to the three traditional vices of aristocratic officers—wine, women, and cards'. Influenced by his deeply religious mother, he early reacted against dissipation and left the army before he was twenty. He had then retired to his huge estate, given up all personal luxuries and, Tolstoy-like, devoted himself to the welfare of the peasantry and the search for what in capital letters he called 'The Meaning of Life'. At the age of thirty his great longing to meet Tolstoy was gratified by a friend, and at their first interview the two men found they agreed upon almost every point. Chertkov felt that his long quest was ended. Here at last was a man—a very great man—who interpreted Christianity exactly as he did himself. To what better use could he dedicate his life than to become his leading disciple and with him work for the furtherance of their ideals? Tolstoy was at once drawn to this striking man, so agreeably unlike the rank and file of his adherents, and a rapid affection and intimacy sprang up between the two.

Sonya's first impression of Chertkov was favourable. He was so utterly different from the 'shaggy Nihilists'. He might be, probably was, a fanatic, but at least he was not a freak. Furthermore, when he chose, he knew how to make himself agreeable, and at first was most anxious to ingratiate himself with the whole of Tolstoy's family, particularly with his wife, against whom in reality he was already prejudiced, for—and this shows the rapid intimacy that sprang up between the two men—Tolstoy had almost at once confided to Chertkov his matrimonial troubles. It had indeed been to him that as early as 1883 he had written the already quoted complaint that Yasnaya Polyana had become 'a madhouse, run by lunatics'. But, to begin with, Chertkov contrived to conceal his animosity, and unconscious of her doom, poor Sonya liked him. She described him as 'tall, handsome,—

clearly an aristocrat from the first glance'. She even pronounced him 'pure as crystal'; still more inappropriately, 'affable'. She seemed, indeed, to have no inkling that of all the men her husband had influenced, here at last was the only one who was to influence him. 'Tolstoy,' declares his biographer E. J. Simmons, 'had found a new saint and Sonya a devil incarnate.'

From Sonya's point of view the villain of the piece had now joined the cast of the Yasnaya Polyana drama. But he had made his entry unrecognized. She had felt no 'pricking of her thumbs'.

For a time the unsuspecting Sonya continued to welcome Chertkov and, as later she was to complain, to treat him almost like another son. Before long, however, her husband's growing dependence on this friend, and apparent blindness to the faults she soon saw in him, began to alarm her. 'Must you,' she asked Tolstoy, 'deliberately shut your eyes to people in whom you don't want to see anything but good?'

Apart from her jealousy of Chertkov, his personality began to get on her nerves. The narrowness of his high forehead, his cold, protruding eyes, overbearing manner and air of conscious authority irritated her. Besides, unlike her endlessly complex husband, he seemed so maddeningly single-minded; untroubled by doubt, self-criticism or indecision. To his chess-board, black-and-white mind everything was clear-cut, simple, obvious. Holding all Tolstoy's, in her opinion, impracticable Utopian views on property, non-resistance, and government, he violently out-Heroded Herod. Added to which he was far more determined to force others into agreement, so much so that, unlike Tolstoy, who prounounced deception to be 'worse than sin', he could not always stick to the truth. Convicted one day of a lie, he naïvely admitted: 'Yes, when I want something very much, I do some-times say the thing which is not.' Yet, fundamentally, Chertkov was sincere. Even Tolstoy's biographer, the infallibly fair-minded Aylmer Maude, despite his unconcealable dislike for Chertkov, admitted him to be 'a man of noble sentiments and high aims'. Though never, any more than Tolstoy, a conscious hypocrite, his humourless fanaticism laid him open to misrepresentation. His theories about money were so irreconcilable with a normal existence that, refusing to touch the horrid stuff himself, he at one time made his wife sign cheques for him and give the money to his secretary, who would then escort him to the station, buy his railway ticket and hand it to him. 'In our movement,' he once said, 'we care for principles, but not persons.'

Chertkov soon became widely known as 'The Czar of all the Tolstoyans', but few men have had bestowed upon them so large a number of conflicting titles. He was 'Tolstoy's heir apparent', 'chief apostle', 'spiritual twin', 'evil genius', 'guardian angel'. Others just called him saint or devil. The simplicity of the last term commended itself to Sonya, who also named him Leovochka's 'black shadow'.

When Chertkov entered the scene, Tolstoy's *What Then Must We Do?* and other controversial books were still banned. Seizing this admirable opportunity to please 'The Master', Chertkov, who possessed a printing press, had these works copied in his own house and organized their unauthorized circulation. He then endeared himself to Tolstoy by financing and managing a pioneering publishing business called *The Intermediary*. This—a long-cherished ambition of Tolstoy's—brought to the people stories in the spirit of his own teaching, by the best writers, and illustrated by good artists. Tolstoy's faith that, if the masses could afford to buy good literature, they would read it, was triumphantly vindicated. In four years the little books, priced at only one and a half kopecks each, sold 12,000,000 copies.

In the first year of this successful venture Tolstoy wrote no fewer than fifteen stories for *The Intermediary*, among them his famous *Where Love Is, There God Is, The Two Pilgrims*, and *What Men Live By*.

The Intermediary led to the first serious clashes between Sonya and Chertkov, who, having constituted himself Tolstoy's literary adviser, now adopted a proprietary attitude and began to requisition, either for publication in *The Intermediary* or to keep as valuable documents, various writings Sonya wanted for her own edition. Too late Sonya realized the situation. The first serious rival she had ever had was now deeply in her husband's confidence and in command of his affections. She could argue, even quarrel, with Tolstoy over the interloper's encroachments, but there was no longer any hope of evicting him. She must learn to make the best both of his presence and of his growing power; and with rising alarm she noticed that now that Chertkov felt his position secure, he was no longer troubling to ingratiate himself with his hostess. Soon, she feared, he would have the audacity

openly to come between husband and wife. 'I do *not* like him,'
she wrote in her diary of March 1886. 'He is clever and sly and
one-sided and he is *not* a good man. It is only his adulation that
makes Leo partial to him.'

For a long time yet Chertkov still continued to fight with
masked batteries, tactics facilitated by the fact that in these
closing years of the 1880s Tolstoy had become much more
settled in his mind, and therefore easier-going than in the years
immediately after his 'spiritual rebirth'. Thanks, however, to
husband and wife's deplorable habit of reading one another's
correspondence as well as diaries, it was not long before Sonya
discovered that Chertkov was working against her. In a letter
rhapsodizing over his joy at finding himself in perfect spiritual
communion with his newly married wife, he commiserated with
'The Master' who, though so much worthier of it, was denied
this happiness.

'This obstinate sly man,' furiously wrote Sonya, 'who swad-
dles Leo in flattery, now wants (Christianity!) to break the ties
which for nearly twenty-five years have bound us together.
This relationship with Chertkov must be put an end to. It is all
false and evil and we must get out of it.'

Too late. The enemy was within the walls. Henceforth in-
ward conflict seethed; but it was still a long time before war was
openly declared.

Chertkov could, when he chose, be good company, and
Tanya and Masha were both at first delighted by so impressive
a new recruit to the ranks of the Tolstoyans; but their brothers
found him too anxious to instruct and improve them. One belief of Tolstoy's he did not share was in the value of physical
work. Nor did he enjoy it. He therefore spared himself bodily
exertion, but looking annoyingly cool and composed, was only
too ready to help on others with advice. This irritated the young
men. Nor did they approve the way in which, because he himself hated 'The Master' ever to step down from the lofty pedestal
on which he had placed him, his presence tended to prevent
Tolstoy from reverting to the playful father of their boyhood.
One bad relapse of Tolstoy's gave his family immense pleasure.
It was a very hot night and they were having dinner on the
verandah; Sonya seated in what was called 'The Chairman's
Place', Tolstoy, as always, on her right, and next to him Chertkov.

All were in a happy mood, joking, and laughing. The only draw-back was the swirling haze of mosquitoes. After a quick amused glance at Chertkov's lofty head, Tolstoy, grinning like a boy, adroitly swatted its bald top. A smear of blood and the crushed remains of a huge mosquito showed how good his aim had been. Everyone roared with laughter, including the swatter, but Tolstoy's laughter abruptly died when gloomily affronted, with-out a flicker of a smile, Chertkov portentously said: 'Lev Niko-laevich, what *have* you done? You have taken the life of a fellow living creature. Are you not ashamed?'

Stifled giggles continued to escape, but everyone felt uncom-fortable.

The year 1888 was notable for two family events. In February Ilya married; and in March, when Sonya was in her forty-fourth and Tolstoy in his sixtieth year, their thirteenth and last child, a small, sickly boy, was born. At the time this further addition to Sonya's load of care may well have seemed worse than super-fluous. Yet the brief life of this Benjamin, christened Ivan, called Vanichka, was to bring her the greatest happiness she had ever known and his death a grief from which she never recovered.

13
'The Kreutzer Sonata'

UNPLEASANT as Sonya had found *The Power of Darkness*, she could not deny that in writing it Tolstoy had, as so long she had urged him to do, reverted from sermonizing to art. The next year, 1888, saw the beginning of another incontestable work of art that was to be a milestone in Sonya's personal as well as in Tolstoy's literary life. The famous *Kreutzer Sonata*, bluntly described by its writer as 'a tale on the theme of sexual love', is a story from which the overworked adjective 'powerful' can scarcely be withheld. Told in the first person by Pozdnyshev, a man whose frantic jealousy of his wife has driven him to murder her, it is a relentless analysis of sex stripped of all the trappings dear to Sonya's heart. No love, in her romantic sense of that word; no illusions; no sentiment. The obsessed narrator is compelled, Ancient Mariner-like, to pour into the horrified ears even of strangers met in the train the story of his anguish and his crime, and frantically to preach his belief that physical love ought to be entirely eliminated from human life. Though craftsmanship made this ferocious story convincing, many readers dismissed it as a mere moral tract in which Tolstoy had used Pozdnyshev to publish his own new ideal of celibacy for the married, as well as for the single. This he had lately been expounding to Vladimir Chertkov in letters, one of which contained his much-quoted dictum 'Except to produce children, sexual relations can have no physical or moral justification.' In the same letters he had frankly admitted his complete failure, so far, to put his convictions into practice, but declared that in the future he hoped to follow what he now believed to be the teaching of Christ.

The Kreutzer Sonata aroused the most violent, prolonged, and varied reactions. The Church condemned it for its implied dismissal of the belief that marriage was a sacrament, and innumerable sermons were preached against it. One archbishop denounced Tolstoy as 'a wolf in sheep's clothing'; another declared him such a menace to society that he ought to be executed. Freethinkers derided the story for what they considered its absurd reversion to the antiquated morality of St. Paul. Lovers of music inveighed against it as a philistine attack on Beethoven. (How dared Tolstoy imply that, as an expression of sensuality, *The Kreutzer Sonata* was an immoral influence?) Others jeeringly declared the true explanation of this virulent attack on sex was that, to an author grown old, the grapes had turned sour.

How had this provocative story come to be written? One evening in the Tolstoys' Moscow house, their eldest son, Sergei, and a professional violinist, had played *The Kreutzer Sonata* with so much feeling that all the company, including the famous painter, I. Repin, and the actor, Andreyev Bulgatov, had been deeply moved. It was suggested and agreed that the three artists present should collaborate to interpret the same theme. Tolstoy was to write a story based on the sonata; Repin to paint a picture inspired by it, and, standing by that picture, Bulgatov would give a public reading of the story. Of the three artists the writer was the only one to carry out this idea. Some time before, he had embarked on a story in which a pathologically jealous husband was to surprise his wife with her lover, a portrait painter. Returning to this story, so far a mere sketch, he now changed the lover from a painter into a violinist, and made him play *The Kreutzer Sonata* to the wife with whom he was in love. The emotional music inflames their passions, and, finding them together, the maddened husband kills his wife. Towards the end of 1889 Tolstoy, after writing eight drafts of the story, finished the final one. He called it *The Kreutzer Sonata* because the narrator curses that piece of music for its evil influence. 'Do you know the first presto of the sonata?' he asks, grinding his teeth. 'Oh-h, what a terrible thing! What a dreadful thing music is! Where does its power come from? In China it is controlled by the State, and so it should be. How can it be allowed that any one person should hypnotize others with it and then do with them whatever he pleases?'

At the instigation of the Church *The Kreutzer Sonata* was banned by the censorship, but vast numbers of lithographed copies, surreptitiously made, were sold in all the bookshops that dared handle contraband literature, and innumerable readings aloud were organized in private houses. No work of fiction has ever been more vehemently discussed. Strakhov wrote to tell Tolstoy that acquaintances meeting in the streets of Petersburg and Moscow, instead of saying 'How do you do?' now asked one another 'Have you read *The Kreutzer Sonata*?'

'It seems indeed,' wrote Countess Alexandra Tolstoy, 'that forgetting all their personal cares people now live only for the works of Count Tolstoy. I doubt whether even the most important public events have ever more completely engrossed everyone.'

Annoyed as Tolstoy was by the public clamour and the various absurd misrepresentations of his story, its effect upon his home life was worse. Though the actual events of the story were clearly not factual, no one, least of all Sonya, could fail to identify Pozdnyshev's diatribes with Tolstoy's own views, or deny that his story denounced the institution of marriage as 'authorized licentiousness'. Ruskin's harsh declaration, 'There is no licentiousness so mortal as licentiousness in marriage', might indeed have been taken as its text.

Sonya was well accustomed to Tolstoy's 'lifting' in his books from real life to an extent which, despite the frequency with which, justly and unjustly, this charge is brought against all novelists, has never been exceeded. This habit of his must often have embarrassed her, not least when, in *Anna Karenina*, he gave his heroine not only the same circumstances and mode of suicide but even the same Christian name as the mistress of a near neighbour, who, out of jealousy, had flung herself under the wheels of a train. At the time of this tragedy, Tolstoy had hurried to the mortuary and stood for an hour gazing at the mutilated body.

But what was embarrassment compared with the anguish of Sonya's wounded feelings over *The Kreutzer Sonata*! Its attack on marriage, until lately sacred to him and still so sacred to herself, horrified her. Worse, the story seemed brutally to assert that love, in the romantic sense of that word to which she clung, did not exist. It was merely an elaborate dressing-up of 'sexual attraction', a mirage-like illusion that, once desire was satisfied, inevitably dissolved, leaving the resentful husband encumbered by a galling fetter, or plagued by a perpetual temptation. Which of these two did Leo consider herself to be? Both!

Not even Tolstoy, she knew, could suspect her of ever having had a lover. But this did not soften the fact that his story divulged not only many intimate aspects, but even actual incidents, in their own married life, such as:

> 'When we were engaged I showed her my diary from which she could learn something of my past, especially about my last liaison, of which she might hear from others and about which I therefore thought it necessary to inform her. I remember her embarrassment, horror, and despair when she learnt of it. I saw that she wanted to give me up. And why did she *not* do so?'

So he remembers that first fatal mistake! thought Sonya, and confesses his motives! What hurt her most was the query: 'Why did she *not* do so?' Clearly there the wish had been father to the thought. Another exposure of family intimacy exhumed his old rancour over her inability to nurse their first baby and the preposterously unfair inference drawn: 'Seeing how easily she abandoned her moral obligations as a mother, I concluded it would be equally easy for her to disregard her moral obligations as a wife. . . .' Later: 'In eight years she had five children and nursed all except the first.' Still harping on that old string? Even to this day did he blame her—think that it had been her fault that she could not nurse Sergei?

Another old grievance was aired, the resented move to Moscow, urged by her for the sake of the children's education in which by then he was losing interest. And what an ugly interpretation was given to this too! 'It is strange what coincidences there are. Just when the parents find life together impossible, it becomes necessary to move to town for the children's education.'

These passages told of actual incidents in their own marriage. How about others yet more wounding? This, for instance: 'In me there often raged a terrible hatred of her. Sometimes I watched her pouring out tea, swinging her leg, lifting a spoon to her mouth, and I hated her for those things as though they were the worse possible crimes.'

Had she got on Leovochka's nerves as badly as that? Most of all she detested his cold-blooded chart of passion and reaction:

'I did not then notice that the periods of anger corresponded quite regularly and punctually with the phases of
what we call love—a period of "love", then a period of
animosity; a violent phase of "love", then a long phase of
animosity. A weaker manifestation of "love" and a shorter
phase of animosity. . . . I did not then understand that this
alternating love and animosity were one and the same animal
feeling only at opposite poles.'

So, that's what he understands now! thought Sonya, writhing
with pain and shame, sickened by the implications that she herself had shared in what he horribly described as a 'swinish life':
'The quarrels between us became frightful, all the more so
because they alternated with similarly violent animal passion.'

Sonya was appalled by this hideous picture of married life:
sheer sex, wholly unsublimated; no sentiment, let alone romance;
no affection; no partnership; no suggestion even of that common
treasury of memories, that can help to save loveless marriages.
Was this how Leo was now trying to make himself see their union
of nearly thirty years of shared labour, laughter, and tears?

The Kreutzer Sonata incited some of the most self-revealing
passages in Sonya's diary:

'Last night while I was correcting The Kreutzer Sonata, it
occurred to me that when a woman is young, she loves a
man with her *heart* and gladly gives herself, realizing what
pleasure it gives to *him*. But as she gets older, looking back
she suddenly realizes that he loved her only when he wanted
her, and always became glum and peevish as soon as he was
satisfied. And when after trying for a long time to ignore
this, she at last begins to feel the same way, her sentimental
love disappears and she becomes like him.'

And again: 'The Kreutzer Sonata is all wrong about young
women. A young woman, especially when she bears children and
nurses them has none of that physical passion. Hers does not
awake until she is thirty.'

Sonya's mind seethed with objections. Even had there been
no personal application in The Kreutzer Sonata its coarseness
would have offended her. Tolstoy had so carefully trained her to

Countess Tolstoy at the time of her marriage

Tolstoy at the time of his marriage

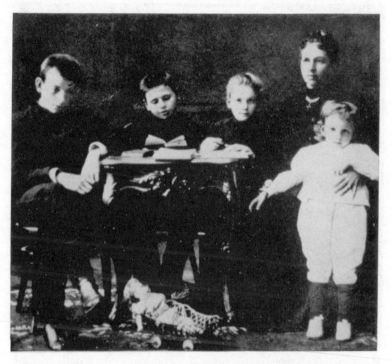

Countess Tolstoy with her younger children

The Tolstoys' house at Yasnaya Polyana

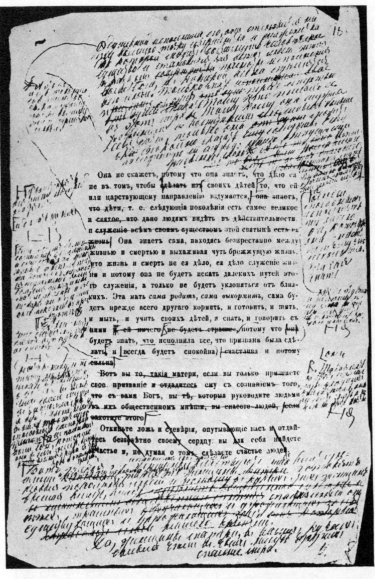

Proof sheet of *What Then Must We Do?* corrected by Tolstoy

Countess Tolstoy in her middle fifties

Count and Countess Tolstoy with their children and grandchildren and the painter N. N. Gay

Count and Countess Tolstoy in 1907

Count and Countess Tolstoy in 1910 — the last photograph
ever taken of Tolstoy

be delicate—more than delicate, prudish—in her tastes. He had even prevented her from reading Zola! She disliked, too, the story's implied indictment of music. Here again perhaps the cap of fiction fitted? If music acted as the match to the tinder, why only in illicit love? Might it not equally well precipitate an honourable proposal? Did Leo now blame music for the mistake of his own marriage? Suppose on that fateful evening long ago Tanya had not sung *The Kiss*, would he then perhaps never have put into her hand his written proposal of marriage?

In answer to the critics' charge that he had accused music of sensuality, Tolstoy declared: 'Music never did, never could express any one emotion in particular. It is an expression of emotion in general, upon which each listener can put his own interpretation.' Nevertheless, Sonya knew that to some extent Pozdnyshev's diatribes did voice his own recently acquired views on music. She remembered how in old days he had often for three or four hours a day played the piano with quite as good a touch, declared listeners, as most professionals, and with far more feeling. But latterly this lifelong lover of music had tended to attack it as a merely sensuous pleasure—a form of self-indulgence much on a par with eating and drinking. 'Do you weep when you eat or drink?' his sister-in-law, Tanya, would ask, at which, to do him justice, Tolstoy would smile. Sonya had always realized that music had a violent emotional effect on him. This was disquietingly evident. While he played or listened, his face, turned pale, would become contorted with—was it pain, or fear? 'What does the music want of me?' he would ask, audibly grinding his teeth. Evidently he did fear the 'depraving power' of music as only something much loved can be feared. 'Tolstoy sat down to play Chopin,' wrote Paul Boyer. 'At the fourth ballad his eyes filled with tears. "Ah, the *animal*!" he cried, and, suddenly rising, left the room.'

Besides being so deeply hurt by *The Kreutzer Sonata*, Sonya was appalled at the thought of the scandal it would let loose. Her fears were fully justified. Both in Moscow and in Petersburg a hideous gabble of gossip broke out. Identifying the writer with the narrator of his story, some readers even took it as tantamount to a confession that if Tolstoy had not already murdered his wife, it was not for want of the impulse. Nor did matters improve for Sonya when to refute a statement that his story advocated free love (how that misapprehension was arrived at is difficult to guess), Tolstoy felt compelled to write *The Postscript to the Kreutzer Sonata*, in which he clearly stated his present views on marriage. 'Marriage,' he explained, 'is a service of self, and therefore not compatible with the Christian ideal which is love of God and your fellow men in general.' Triumphantly asked by many whether obedience to his teaching would not end the human race, he disconcertingly replied: 'And why should it continue?'

The title *The Postscript to the Kreutzer Sonata* released a jabber of malicious jokes. 'The real postscript to *The Kreutzer Sonata*, declared scoffers, 'is little Vanichka, the latest born child of the Tolstoys.' This was not in point of fact true, for the boy had been born before his father began to write *The Kreutzer Sonata*. But it could have been true; for that Vanichka might have had many younger brothers or sisters, there can be no question. Told of this jeer at 'The Great Christian who preaches celibacy', the hapless Sonya became more than ever afraid of starting yet another baby. To clear her reputation, she now took up her own pen and wrote *Whose Guilt Is It?* a story with precisely the same situation as *The Kreutzer Sonata*, but laying the blame, in that work shared by husband and wife, upon the husband, a brutal sensualist who at the age of thirty-four marries a girl of eighteen and frightens and disgusts her by his coarseness and violence. The purely platonic love of a young artist for the innocent young wife arouses the suspicions of the husband, and in a fit of passion he murders her.

Sonya read her self-exonerating story to anyone whose attention she could capture, and she wanted to publish it, but fortunately allowed herself to be dissuaded. Denied this outlet, self-pity gushed out.

> 'Everyone from the Czar downwards,' she wrote in her diary, 'feels sorry for me. But what's the good of quoting other people, when in my own heart I know that the story *was* aimed at myself? It has humiliated me in the eyes of the whole world, and has destroyed the last remnant of love between us, and all this despite the fact that in the whole of my married life I have never done anything wrong.'

It was not true that the 'last remnant of love' had been destroyed. Affection as well as passion still survived. Three months after writing that lament, Sonya, half pleased, half contemptuous, and further embittered, wrote:

'Leova is unusually kind, pleasant and cheerful. But all this, alas, is due to the old cause. If only those who swallow *The Kreutzer Sonata* with such veneration could for one moment see the life their teacher leads himself—and which alone makes him happy, they would hurl their tin god off the pedestal on which they have placed him. And yet I love him best when he is weak, kind, and normal in his habits. It may not be good to be an animal, but neither is it any good to preach principles you can't practise.'

In this characteristic jumble of resentment and leniency, self-deception, too, played its part. Sonya knew perfectly well that when Tolstoy enjoined complete chastity, he was preaching and striving after an ideal he fully recognized to be unattainable. On that point he had no self-delusions whatever. Again and again he declared this in print as well as in talk: 'The ideal of neither the material nor the spiritual life can be recognized by the earth-bound. The whole point is in the continual effort to approach the ideal. If the ideal were attainable, it would cease to be an ideal.' Elsewhere, more figuratively, he wrote: 'A man striving after Christ's ideal is like a man carrying a lantern on a long stick. The light will always be ahead of him, and yet it will shine in the dark and show him the right path.'

Sonya's more matter-of-fact mind could never really approve of her husband's preaching ideals he knew himself to be unable to put into practice. Nor had she much patience with asceticism carried to extreme. 'You do not smoke,' she had written shortly before the bursting of *The Kreutzer Sonata* bombshell, 'you work beyond your strength. Your brain is not sufficiently nourished. Hence the drowsiness and weakness. How stupid vegetarianism is! Kill life in yourself, kill all impulses of the flesh, all the needs. Why not kill yourself altogether? After all, you are committing yourself to slow death. What's the difference?' Above all she could not bear that sinister complete change in his outlook which was to make him describe beauty as coming, not from God, but from the devil.

At the beginning of 1891 Sonya decided to ask for an audience

with Alexander III. She wanted to try to persuade him to lift the
ban on *The Kreutzer Sonata*, so that it could be published in the
thirteenth volume, then under preparation, of her complete
edition of Tolstoy's works. People were surprised by this apparent
inconsistency. If she so much disliked the story and its implications, why agitate to procure its publication? Had her resentment
cooled? Did she urgently need the money the sale of the story
would bring in? Her motives were copiously mixed and her
diary reveals the disingenuousness of one: 'Surely people will
look at it in this light? If I had really thought the story had been
written about myself and my own married life I would not have
asked the Emperor to release it.'

In her letter to Alexander III she wrote:

'I have the audacity humbly to beg Your Imperial Majesty
to allow me to place before you my request on behalf of my
husband L. N. Tolstoy. Your Majesty's generous attention
will allow me to explain the circumstances which might help
my husband to return to his former literary work, and also to
show that certain allegations made against his present activities are so false and painful that they undermine the spirits and
energies of the Russian writer, whose health, as it is, is none
too good, but who perhaps could still work for the glory of
his country.
                    Your Imperial Majesty's humble servant
                                    Countess Leo Tolstoy.'

Granted an audience on the appointed morning, Sonya,
dressed in her best, a black gown and a black hat with a lace veil,
set out from her sister's house for the Palace. Her heart was thud-
ding with excitement. She had to wait downstairs for a long time
before a handsome gold-laced gentleman of the Court appeared.
After a few words he ran very fast up a steep flight of stairs, and
Sonya, supposing it necessary to keep close to him, ran so fast
herself that when with a low bow he left her in the ante-room
she found she was terribly giddy.

'I thought I should die,' she wrote with probably unin-
tentional humour, 'I was in a terrible state and the first thing
that occurred to me was that, after all, the whole affair was

not worth my life, and that when the Gentleman of the Court came back to fetch me, he would find me dead! At all events I would not be able to utter a single word. My heart beat so violently that I could neither breathe, speak, nor even cry for help. After resting for a while I wanted to ask for water, but couldn't move. Then I remembered that when a horse is overworked it is taken for a slow walk to recover. So I got up and began to pace slowly round the room. But for a long time it made no difference. I carefully loosened my stays and sat down again, rubbing my chest and wondering how my children would take the news of my death.'

Fortunately the Czar, who was giving another audience, was unable to receive Sonya for a quarter of an hour, so it may be hoped that before she was summoned she had had time to readjust her stay-laces as well as to recover her breath. When at last she was ushered into the Imperial Presence the Emperor received her most graciously. 'Tell me, Countess,' he asked, 'why you are making such persistent efforts to obtain permission to publish The Kreutzer Sonata? I should have thought that, aimed as the story is, against marriage, you would not have liked it. Indeed, as Tolstoy's wife, I would have expected you to find it most distasteful.'

'Your Majesty,' replied Sonya with quiet dignity, all her nervousness dispelled, 'I am asking permission to publish it not as Tolstoy's wife, but as his publisher, and to publish his works well means to publish them complete.'

Favourably impressed, the Emperor was delighted when Sonya told him that she had lately noticed a tendency in her husband to go back to writing literary works, and that she hoped and believed another great book like War and Peace was germinating in his mind.

'What a blessing that would be!' exclaimed the Czar. 'Such a wonderful, wonderful writer!'

Pursuing her advantage, Sonya now tried to explain (how, it is difficult to guess) that in reality The Kreutzer Sonata really upheld the institution of marriage. Puzzled, the Emperor suggested that perhaps the actual writing of the story might be a little modified. That, she assured him, was impossible. 'My husband can never alter anything in his books,' she maintained. (As a matter of fact, in her own publication, the story was very much toned down.)

This successful audience lasted nearly an hour, the upshot being that the Emperor agreed to lift the ban on *The Kreutzer Sonata* on condition that it was printed only in the thirteenth volume of the complete edition of Tolstoy's works, and not sold separately. This, he thought, would make the story too expensive for more than a few people to be able to buy it. Fervently grateful, Sonya exclaimed: 'Oh, your Majesty, if my husband does return to pure literature, I should be the happiest woman alive if I knew the final judgment on his works were to rest with Your Majesty's decision.'

'You can rest assured, Countess Tolstoy,' said the Czar, 'everything will be well looked after.' He then made many enquiries about Sonya's family, and arranged for her to be received by the Empress. He had made no allusion to the unanswered letter Tolstoy had written exhorting him in the name of Christian charity to pardon the assassinators of his father. Jubilant, Sonya sailed out of the palace, her wounded vanity soothed by the success of her mission—surely, she told herself, no inconsiderable tribute to her personal charms? Latterly her self-confidence had been seeping away. 'I seem,' she had written in her diary, 'to have lost that personal power over people which not so long ago I could strongly feel.'

For a woman approaching fifty Sonya gave herself ample exercise that day. 'The coach,' she wrote, 'took me back from the place to my sister's house, and I ran like wildfire up the four flights of stairs and told my family everything. They all shared my joy and congratulated me.'

But alas, the one person who mattered did not congratulate her. The author of the released book was not grateful. 'Her wheedling of the Emperor was most distasteful to me,' he jotted down in his diary. By this time all the commotion over the denounced book and the various absurd misconstructions put upon its meaning had turned him violently against his own work. 'There must have been something nasty in *The Kreutzer Sonata*,' he wrote to Chertkov. 'Every reminder of it has become revolting to me. For it to stir up so much evil there must have been something wrong in my motives for writing it.'

Sonya's success with the Emperor had an unfortunate sequel.

Not long afterwards Tolstoy published a renouncement of all
rights in everything he had written after 1881. (The earlier books,
it may be remembered, had already been made over to Sonya.)
The inevitable result was that, seizing their opportunity, various
publishers raced one another to rush out *The Kreutzer Sonata* in a
separate volume. For this Sonya was in no way to blame. On the
contrary, from every point of view, the financial included, she
was furious to see the bookshops piled high with pirated copies
of her husband's book. The Head of the Holy Synod Pobedonostov, who had been tutor to the Czar, lost no time in writing
to tell him that the immense sale of the book was doing untold
harm to students, young girls and the 'ignorant masses'.

> 'The Tolstoyan gospel,' he declared, 'with its repudiation
> of the Church and Holy Matrimony, and its socialistic doc-
> trines, is spreading an epidemic insanity, which, poisoning the
> minds of both the educated and the uneducated, is infecting
> the whole population with the most perverted notions on
> Faith, Government, and Society.'

Vexed by this apparent abuse of his sanction of the book's
publication, the harassed Emperor was disillusioned about the
guiltless Sonya. 'Well, if *that* woman has deceived me,' he sadly
exclaimed, 'I really don't know who I can trust!'

Other consequences of *The Kreutzer Sonata* were worse. It
had inflamed the relationship between husband and wife. Tolstoy
had turned so many somersaults since their marriage. But of them
all, to Sonya this, his latest, over holy matrimony, seemed the
most violent. How many readjustments had she been asked to
make since thirty years ago, 'a little girl in a yellow dress', she
had first come to Yasnaya Polyana! To comply with all, she would
have needed to be made of wax; whereas by now, her mind,
perhaps never very flexible, was becoming less so. Tolstoy's old
game, The Charge of the Numidian Cavalry, came into her head.
Was she all her life to be expected to play mental, moral, and
spiritual 'Follow My Leader'? She remembered her very first
letter to him in which she had expressed the hope that he would
always 'look on the world with the same eyes as now'. That wish
had assuredly not been granted.

Not only did this latest development blight the present, it

damaged the past. Still worse, it cast a dark shadow over the future. Since Tolstoy had openly declared his allegiance to the Pauline doctrine on sex, Sonya had become convinced that he had really always felt physical love to be degrading, and in yielding to it had succumbed to a temptation he only wished he could resist. Inevitably therefore, she argued, he must associate his wife with his falls into sin! This produced a revulsion on her part that made it difficult to respond to his still continuing passionate demands upon herself. Her old fear, originally implanted by his diary, that he had been only physically in love, revived to torment her. For many years she had lived in perpetual dread of childbirth, but had with occasional protests continued to run risks. And what was her reward as a submissive wife? Where was his gratitude? 'Man,' he was telling the whole world, 'survives earthquakes, epidemics, terrible illnesses, and every kind of spiritual suffering, but always the most poignant tragedy was, is, and ever will be, the tragedy of the bedroom.'

Because Yasnaya Polyana had at the time been overflowing with guests, by a curious irony it was in the very bedroom Sonya shared with Tolstoy that the first reading of *The Kreutzer Sonata* was given. A young actor was asked to read aloud the story. Embarrassed by its theme and the uninhibited way in which it was written, he had soon faltered, and before he would go on, the women had to be asked to leave. Silence followed the reading, as one by one listeners left the room to reassemble elsewhere to discuss what they had heard. Bathos ensued. Feverishly anxious to know whether or not his story had conveyed its, to him, vitally important meaning, Tolstoy was found by the embarrassed tutor listening outside the door!

14

Renouncement

The *Kreutzer Sonata* was far from being Sonya's only trouble in the early 1890s. Every variety of worry harassed her. Tolstoy was hating the thought of still possessing property, and hideously embarrassed too, for though he had made Sonya take over the control of his land and houses, he was still their legal owner, and for that accused of hypocrisy. Meanwhile Sonya was suffering from a sense of martyrdom at being the unthanked drudge of the whole family:

> 'It is always *I* who have to decide everything. I feel as though I had been caught in a trap and the task of running this *Christian* household is the greatest curse that God has sent me. If spiritual salvation consists in killing the life of your neighbour, then Leo is certainly saved.'

Sudden estate trouble plunged Tolstoy into shame and determined him legally to rid himself of his property. Certain peasants had got into the way of felling trees in a forest that belonged to him and carrying off the timber. After this pillaging had been going on for some time, Sonya decided that it must be stopped, and filed a complaint at Tula. The culprits were arrested, tried, and sentenced to six weeks' imprisonment. Sonya's wish to give them a salutary fright achieved, she, in ignorance of the law, immediately demanded their liberation. But this had been a criminal case, and once the Court had passed sentence it was not in the plaintiff's power to withdraw the charge. Tolstoy was appalled. Thanks to his accursed property, fellow men were now languishing in gaol. And at the instigation of his wife! It was not the peasants, no doubt desperately in need of fuel, who were 'thieves'. It was the owners of property. In self-defence Sonya told him that he had himself sanctioned her act by replying when asked what should be done: 'I think we ought to scare them and then forgive.' Frantic with anger and shame, Tolstoy rampaged round their room nearly all night, railing against Society and reproaching Sonya, according to whose diary his reproaches were 'terribly brutal'.

Early in 1891 Tolstoy decided finally to extricate himself from his anomalous position as a landowner, and after long confabulation and dispute his estates, divided into ten equal parts, were legally made over to Sonya and the then nine surviving children. As a Tolstoyan, Masha refused to accept her share, but Sonya, predicting that she would later change her mind, kept it in trust for her. The house and estate of Yasnaya Polyana went to Sonya and the youngest child Vanichka. All this business had fallen very heavily on Sonya. Annoyed one very hot day by Tolstoy's attempt to shirk facing the problems by making boots, her general discontent boiled over in her diary:

> 'I should like to see him in good health, but he is ruining his digestion (so the doctor says) with a lot of harmful food. I should love to see in him the artist, but he spends his time writing sermons. I should be happy if he were kind, or friendly, or sympathetic, but he is either sensual or coldly indifferent. . . . He worries me dreadfully, and always will with his restless moods and nature.'

By the early autumn the whole of Tolstoy's landed property had been transferred. From now on he lived as the guest of his family. But this transaction could not really ease his mind for he knew how many people considered it merely a farcical evasion that still left him wide open to the charge of hypocrisy. But what more could he do? His wife and family could not be left roofless. Yet something more, he determined, must be done. There was still all the income from his books. It was a long time now since he had declared in print that to write for money was prostitution, yet, astutely handled by Sonya, his works were regularly bringing in very large sums of money. True, he had made Sonya accept the copyrights in all his books written before 1881, and these included the immensely lucrative *War and Peace* and *Anna Karenina*. But as the profit on them paid for the upkeep of the houses in

which he lived, he none the less benefited by their sale. He now
decided to give up all profits from his books. Literary property
proved far more difficult to deal with than landed estate. His wish
was to renounce all copyright, so that anyone who chose could
publish his books without paying any royalty. Told of this decision, Sonya, horror-stricken, did her utmost to dissuade him.
The royalties on his books were, after all, the main source of the
family income. Apart from them, indeed, very little now came
in. No one had a greater respect for literary genius than Sonya,
but she did not in the least agree with Ruskin's dictum that
'genius must not be sold'. She has been harshly criticized for
opposing her husband's wishes in this matter. But how many wives
of 'best-sellers'—and, incidentally, Tolstoy was a best-seller—
would meekly acquiesce in their family's being reduced to
poverty? Like most mothers, she wanted to see her children
properly educated and not to have to lie awake worrying about
their futures. Her husband would get all the credit for the sacrifice, but she would still have to pay the bills! As for the 'simple
life' which he enjoined, he never gave her any practical advice as
to how it was to be achieved. To begin with, how without
money or staff was she to feed his ravenous rabble of Tolstoyans?
More important, where, and on what, were her children to live?
What were they to be taught, and by whom? To such questions
he gave no answer.

Nor were Sonya's motives entirely self-interested—if a
mother's concern for her children be self-interest. 'It is not,' she
rightly argued, 'the *poor* who would benefit by such a sacrifice.
It is the already rich publishers.' Herself a publisher, she knew
how detrimental to Tolstoy's work the proposed renouncement
would be. Liberty to scramble for the latest book by a world-
famous author would inevitably result in its being rushed out
without proper care for production. But deaf to all Sonya's
arguments and protests, Tolstoy, in July 1891, firmly declared
his determination to write a letter to the Press renouncing the
copyrights in everything he had written since 1881 and all that
he might write in the future. This brought on a violent quarrel
in which he called Sonya a greedy, stupid woman 'out for money'
with which morally to ruin his children. She retaliated by
accusing him of egotism and vainglory (he wanted—she alleged
—to be called 'a saint'), of trying to humiliate her on every

possible occasion, and of driving her crazy with his 'Dark People'.

'Leave me alone! Leave me alone!' shouted Tolstoy, his fingers to his ears. Taking him at his word, Sonya rushed sobbing into the garden, but, embarrassed at being seen in tears by the gardener, fled on to the orchard, where sitting on the wet grass by a ditch, she wrote in her notebook that she was going to the railway station to kill herself, her intention being, like Anna Karenina, to fling herself under the wheels of a train. But as, with so terrible a headache that she thought 'her head must burst', she was making her way to the station, she saw coming towards her a man in a peasant's blouse. For a moment she was overjoyed. She thought it was her repentant husband seeking her to make things up. But the approaching figure turned out to be her brother-in-law, Tanya's husband, Alexander Kuzminsky. Seeing how distraught she was, he firmly refused to leave her until at last he succeeded in persuading her to return with him to the house.

This crisis was inevitably followed by yet another reconciliation, once again sealed with the 'sham cement of kisses'. Unconvinced but defeated, Sonya told Tolstoy to have done with it—to publish his letter of renunciation to the Press and never, never again to mention the matter. He said he would not do this until he felt that she really understood that it *ought* to be done.

'I said,' wrote Sonya, 'that I could not tell a lie and that I could not understand why it ought to be done. This day has broken something within me, and I feel old and dejected.'

Not long afterwards Tolstoy sent Sonya, then in Moscow on publishing business, a statement of renunciation, and asked her to publish it in the newspapers: 'Please, darling,' he wrote, 'reflect well with God and do this for me with good feeling, and with the consciousness that for you yourself it is a happy thing, because by doing it you redeem from a grievous situation a man whom you love.'

Submitting to the inevitable, Sonya sent off the statement, but she was not, nor did she ever become, reconciled to her family's being thus deprived of a large income. She did, however, believe, and this was some consolation, that this public surrender of all profit from his writings must convince people of her husband's sincerity.

Had she not met her brother-in-law, might a genuine attempt have followed her declared intention to commit suicide? Perhaps more nearly so than on any previous occasion. Her diary for that excruciating day remembers how in youth she had often contemplated suicide, but had always felt that she could not really do such a thing. But this time, she wrote, she *would* have done it, had it not been for the accident of meeting her brother-in-law. Whatever her intention, she was evidently quite ready to be dissuaded.

Sonya's home life provided no tranquil background to the stresses over *The Kreutzer Sonata*, her husband's ethical convulsions, and his expensive ways of soothing his conscience. All the while she staggered under a load of other family cares: 'This chaos of worries, stumbling over each other, drives me to a state of complete bewilderment and I lose all my balance.' The married son, Ilya, was living beyond his means; Leo, sickly, nervous, unsettled, was the cause of continuous anxiety. Both ceaselessly plagued her with demands for money. Masha's perpetual state of indecision as to whether or not she should marry Tolstoy's disciple and future authorized biographer, P. I. Birukov, annoyed Sonya, who had decided her daughter's supposed love for this excellent man to be purely imaginary. Meanwhile, spiritually aflame, the tiresome girl was all day destroying herself with overwork, and in the evenings beautifully copying out her beloved father's writings. Now that Tolstoy's pen had deserted creative work for sermonizing, Sonya no longer cared to copy his manuscripts, but this did not prevent her from being jealous of her daughter's taking her place.

Still charming and with hordes of suitors, the cherished Tanya could find no man she really wanted to marry, and her life at home had become difficult. Devoted to both her parents, yet not like Masha, a whole-hearted Tolstoyan, she was torn between the two, for ever trying to find a solution to their conflict. She did fully realize her mother's difficulties, but thinking her father the most important, pleaded with her to make as many concessions as possible.

The eldest son, Sergei, always rather detached, tried to keep out of family disputes, and was therefore little help to his mother. The youngest boys, Andrev and Misha, were neither of them doing well at school; and all the while the precious Benjamin of the family, little Vanichka, now become the centre of Sonya's existence, was alarmingly delicate. Then there were the constant nagging worries of an over-driven domestic staff, estate management, publishing cares, the Dark Ones, and the steady encroachment of Chertkov. Nor was there any respite for Sonya as housewife and hostess. The house teemed with children, governesses, tutors, servants, and dogs. Every day at least fourteen people sat down to each meal at the long narrow table in the dining-room, which, otherwise sparsely furnished, surprisingly held two pianos and a chessboard. Neighbours, pilgrims, and beggars constantly called and a perpetual kaleidoscope of guests came to stay—the 'Dark' and the 'Bright' people—the children's friends, and various distinguished foreigners. The hostess planned picnics, riding, and walking parties, and in the evenings organized games, presided over singing, piano and guitar playing, readings aloud or general conversation. In the mornings, while Sonya battled with the squabbles of nurses and governesses, the sicknesses of children and the complexities of household accounts, Tolstoy, at that time writing *The Kingdom of God is Within You*, withdrew to work in the vaulted ground-floor room that was now his study. Its walls were so thick that nearly all sound was shut out and light filtered in only through two high narrow grated windows. Very little furniture: a large writing-table, worn chairs covered in black oilskin, a bookshelf, and that curious very hard and narrow leather couch on which Tolstoy and all his children had been born. Two portraits, one of Charles Dickens, the other of Schopenhauer, and in a recessed niche a bust of Tolstoy's favourite brother, Nicholas. A scythe and a saw were propped against a wall, and a basket of cobbling tools stood on the floor. When her husband was ensconced in this fastness, Sonya seldom ventured to disturb him. Artists, however, were allowed to paint or sculpt him as he wrote, and it was in this famous setting that Gay, Repin, Ginsburg, and others did their best portraits of him. Tolstoy did not like sitting, but seldom has anyone more often submitted to painters and sculptors. He was irritated by what he considered Repin's sentimental pictures of him tilling the soil or making shoes. 'Repin even took my boots off. That was going too far—I never go barefoot,' he jokingly complained. 'It was lucky he left me my trousers!'

While Tolstoy wrote and artists reverently depicted him,

Sonya, exhausted and wholly unable to find a Kingdom of Heaven 'within herself', toiled about the house feeling a mere unregarded Martha. Her once superb health was failing. Nor did she feel any better for being told she had now entered into the 'critical period of life', a phrase which from now on repeatedly occurs in her diary. Not surprisingly she wrote:

> 'I am losing my balance. I know that this is an easy enough excuse; but really there is nowadays no single moment in my life which is not taken up with the health and depression of my husband, the nursery, the education and illness of the children, the grown-up sons and daughters and all their troubles; servants and debts.'

Except for Tolstoy's excommunication, an ordeal yet to come, all the practical consequences of his 'spiritual rebirth' had by now fallen heavily upon Sonya's shoulders. She can scarcely be blamed for succumbing to the eighth deadly sin of self-pity. No one, she felt, realized the weight of her burden—the complexity of her problems. As the wife of a genius, she seemed to be allowed no existence in her own right. Whatever was put upon her in 'The Master's' service, Chertkov and his myrmidons expected her to accept as a privilege of which she was unworthy. Wife, mistress, housekeeper, sick nurse, watch-dog, she must also be a perpetual scapegoat; and all the time there seemed no hope of a truce in the unending conflict between those two halves of herself—the wife and the mother.

15

Famine

SHORTLY after the division of his property Tolstoy plunged into a wholly new kind of work that left him practically no time to write either sermons or fiction. Early in the summer of 1891 it had become clear that the famine impending in the central and south-eastern provinces of Russia threatened the lives of thousands of peasants. Tolstoy was at once approached. Would he come to the stricken area and help to organize the relief work? At first he refused point blank. Active intervention would be a breach of the principle of non-resistance even to evil, and in any case he disapproved of the 'pseudo goodness' of philanthropy, against which, to Sonya's irritation, he continually inveighed as 'the hypocritical pretence of the privileged minority to save the majority which it has itself deprived of everything'. But as the famine spread, as so often happened, Tolstoy's heart overcame his scruples. At the entreaty of his neighbour and great friend I. I. Rayevski, already at work in the province of Damosky, he set out with Masha to see the state of affairs for himself. He was horrified by what he found. Scores of peasants had already died. Those still able to stagger about swayed on their feet. There was no firewood, the only way to get any warmth was to burn the thatch off the roofs, and the sole procurable food was black bread made out of goose-foot. Whimpering children—skeletons with unnaturally swollen stomachs—tottered on matchstick legs. Horses lay dead in the fields. The overcrowding sickened Tolstoy. In one tiny filthy hovel he found huddled together for warmth a man, his wife, four children, their grandfather, a colt, a foal, and three sheep.

Shocked pity now took command of Tolstoy. Defying his own disapproval, he decided to spend the whole winter in the stricken area. Tanya was summoned to join him and Masha, and

the three of them hurled themselves into unceasing relief work
that was to continue for nearly two years. Very soon, except for
the four youngest children, every member of the Tolstoy family
was actively engaged in fighting the famine. Sergei and Ilya
organized food kitchens in the province of Tula and, abandoning
his studies at the university, young Leo rushed off to help in the
Samara district.

Tied to the small children, Sonya could not leave Moscow,
where Tolstoy had just promised to spend the winter with her.
She was dismayed to hear of his decision. Without her to look
after him and see that his everlasting faddy vegetables were
properly cleansed and sieved, what would happen to Leo's always
precarious digestion? Who would, as, unsuspected, she did, slip
meat-juice into his silly mushroom soup? Indeed, what decent
food would be available in such a plague-stricken wilderness?
And what kind of a life would this be for her young daughters!
Her fears were well-founded. Typhus, smallpox, and cholera
raged, and the general conditions were shocking. But again in
Sonya, as in Tolstoy, compassion prevailed over self-interest. 'I
am now entirely in sympathy with your new activities, Leo,' she
wrote.

Without any protest or fuss she at once agreed to Tolstoy's
appropriation of whatever money she could scrape together, and
this, in her favour let it be remembered, was just after he had
given away his copyrights. In this new seraphic mood, temporarily, she became almost a convert to Tolstoyism:

'As I sat down to dinner with the children today,' she
wrote, 'it struck me how egotistical, fat, and soporific the
existence of our bourgeois society is. No contact with the
people, no sympathy, no help for others! I could scarcely eat.
I became so haunted by those who are dying of hunger while
I and my children are morally perishing in this dead atmosphere.'

Sonya quickly found an invaluable part to play. She wrote a
masterly description of the conditions in the famine district, the
work her family was doing, and appealed for help. Sent to the
editor of *The Russian Gazette*, her letter was at once published,
reprinted in all the Russian newspapers and translated into the

European and American Press. Gifts of money, clothes, and provisions poured in, and very soon she was able regularly to send her husband large supplies of money, linen, and medicines. Thanks entirely to her enterprise, shiploads of grain arrived from America and large donations of money from the Society of Friends in England. With unfailing punctuality, she now coped with an immense correspondence as well as with the continual buying and despatch of provisions for the starving.

Before long the 'Thirteenth Apostle', as Tolstoy was now called, wrote from the tiny uncarpeted, uncurtained, and, save for an iron bedstead, unfurnished bedroom in which he now lived, to tell Sonya that he had organized thirty kitchens in which 1,500 people were being regularly fed. And this was only the beginning. Ultimately, he established 246 eating-houses for adults, and 124 for children, in which, twice daily, over 13,000 were fed. He set up feeding stations for the cattle too. And all the while, at the age of sixty-four, he worked with a fury of which no one else was capable. Every day from morning to night he travelled on horseback or in a rough cart from one village to another, organizing, superintending, inspiring, and himself doing an immense amount of physical work. To his great grief his friend, Rayevski, exhausted by overwork, died of influenza. Sorely missing his companion, he battled on alone month after month, and all this work was done with remarkable economy as well as efficiency. 'Tolstoy,' wrote Chekov, who was also fighting the famine, 'in these days he is not a man but a superman—a Jupiter!'

But poor 'Jupiter' was not pleased with himself. Far from being proud of saving thousands from starvation he still condemned his work as a 'weakness' of which he felt ashamed. Suffering indeed from a genuine sense of guilt, he wrote:

'There is so much about it that is all wrong. There is my wife's money and all the subscriptions. There is the relationship between those who feed and those who are fed. There is sin without end. Yet I CAN'T stay at home and write. I feel the necessity of *doing* something. . . . It is unsuitable for me to feed those by whom I myself am fed, but I've been dragged into it and I find myself distributing the vomit thrown up by the rich.'

Mercifully for the peasants, Tolstoy persisted in his evil ways. For nearly two years this novel kind of sinner continued to violate his conscience by self-indulgently intervening between Man and calamity, aided and abetted by misgovernment.

In the very little spare time Tolstoy had he was still writing *The Kingdom of God is Within You*. He was only occasionally able to return to Moscow for a few days to see Sonya, but early in 1891 she came out to the scene of his activities. Shocked by the dirt and disorder of his staff headquarters, she swept through the premises like a hurricane. Having put everything to rights, brought the accounts up to date and even found time to help the so-called tailor make coats for twenty-three village boys, she whirled back to her own nursery, leaving the workers gasping at her efficiency and preternatural energy.

In the second year of the famine political complications arose. To save Russia from being discredited in the eyes of Europe, the Imperial Government had at the very beginning of the trouble issued the declaration: 'There is no famine in Russia. There are certain localities which have suffered from failure of the crops.' Incredible as it may seem, the word 'famine' was banned from all the newspapers; the absurd euphemism 'failure of the crops' substituted. The Government grew increasingly uneasy about the limelight the various charity organizations had thrown on the calamity; and as Tolstoy was now an international figure, his activities were what most displeased them. Led by his arch-enemy, Pobedonostov, Procurator of The Holy Synod, the Church had long fulminated against Tolstoy's attacks on nearly every established institution. And now he was rousing the indignation of all Europe and incidentally making himself more popular than ever. But the authorities agreed that any open steps taken against him would only further gild his halo and draw still closer attention to the shocking conditions in Russia. They therefore put up with what they deplored. Before long another development inflamed the situation. Under cover of the necessary accounts of the money he had received, Tolstoy, thanks to whom the famine had become world front-page news, was now writing brilliant articles in which he aired some of his Christian Anarchical views. In Russia, needless to say, these articles were lopped into harmlessness by the censor; but translated into English by Dr. Dillon, they appeared in full in the *Daily*

Telegraph. According to a statement later made by Tolstoy, but denied by Dr. Dillon, a mistranslation of a phrase in one of these articles gave the erroneous impression that the Russian peasants were being incited by Tolstoy to rise against the conditions that had made such a famine possible. The *Moscow News* drew attention to this in tones of outraged patriotism. Such treason, they declared, was not to be tolerated. The Archpriest of Kharkov pronounced a public anathema upon Tolstoy and a storm broke out in St. Petersburg Government offices. What was to be done with Tolstoy? Try him? Arrest him without trial? Impossible! He was much too greatly loved in Russia, and far too famous a figure both in Europe and in America. Someone suggested that he should secretly be incarcerated in the Zuzdal monastery; an ecclesiastical Bastille, in whose appalling dungeons enemies, or supposed enemies, of the Russian Orthodox Church were imprisoned without trial; and it was decided that a proposal to this effect should be submitted to the Czar.

Meanwhile the air buzzed with sinister rumours, and Sonya became frantic with alarm. Blaming Tolstoy for this fresh trouble, she dashed off a letter to him: 'You will destroy us all with your rash articles! Where, indeed, is your love of peace and non-resistance? As the father of nine children you have absolutely no right to ruin them and me.'

Even Tanya, devoted daughter as she was, exclaimed that she was tired of being the daughter of a great man. 'Ah! and how weary I am of being the wife of a great man!' groaned her mother.

Fortunately the conspiracy to incarcerate Tolstoy reached the ears of Countess Alexandra Tolstoy ('Grannie'). No one had more influence at Court than this 'chivalrous Dame of the Order of St. Catherine', who, having educated the Czar's sister, had known him since his boyhood and was still a close friend. The Czar had recently given her an opening by asking her who she believed to be the most popular man in Russia. (She need not, he added, go through the farce of mentioning his own name.) 'Leo Tolstoy,' she had replied without a moment's hesitation. Knowing of her devotion to her cousin, the Czar had smiled indulgently and said: 'I think you are absolutely right.'

As soon as Countess Alexandra heard of the plot against her cousin, she asked for an interview with the Czar. He at once

came to see her. 'Sire,' she said, 'in a few days you will be asked
to sanction the confinement in a monastery of the greatest genius
and best-loved man in Russia.'

'Tolstoy?'

'You have guessed it, sire.'

'Does that mean he is plotting against my life?'

On this point it was easy to reassure the Czar, and when
shortly afterwards he was approached by the Minister for the
Interior, he said firmly: 'You are not to touch Tolstoy. I refuse
to make a martyr of him, and draw universal indignation upon
myself.'

Had it not been for Countess Alexandra's intervention Tolstoy
might well have been interned for life.

Sinful though he thought it, Tolstoy's famine work had a
wonderfully salutary effect on his relationship with Sonya. Bodily
separation healed their lacerated nerves, and a shared compelling
purpose united their minds and spirits. At the height of his
labours, the 'Thirteenth Apostle' wrote to Aylmer Maude: 'I have
not been so close to my wife for ten years and that is more important than anything else'; and, writing in a fit of loneliness to
beg him to come home, she exclaimed: 'What a misfortune at my
age (48) to love a man like you!'

'I know only two things,' her husband answered, 'that I love
you with all my soul, and that I long to see you and to calm you.'

But the summer of 1894, spent together at Yasnaya Polyana,
was for Sonya clouded by Chertkov, who with his wife had
taken a house for a short time in the nearby village of Dyomenka.
Tolstoy was delighted to have his 'spiritual twin' within such
easy reach, but Sonya was jealous of him and deeply oppressed
by the 'Dark Ones'. 'They are so repulsive to me,' she wrote to
her sister, 'that at times I want to use a pistol on them or feed
them arsenic. Pharisees, cheats, dissimulators with harmful
theories; nothing more!' Tolstoy, again finding family life un-
conducive to serving his God in the way he wished, characteristically wrote in his diary, which unfortunately Sonya still
read: 'If husband and wife cannot agree on a way of life, then it
is necessary that the one who thinks less should submit to the one
who thinks more. How happy I would be to submit to Sonya,
but this is really as impossible as for a goose to go back into its
own egg.'

On the top of family cares and disagreements, Sonya was now feeling very ill. Latterly she had suffered from what she called her 'periodic madness', an abnormal mental and physical disturbance that, she complained, afflicted her every autumn. This year she wrote to her sister:

> 'Day and night I feel as if a stone pressed on my breast and I simply have no strength. This evening I was alone (indeed Leovochka is now seldom with me; he is either sleeping, walking or visiting the Chertkovs in the evening) and I was filled with such anguish that I at once thought of you and wanted to cry out: "Tanya, Tanya!"

The year 1895 began with an absurd quarrel over a photograph which Chertkov had persuaded Tolstoy to have taken with himself and four other disciples. Detesting the idea of this photograph being published, Sonya got hold of the negative from the photographer, tried to cut out her husband's face with a diamond, and then destroyed the plate. Not unnaturally Chertkov was deeply offended, and the latent hostility between him and Sonya deepened. The 'Dark Ones' were at this time giving plenty of trouble. One of the most squalid of them, a creature covered with lice, fell in love with Tanya, and took to awakening the whole household at four o'clock in the morning to urge his suit. Fortunately this madman's courtship was brief, for he was removed to a lunatic asylum.

At this period Sonya's now very acrimonious diary repeatedly complains of how much Tolstoy's strivings after the 'simple life' are complicating her own. 'His vegetarianism means having to cook a double dinner which causes more expense and gives more work. His sermons on universal love have resulted in indifference to his own family and the intrusion of all kinds of rabble.' Yet her diary still occasionally breaks into happiness, tenderness, even what she calls 'stupid sentimentality'. 'My relations with Leo are fine and *passionate*'; and she tells how when she is ill he brings her 'two lovely apples', and she, to commemorate this gallantry, plants their pips.

A violent quarrel broke out over the publication of Tolstoy's story *Master and Man*, which he gave to Lyubov Gurevich, the editress of the *Northern Messenger*, to publish. Sonya badly wanted this story for the thirteenth volume of her edition of Tolstoy's work, and annoyed him by her feverish haste to get hold of a copy of the manuscript in time to publish it before it appeared in the magazine. Angry words flew backwards and forwards, and finally Tolstoy, enraged, ran up to his room, declaring that he would leave the house for ever. Seized by the absurd suspicion that he intended to leave her for the reputedly attractive editress, Sonya, in only her dressing-gown and slippers, rushed out into the street, deep in snow. Tolstoy dashed after her in his dressing-gown, and dragged her back to the house, but not to peace. Next day the quarrel broke out again. Once more Sonya left the house, apparently determined to freeze to death. This time Masha followed her and persuaded her to return. The result of these crazy escapades was a severe chill. Illness of either husband or wife invariably induced reconciliation. Tolstoy knelt beside Sonya's bed to ask for forgiveness and gave her *Master and Man*.

'I'm correcting the proof with joy in my heart,' wrote Sonya, 'and perceive with emotion the artistic greatness of the story. My eyes fill with tears of happiness over it.'

16

Vanichka

THE KREUTZER SONATA, the crisis over the copyrights, the long drag of the famine, and her own failing health had made the first years of the 1890s very painful for Sonya. All through this difficult time she had, however, had one great support and refuge—her passionate and reciprocated love for the baby of the family, little Vanichka. Like all but the wisest and rarest of women, Sonya was happiest and best in the early stage of motherhood when her duties were still clearly defined, her responsibility indisputable, her hopes undisappointed. As playfellow, teacher, and sick nurse, she was well equipped to preside over the daily destinies of small children. Like many worse and some better mothers, as they grew older she missed their first unquestioning dependence upon herself and quicksilver responsiveness. With the exception of her two younger daughters, Masha and Alexandra, both of whom she had avowedly loved less than the others, all her children had in their infancy enchanted her. But this last-born child seemed in his frail self to unite all the charms and virtues his older brothers and sisters had shared between them. But that was only one aspect. Other qualities, all his own, could not be defined. Some mysterious intuitive understanding made this radiant child not only the 'perfect plaything for an hour', but a friend to whom Sonya could talk as though he were mature, and in whose presence she could find relief from almost everything that perplexed or grieved her. More than that, he made her feel blessed among women—singled out as one upon whom a sacred trust had been laid, for to her eyes this little being had the look of one come on a mission to earth.

It is easy enough to idealize out of all semblance of reality children who die young. Many who, had they survived, would have dwindled into quite ordinary mortals are for ever mourned for what they might have become. But this son of two remarkable people struck everyone as being endowed with rare gifts of mind, heart, and spirit. 'The first time I ever saw him,' said the famous Russian scientist, Mechnikov, 'I knew that he would either die or become a greater genius than his father'; and many others wrote, not after but before, Vanichka's death, to tell his mother of the remarkable impression made upon them by her brilliant, ethereal, yet so determined-looking little son.

Sonya did not attempt to conceal her idolatry of Vanichka. When he was in the room she could never take her eyes off his face, nor refrain from rhapsodizing about him and shamelessly showing him off. But he was unspoilable, and her friends were never bored. Many remembered him at a party, beautifully dancing the mazurka. The tiny graceful figure, so light that it seemed to defy the law of gravity, flew round the room, his feet scarcely touching the polished floor until, correctly clicking heels, he dropped on one knee, and then rising on to the very tips of his toes, with a low bow gave his hand to his partner, the tallest girl at the party, and flushed and shining-eyed, proudly promenaded her round the room. His youngest sister, Sasha, remembered how, driving home after the party, his peaked little face waxwhite again, he curled up on his mother's lap and fell asleep in her arms.

Of all the Tolstoy children, Vanichka was in appearance, though much better-looking, the most like what his father had been at his age. The same pensive penetrating eyes and look of preternatural sensitivity. Everyone was struck by the resemblance; and one day while Sonya was combing Vanichka's long curly hair in front of the looking-glass, he turned his face up to her and gleefully said: 'Mummy, I feel I really *am* like Papa!'

Vanichka was as unmistakably his father's as his mother's favourite. The other children did not seem to resent this; not even Sasha who, less than four years older than he, might well have felt left out. A look of melting tenderness came into Tolstoy's face whenever his gaze fell on Vanichka, so young, so tiny, yet able to talk to him like a contemporary. There was foreboding, too, in the father's eyes. The child looked so fragile, and after any exertion or excitement (and what did not excite him!) his milk-white skin would become even more transparent, the dark half-circles under his eyes deeper, the blue vein on his high-domed forehead more prominent. Solemnly, seriously, the sixty-five-year-old man and the five-year-old child would debate every kind of question; and it was noticed that the son had either inherited or imbibed many of his father's opinions. For instance, when Sonya, walking with him in the garden, told him that some day the house, its grounds and everything that he could see from them would belong to him, his little face clouded over and, stamping his foot, he cried: 'No! Mama, don't say Yasnaya Polyana will be mine. Everything is everyoneses'!' And though he would obey his mother's wishes, he would have liked to refuse the meat with which, in the hope of strengthening him, she piled his plate. Surely it couldn't be right that animals should be killed to give him food?

Though Vanichka's intuitive wisdom made him seem much older than his years, he was not in the least unchildlike, but romped and joked as gaily as the most robust and ordinary boy. He could, however, never be happy if anyone about him was not, and if others were sad or worried he invariably knew. 'Are you ill, Mamma?' he asked, stroking her head, after she and his father had had a quarrel. 'You are not quite your real everyday self today.' Neither could he bear to see anyone angry. Why, he wondered, must people so often spoil things for themselves as well as for others? If his sister Sasha was scolded he burst into tears, and the evident fact that she was loved less than himself by their mother hurt him far more than it hurt her. 'And Sasha?' he would softly ask if a toy or a sweetmeat was offered to him and not to her.

Vanichka's gentle radiance and instinctive ethical sense gave him influence over others. In one of Sasha's two books about her father, she tells that whenever she did anything wrong it visibly gave her little brother so much pain that she always felt impelled hurriedly to put things right. Despite Vanichka's sympathy with his father's disapproval of private ownership, he was very fond of some of his childish belongings; yet he often wanted to make presents of them to those he loved. A few days before his death this impulse to give everything away became irresistible. Tying little labels to all his possessions, he wrote on them 'To Masha from Vanya', 'To our chef, Simon Nikolaevich, from Vanya', and so forth. He then took all his framed pictures down from the walls, asked for a hammer, and nailed them up in his favourite brother Misha's room.

For years Sonya paid the inevitable toll of obsessive maternal love—perpetual anxiety; rational enough, for Vanichka, often alarmingly ill with high temperatures, was a very delicate child. But her fears were superstitious too. Surely this sprite did not look like a boy upon whom shades of the prison house could ever close? 'He was so slender and bodiless,' she wrote, 'he was all soul; such a gentle sensitive being. He was made of the finest spiritual stuff—and he was *not* made for this world.' Her haunting dread breaks out in snatches in her diary: 'This tiny flicker of life in Vanichka.' 'He has suddenly become so thin and pale that it breaks my heart to see him.' 'Many times a day I feel his poor little cold hands and feet, and I am filled with anguish. When he eats so little I can't eat anything either.' She counted every ounce he swallowed; watched every breath he drew.

Sonya's suspense was not prolonged. Tragedy swooped. On the morning of a day just one month before his seventh birthday Vanichka did not feel well. Before evening his throat was sore and he was burning hot. The thermometer confirmed Sonya's fears, and the hastily summoned doctor diagnosed a pernicious form of scarlet fever. Even then the stricken child still thought of others and tried to soothe his terrified mother and weeping nurse.

'It isn't really anything, Mamma,' he hoarsely assured Sonya. 'It will turn out all right. Why are you crying, Nannie? Don't cry. . . .'

In less than thirty-six hours Vanichka was dead.

His sister never forgot the sudden deathly stillness that fell on the house, and then how it was rent by a woman's wild shrieks of despair. Later she remembered her mother dementedly tearing her hair, beating her head against the wall, and crying out: 'Why has he been taken from us? It can't be true! Tell me it isn't. Why don't you speak? He isn't really dead, is he?'

Grief drove Sonya very near to madness. At first she could scarcely even try to control herself. Yet she could not weep. Tears would not come.

'February 23rd, 1895. My Vanichka died in the night. My God! To think that *I* am still alive!'

After that brief entry it was more than two years before Sonya again wrote a single word in her diary. 'I stagger from room to room,' she wrote to her sister Tanya. '*Can* one live long in such anguish? Everything has gone out of me.'

Tolstoy's very different grief was scarcely less pitiful. He had long tried to persuade himself that love for any one particular human being was wrong. To mourn for the dead, he told himself, was sinful. But once again emotion overcame principle. Unable to restrain his sobs, he faltered out: 'And I had dreamed that Vanichka, alone of all my sons, would carry on my task after my death.' 'For the first time in my life I have lost heart,' he confessed. Other laments escaped his clenched lips and when, shaking and suddenly bowed, with his elder sons, he carried the little coffin to the grave, the tears streamed down his ravaged face. 'Why do children die?' he wrote to Countess Alexandra. 'Why did this particular child die who, sent like a harbinger to a world not yet ready to receive him, froze like a swallow coming too soon?'

It was not without credit to Sonya that, even in the first frenzy of her gief, she still had eyes to see, heart to feel for the father of her lost child. 'Leovochka has grown all bent,' she wrote to her sister. 'He wanders about with an infinitely sad look in his bright eyes, and it is clear that the last shining light of his old age has vanished. It is painful to look at him. Terrible! This sorrow has crushed him.' She described, too, the touching way in which, as they drove to the funeral, he had tried to comfort her with tender words. This, he reminded her, was the very road to Potroskoye along which, thirty-three years ago, he had so often journeyed to court her when he loved her so much that he had not dared tell her of his love. Sonya was deeply moved. She too remembered the romance of that far-off time, the magic thrill of her first visit to Yasnaya Polyana. But where, now, was the slender bright-eyed girl of whom he spoke—the 'little girl in the yellow dress', who had slithered down the haystack? She no longer existed. She too was dead—as dead as Vanichka.

For a long time after the coffin had been lowered the mother stood in a stupor by the open grave. Joyful cries brought her back to earth. Vanichka's Nannie was handing the village children cakes and sweets—a Russian custom at funerals. Sonya had remembered how Vanichka had loved to give the village children sweets and suddenly, to everyone's relief, for the first time since his death, she burst into tears.

4

With characteristic optimism Tolstoy soon began to console himself with the thought that Sonya was being uplifted by her grief.

'Motherhood,' he wrote, 'has kept her receptive to spiritual truth. I'm deeply impressed by the purity of her soul and by her humility. She is still seeking, and so sincerely that I am confident that she will find. She submits to the will of God, only praying Him to show her the way to live without the little being she so greatly loved.'

He was convinced that something very great was working in her soul.

For a time shared grief did seem to unite more closely than ever these 'two winged falcons in a snare'. 'I've never loved Sonya as I do now. Never before have we felt so near to one another,' he wrote to Countess Alexandra Tolstoy, and this was *not* written to be passed on to Sonya. All his life Tolstoy had treated his clever cousin as a kind of mother confessor. It would not have been possible for him to write her an untruth. For a time he did genuinely believe that sorrow had engendered in Sonya a spiritual awakening. 'Now that she is suffering so much,' he wrote to his translator and biographer, Aylmer Maude, 'I feel with every nerve of my body the truth of the words that a man and his wife are not two separate beings, but one.'

Meanwhile he devoted himself to Sonya's wellbeing. It was nearly thirty years since he had been out of Russia. Nor did he wish to go now, but thinking Yasnaya Polyana, where at every turn the mother must miss that beloved little figure, for the present too poignant, he considered taking her abroad for a complete change of scene. But he was told that if he left the country he would probably never be allowed to come back, so the plan had to be relinquished.

The preacher in Tolstoy still persevered, but as the months passed and Sonya remained sunk in grief, his hopes for her spiritual rebirth gradually waned. Every moment she missed her child too agonizingly to be conscious of anything but 'one burning sense of anguish—of hopeless grief'. Without the immediate delight of Vanichka's presence and all her hopes of what he was to become, the present was unbearable; the emptied future stretched bleakly ahead. Remorse troubled her too. 'What is so terrible,' she wrote, 'is that, though eight children still remain, I feel utterly alone in my grief, and though they are all very kind and loving to me, I cannot enter into their existence. Life seems to have come to an end.'

Her thoughts toiled back through the years to the deaths, so terrible at the time, of her other little boys, darling little Peter and Alyosha. They, too, had been adorable, but they had been just children; not preternatural beings. Her one comfort was in Leovochka's revived tenderness towards herself. Even more she valued his new understanding and consequent tolerance of her failure to share his doctrines. For the first time he even expressed respect for the intellectual integrity that had kept her independent.

'I understand everything now,' he wrote. 'I realize that you *could* not come to me, and for that reason you have had to remain alone. But you are not alone. I am with you. I love you just as you are, and shall love you to the very end as hard as it is possible to love.'

Grateful for this belated recognition of her right to think for herself, Sonya wrote to say how happy his letter had made her, and how fully she realized that not one of their quarrels had ever really mattered.

'The basis of our relationship,' she wrote, 'an inner feeling for one another, is still serious, strong and harmonious. We both know what is good, and we both love one another. Thank God for this. And the eyes of both of us are turned in the same direction—towards the exit door of life, and neither of us fears it.'

It began to look as though there was real hope for the future, and the chances were strengthened by Tolstoy's occasional enforced absences. These gave him opportunities to write to Sonya, and to the highest degree he possessed that unfair advantage of the literary artist, the power to put almost anything right with his pen. Wives of literary geniuses would be well advised to give themselves frequent spells of grass-widowhood. Tolstoy

often sneered at the 'sham cement of kisses'. Did he realize that
the true cement of his marriage was in his letters? About eight
months after Vanichka's death came one of Sonya's most precious possessions, Tolstoy's beautiful letter about his new feeling
for her. This, he said, was really too sacred to be spoken of, but
he knew that she would be glad to know of it, and that, once
expressed, it would not fade.

'Strange,' he wrote, 'is this new feeling now binding us
together. It is only occasionally that the clouds of our failure
to understand one another obscure the light. But I hope that
before nightfall these clouds will disperse, and that our sunset
will be quite clear and limpid.'

Sonya wept with joy. A shared sunset 'quite clear and limpid'? Might such happiness really still be theirs? But meanwhile
the long heavy hours of afternoon stretched in between. These
still had to be lived through. And where, now, was the realm of
her thirty-three years' reign? The nursery no longer existed.

17
Infatuation

Nor long after being made so happy by Tolstoy's letter, Sonya was bitterly hurt to read in his diary: 'Sonya is suffering as much as ever and is unable to rise to a religious level. The reason is that she has confused all her spiritual powers with her animal love for her children.' 'But why *animal* love?' demanded Sonya's diary.

A 'sunset quite clear and limpid'? The tranquillity of that prospect had receded into a remote future, for the great wave of tenderness felt by Tolstoy for Sonya after Vanichka's death had crested into a violent resurgence of physical passion.

'Read this when you are alone,' Tolstoy began a letter that ended, 'this is a man of sixty-nine who writes to a woman of fifty-three!' and at about the same date Sonya entered in her lately resumed diary for 1897: 'Leo is joyously happy and was madly passionate last night.'

For a would-be ascetic, craving tranquillity in which to draw nearer to God, to be 'mad with passion' was in itself a predicament; but soon an even worse fate befell Tolstoy. He became tormented by jealousy. Bereft of her best-loved child, ailing and bewildered, Sonya found distraction and solace in a platonic attachment to a man twelve years younger than herself. For the summer of 1898 the distinguished pianist and composer, S. I. Taneyev, had rented Kuzminsky House which that year Tanya and her family were not occupying. The tenant delighted the family with piano recitals, played duets with Tolstoy, gave his hostess lessons; and in the aching void left by her child's death, Sonya's love of music, stimulated by Taneyev's beautiful playing, became an unslakeable passion: 'I played the piano for hours and hours. It gave my soul a rest.' Her stiffened fingers endlessly practised scales or raptly pounded out whatever she had recently heard Taneyev play; and guests, whether or not musical, were cajoled into playing duets with their hostess, their combined efforts sounding more like conflict than collaboration. She attended nearly all the concerts Taneyev gave in Moscow, and as often as she could capture him, took him out for drives; for by a kind of transference he had become to her the personification of music, and she craved for his company as much as for his playing. Judging by descriptions of the amiable little musician, no little power of sublimation was needed to invest him with personal glamour. His plump body bulged in tight clothes; his eyes were slits, his snub nose red-tipped, his voice a tinny falsetto. 'My affection,' credibly stated Sonya's diary, 'was due not to his appearance, but to his wonderful musical genius. The noble earnest part of his music came from his soul.'

There being nothing culpable in Sonya's feelings, innocence made her careless of appearances; soon everyone, except the object of it, was amusedly aware of her infatuation.

It was a great pity that Tolstoy, who at first had greatly enjoyed Taneyev's music, could not smile indulgently at Sonya's innocent starry-eyed devotion to the man whom in her stricken state she confused with the art of which he was master. But, at first merely bored by the musician's too frequent visits, he soon became not only irritated but hurt and jealous. Again the fatal habit of reading Sonya's diary was probably to blame. Passages, written in depression and taken out of their context, could be most misleading; for instance, this one written years before she met Taneyev: 'Would it not be better to have memories of love —even of a sinful love—than this present vacuum of a spotless conscience?' Even had Sonya, which she certainly did not, felt any hankerings after 'sinful love', she would not have turned to Taneyev, who was notoriously indifferent to women. Naturally amiable and socially inclined, he may at first have seemed to respond to Sonya's craving for a sentimental friendship, but even on that plane it is probable that the encouragement he gave was meagre. Sonya's diary tells that whenever he played Mendelssohn's *Songs Without Words* (any song there may have been in Taneyev's heart was certainly without words) her 'heart turned right over'. As for the sixty or so letters she wrote to him, scarcely a line is more intimate than an invitation or an enquiry after his health. The most personal passage is: 'How vexatious that we don't see each other! Won't you come this evening instead of taking your walk? I shall be at home and alone. I shall be infinitely more gay with you than by myself.' Yet even so one-sided a relationship, their wholly uncompromising meetings, and her rapturous enjoyment of his music, had a perceptibly tonic effect on Sonya. Renewed zest for life brightened her eyes, made her walk with a springier step.

Few daughters care to see their mother reanimated by the real, or supposed, attentions of a stranger, and the slightest suggestion of archness is odious to them. The youngest of the family, the fourteen-year-old Sasha, instinctively resented her mother's manner to Taneyev and the delight she took in plying him, not only with caviare, but with bon-bons for which the child felt she herself could have found a better use. In fact she soon had a violent dislike for the kindly, inoffensive little man, who, beaming with good nature at sight of any child, loved to play battledore-and-shuttlecock with her, a game she too enjoyed at first, especially the way he would cackle with laughter at his own clumsiness. But soon everything about him began to exasperate her. One day Sonya recited to this captious daughter Tintchev's lines:

'O how in our declining days
We love more tenderly and sadly.'

Associating it with Taneyev, Sasha hated this rather mawkish poem, and was delighted to find her father agreed. 'A repulsive poem,' he declared, 'praising drivelling old-age love!' By this time he had become rabidly jealous, and his sense of propriety, always hypersensitive where his family was concerned—indifference to opinion being one of the lessons he could never teach himself—was offended by his wife's 'public pursuit of a well-known man'. On the other hand, Sonya, her conscience clear, had no objection whatever to being seen about with the famous musician. Precisely because there was no fire, there was smoke, and ribald gossip broke out over this enacted skit on *The Kreutzer Sonata*, now jubilantly declared to be prophetic as well as retrospective. What an irony that its author should find himself in the same plight as its hero—'betrayed by his wife for a musician!' Enraged by sniggers, Tolstoy cannot have been soothed by reading in Sonya's diary: 'Gossip doesn't worry me. I'm even proud to be connected in people's minds with such a wonderful, kind, moral, and talented man.' Put on the defensive, she was later to write:

'Taneyev has given me a rich joyful gift. He has opened the doors of music for me. His playing brought me back to a life I had left after Vanichka's death, and his meek and gentle presence is balm to my spirit. After seeing him I feel serene and happy. Yet they all believe I'm in love. How vulgar they are! I am too old—such words and thoughts no longer apply to me.'

Tolstoy's sufferings over what he called 'this degrading madness' were frequently bemoaned in his diary, though unusually guardedly, for he did not mention Taneyev's name: 'June 12th, 1897. Early morning. I can't sleep for anguish. . . . Here there are nothing but pastimes of all kinds and guzzling and senile flirtations and worse.' Only once did his hostility vent itself in open abuse of the musician by name: 'Taneyev disgusts me with his self-satisfied moral and (though it seems absurd to say this) aesthetic stolidity, and his position here as *coq de village*.'

Tolstoy's expressions of disgust were not confined to his diary. When Sonya left for Petersburg, ostensibly to visit her sister, but really, he felt sure, to attend a concert of Taneyev's, he broke out in a letter:

'It is terribly painful and humiliating to think that a complete outsider, an unnecessary person, rules our lives. . . . It is frightfully disgusting and shameful, and this is happening just at the end of our lives—a good life lived cleanly together—just at the time when we were coming closer and closer in spite of all that might have divided us, and now suddenly, instead of the natural good and happy conclusion of thirty-five years of life together, here's this vile abomination that leaves its horrid stamp on everything. You too are suffering because you love me, and you want to be good, but up to now you have been unable to be so, and I'm terribly sorry for you, for I love you with the best love of all—not of the flesh and not of the mind, but of the soul.'

'It is frightfully disgusting and shameful' was surely as hysterical an overstatement as any ever penned by Sonya, and how could she be expected not to smile over the claim that *his* love was 'not of the flesh'? Besides, was he not asking too much of her? Why should she give up her friendship? Recriminations continued; quarrels blazed, subsided, revived; and the tragicomedy reached its climax when at dinner one day Sonya casually announced that Taneyev was coming to stay. Tolstoy's smouldering wrath flared up, and there was a terrible scene. He declared that if ever Taneyev entered the house he would leave it and never return. When the visitor arrived, however, the host behaved studiously well, but Sonya's happiness in her new friendship was being destroyed by her husband's attitude. Though her conscience was clear, she began to suffer qualms about the effect on him of her affection for the 'unnecessary person'; for however unreasonable she might think Tolstoy, she could never help worrying about him: 'Sometimes Lev really frightens me with his thinness and his headaches—and oh, that jealousy! When I became friendly with Taneyev I thought it would be a good thing to have such a friend in one's old age, a gentle kind and talented man. And see what has happened!'

A new friendship mingled with music was, indeed, exactly what a psychiatrist would have prescribed for an ageing bereaved woman sorely in need of distraction and the renewing effect of seeing herself through a fresh pair of eyes.

'Taneyev left today,' she wrote, 'and Lev is happy and quiet, and I am contented too, because I have seen my friend. There is only one reason why Lev should demand that I should give up such a friend, and this is his own pain. It would give me such pain to give up my friendship in which there is nothing sinful but such calm joy. I couldn't cut him out of my life.'

Far from attempting any such sacrifice, she invited Taneyev to come again the very next month, but having done so felt terribly uneasy:

'July 3rd, 1897. He is coming tomorrow. I haven't told Lev yet. My God! Will he be jealous again? Wouldn't

Taneyev be astonished if he knew. Yet I can't help rejoicing
at the prospect of so much lovely music and some pleasant
conversation with such a cheerful, charming man.'

Sonya's defiance of his expressed wishes incensed Tolstoy all
the more because it aggravated his uncomfortable sense that,
having handed over his property, he was no longer the master of
the house. 'At dinner,' wrote Sonya on July 4th, 'Misha referred
to Taneyev's approaching arrival. Leo grimaced and exclaimed:
'*I* didn't know about that!' The next two hundred words of
Sonya's diary were omitted by its editor, her son Sergei, as 'un-
printable'. The following day she wrote: 'All my cares, all my
affections, all my patience at his coarse reproaches cannot calm
his anger at Taneyev's arrival.' Next day was no better. 'He was
irritable, most disagreeable. My gentle words had no effect whatsoever.' Here again several passages have been cut out. Indeed, long
deletions in the text of the diary have by this time become frequent.
Taneyev stayed a whole week, and for all Sonya's natural
delight in his company, his visit, detested as it was by Tolstoy,
proved a great strain. But the last day of what must have seemed
an interminable week went well.

'Leo suddenly grew quiet and friendly,' wrote the relieved
hostess. 'He went riding and cycling and has not been at all
angry with me. As if there were any reason why he should
be! What evil can there be in my friendship with such a kind,
pure, and talented man? What a pity Lev Nikolaevich's
jealousy should have spoilt our friendship.'

Innocent as were Sonya's feelings for Taneyev, it cannot be
denied that they were morbid. She was in a pathological condition, and in her dreams the child she had lost and the new
friend at whom she was clutching, fused, and appeared together.
One night she saw her dead son seated on the musician's knee; in
another both stood with their arms outstretched towards her.
Troubled, she began to wonder whether the spirit of Vanichka
disapproved of her hurting his father's feelings: 'Today Vanichka
seemed to be trying to turn me *away* from Taneyev. He must
have felt sorry for his father; but yet I know he can't blame me,
for it was he who sent me Taneyev.'

On July 8th of this painful year (1897) Tolstoy, nauseated by Sonya's infatuation, wrote her a letter in which he again declared his intention to leave home. But he did not give her this letter. Nor was it destroyed. He hid it inside the upholstery of one of the chairs in his study, and years later, hearing that the furniture was to be re-covered, extracted it from its hiding place and wrote on the envelope 'To be given to Sonya after my death.' After he died Sonya read two letters, one intended for her eyes only, which she tore into tiny shreds, the other, if she wished to publish it, for the world. In the second, which she did publish, Tolstoy reminded her that for years he had been tormented by the disparity between his life and his beliefs, but had realized that it was not possible for her to change her ways. Nor had he been able to leave her. Besides, so long as their children were still young he had not thought it right to deprive them of whatever influence he might still have. But, now, he had made up his mind to what he had long wanted to do:

'Hindus, when they neared their sixties, retired into the forest, and as every religious old man desires to dedicate the last years of his life to God and not to jokes, puns, gossip, and lawn tennis, so I, who am now entering upon my seventieth year, yearn with all the strength of my spirit for that tranquillity and solitude.'

This letter implored Sonya to let him go of her own free will, and neither to condemn, nor to seek for him. His leaving home did not, he assured her, mean he was dissatisfied with her. He knew that she could not, literally could not, see and feel as he did, and hence could not alter her life and make sacrifices for the sake of something in which she did not believe. He was not reproaching her, but on the contrary remembering with love and gratitude their thirty-five years of life together: 'I cannot blame you for not having followed me, and I thank you, and lovingly recall all that you have given. Goodbye, dear Sonya.'

Needless to say, Tolstoy did not retire like a Hindu. Instead, he stayed on at Yasnaya Polyana till nearly the end of the year. In August Sonya wrote: 'I shall soon go to Moscow and I'll hire a piano, and I hope Taneyev will come and play to me. The very thought gives me a new lease of life'; and when an illness of

Taneyev's postponed this expected treat, her scurrying pen wrote: 'Oh, what a terrible violent hopeless desire to hear that man play again! Will I *never* hear him?'

The next twist in this tragi-comedy, now rapidly degenerating into farce, was that, in her turn, Sonya became racked by jealousy. Tolstoy sent an article to Lyubov Gurevich, the woman editor of *The Northern Messenger* who in 1895 had aroused her jealousy, and this was taken as evidence that he was in love with that 'scheming half Jewess'! 'For a moment,' wrote Sonya, 'I wanted to take my life. I then played the piano for five hours, ate nothing all day, and slept in the parlour as sleep only those who sleep after great agitation. I dropped down like a stone.'

As a protest Sonya left Moscow the very day Tolstoy was expected there, but a telegram brought her back post-haste to the enjoyment of an highly emotional reconciliation: 'L.N. met me at the door with tears in his eyes. We threw ourselves into each other's arms.' So happy indeed did this reunion make her that deciding henceforth to devote herself entirely to her husband's happiness and peace of mind, she impulsively promised never again intentionally to see Taneyev. 'It was easy for me then to promise anything,' she wrote, 'for I so deeply and warmly loved Leovochka.'

An unlucky dip into Tolstoy's diary shattered this lucid interval. Sonya read of his gladness because for the first time she had 'admitted her guilt'. 'My God!' spluttered her pen. 'Help me to endure this! Again, to the eyes of posterity, Leo must make himself out to be the martyr and me the one who is to blame! But in *what* am I to blame?'

Unable, or no longer desirous to keep her hasty promise, she did not cease to see Taneyev 'intentionally', and frequently travelled all the way to Petersburg to hear him perform.

Tolstoy's diary of the early months of 1898 contain far fewer outbursts about his own feelings, but resentment of Sonya's behaviour is repeatedly betrayed by bitter attacks on her sex in general: 'Women do not use words to express their thoughts but to attain their ends. . . . When falling in love breaks out after marriage, it is out of place and disgusting. . . . Woman is the tool of the devil. She is generally stupid, but the devil lends her brains when she works for him.' These diatribes give a wholly misleading impression of Tolstoy's real opinion of women,

whom, both in conversation and in writing, he often declared
to be the 'better half of the human race'.

In April 1898 Tolstoy's departure to help fight another
famine brought about a domestic truce. But on his return, exhausted, fresh conflict broke out. To his disgust Sonya went off
to stay in a house where Tolstoy knew Taneyev was also to be a
guest. Tanya Kuzminsky was there too, and Sonya was bitterly
hurt when concern for Tolstoy's peace of mind made this dearly
loved sister criticize her continued pursuit of the musician.

A few days after Sonya's return she was subjected to one of
the most violent curtain lectures on record, the gist of which,
oddly enough, Tolstoy wrote down in a dialogue intended for
his sister-in-law Tanya, but never gave to her. The trouble began
when Sonya reproached him for discussing her and Taneyev with
her sister. Tolstoy begged her to change the subject. He did not
wish to talk of what he hoped would soon come to an end. How,
asked Sonya, could she help talking about it? It was not possible
to go on living in trembling suspense, and she was sure that if
Taneyev should happen to come again it would start all over
again. The phrase 'if he should happen to come', always used by
Sonya about Taneyev's prearranged visits, exasperated Tolstoy.
He told her that she must acknowledge her feeling for Taneyev
as a 'bad' one, and 'repent of it in her soul'. She indignantly protested that she had nothing whatever to repent of, and was not
soothed by Tolstoy's retort: 'The exceptional feeling of an old
married woman for a stranger *is* a bad feeling.'

'The old married woman' maintained that her great grief had
made her turn to music, but without any particular feeling for
the man who played it. Why tell an untruth? asked Tolstoy.
What, then, she demanded, was his conception of her feelings for
himself? How could she love him if she loved another? Tolstoy
insisted that she must recognize her feeling for Taneyev for what
it was. Only by recognizing an emotion or a habit to be wrong
could one ever free oneself from its hold.

Driven desperate, Sonya cried out: 'The same thing over and
over again! It's simply torture!' All she wanted, she assured him,
was that Taneyev should come about once a month and play to
her as he might to any mere acquaintance.

'Your words prove that you do have a very special feeling
for this man,' declared Tolstoy. 'There is, after all, no other man

whose occasional visits could give you joy. If a monthly visit is so enjoyable, how much more so would be a weekly or a daily one? You have involuntarily admitted your feeling for him. And until you recognize it to be a bad feeling, nothing can be altered.'

This futile argument went on until after prolonged shouting followed by exhausted silence, Tolstoy tardily 'remembered God' (his own words) and, beginning to reproach himself, ceased to reproach his sobbing wife.

'I prayed and thought to myself,' he later wrote, 'she can't renounce a *feeling*. With her, as with all women, feeling predominates, and any change that takes place in her emotions will be independent of her mind. Probably Tanya is right and this will gradually come about in a mysterious feminine way quite incomprehensible to me. . . . Full of pity and a desire to soothe her, I told her that probably I had made a mistake in my way of arguing.'

Too late! Sonya, worn out, ill, was no longer in any condition to be soothed. Laughing, sobbing, gasping for breath, she became violently hysterical. 'I held her,' wrote Tolstoy. 'I know that always helps. I kissed her brows. For a long time she could not get her breath. Then she began to yawn and to sigh and at last she fell asleep.'

Sonya described her own hysteria.

'At night the same jealousy talk began again. Shouting, abuse, and reproaches. My nerves simply could not stand it. Something that keeps the balance in my brain gave way and I lost self-control. I had a terrible attack of nerves. I trembled all over, sobbed, raved, and kept starting up in my fright. I don't really remember what happened to me, but I know it ended in a kind of numbness.'

Not long after this climax husband and wife enjoyed one of their happiest armistices; and once again Tolstoy's envisaged 'sunset quite clear and limpid' seemed a not impossible dream. For a few days spent alone together after a separation they were so happy that both wept at parting, and Sonya wrote: 'It is lovely that he cares about me so much, guards me so jealously, and is so afraid of losing me. But he need have no fear. Whomever I might love, there is no one else in the world I could even compare with my husband!'

'Guards me so jealously' betrays that, as might be supposed, Sonya would really have minded if Tolstoy had not been jealous of Taneyev. How gratifyingly jealous he had been it would be difficult to exaggerate. Sonya's diary tells that, in between the pages of a book, she came upon an unposted letter from him to herself; and upon the envelope he had written that he had resolved to kill himself because she loved another. Seeing the envelope in her hands Tolstoy snatched it from her and tore it to tatters.

Gradually the affair that had never really existed petered out. Not because Sonya could be brought to admit any sense of guilt or to consent to break off her friendship, but because Taneyev, who had probably heard of Tolstoy's resentment, became more and more elusive until she could no longer shut her eyes to the fact that he was deliberately avoiding her. For several years, however, Sonya, as the malicious put it, 'kept up the chase', attending innumerable concerts and going wherever there was hope of meeting the fleeing musician. But when in 1904 he deliberately left her box at a concert to go and sit in the gallery, it was impossible to ignore his wish to disentangle himself. In answer to her written enquiry as to why he had done this, he gave the preposterous explanation that he found her presence preoccupying and valued the Tchaikowsky music more. This chilling proof of his indifference destroyed whatever happiness the friendship had ever brought her.

Tender memories, however, survived, and when, after an interval of nine years Taneyev came back to stay at Yasnaya Polyana, Sonya's still critical daughter Sasha, now twenty-four, was again exasperated by her mother's heightened animation and the way her 'great eyes glowed'. Plumper than ever, and quite unconscious of the surrounding tension, Taneyev settled himself at the piano and began to play Sonya's old favourite, one of Mendelssohn's *Songs Without Words*. After the first few notes Sonya burst out sobbing; the musician sprang up from the piano and nervously walked up and down rubbing his hands together. No one knew which way to look.

At sixty-four Sonya's complexion was still fresh, and her eyes bright, but latterly her head had begun to shake and for the first time the hostile daughter, struck with sudden compassion, saw her mother as an old woman. Sonya repeatedly begged Taneyev to play the *Song Without Words* again, the tone of her voice implying that for him and herself that title was invested with some mysterious significance. Everyone present, most of all the musician, was hideously embarrassed, but throughout this painful visit the host treated Taneyev with frosted civility. Sonya's diary betrayed her revived susceptibility: 'The day of the heart's emotion. Oh that *Song Without Words!*' She was even inspired to write a short story called *The Song Without Words*, which she gave Tolstoy to read and was surprised as well as hurt because he did not like it.

Taneyev's return to Yasnaya Polyana was followed by at least one more meeting with Sonya. Two weeks later she wrote in her diary: 'This morning I was at Taneyev's. I gave him the album of photographs. We were both restrained and unnatural.' Restrained? Taneyev had never had anything to restrain, and Sonya was applying artificial respiration to what had never really come to life. Years later when the mirage had quite faded and she had disentangled from his glamorous music the rather arid personality of the man, she wrote:

'At one time I had only to meet Taneyev, hear his unimpassioned quiet voice and I grew calm. My condition was abnormal. It coincided with my critical period. Taneyev's personality had almost nothing to do with my feelings. Externally he was uninteresting, always equable, extremely secretive, and to the end a man wholly incomprehensible to me.'

Sonya was not the only member of the Tolstoy family to strike onlookers as being the victim of infatuation. Puck—'Lord what fools these mortals be!'—was as busy with his magic juice at Yasnaya as in any wood near Athens. He did not even spare the spiritual, usually clear-sighted eyes of Masha. In 1897 this saint-like creature, who dedicating herself to her father and his work had renounced her inheritance, fell headlong in love with the most incongruous being. Prince Nicholas Obolensky, a distant cousin of Tolstoy's, had come to lodge with the family in

Moscow while he was at the university. Handsome, graceful, innately lazy, this sybarite liked to get up just in time for the middle-day meal, and, shirking lectures, to lie in bed, a perpetual cigarette in one well-manicured hand, a novel in the other. He did, however, just manage to scrape through his examinations. No one could deny that he had a sweet disposition, and as he neither drank nor gambled, in Tolstoy's eyes he did at least possess negative virtues. But everyone would have expected Masha gently to dismiss him. Instead, she began to moon about the house with a rapt, entranced look; a shining light came into her wide grey eyes, a surreptitious, almost guilty, smile played about her lips; and before long, to the pain and bewilderment of the family, she announced her intention of marrying the young man. Tolstoy was stunned, but afraid that the devastating loss of his closest companion and irreplaceable helper might be affecting his judgment did not attempt to dissuade her. He did, however, write her a solemn letter warning her of inevitable money difficulties: 'Children,' he declared, 'spell need. . . . Do you intend to ask that your inheritance be given back to you? Does he mean to take a job, and if so, where?' He assured her, however, that should she decide to reclaim her inheritance it would not affect his opinion of her.

Apart from apparent incompatibility, there were practical difficulties in the way of this marriage. Not only did Prince Obolensky have no money, he seemed without either inclination or capacity to earn any. Shamefacedly, Masha was obliged to ask for her renounced share of the family inheritance. If her father was mute, her mother and her brothers were not, and the extrication of her former share of the property entailed financial loss to both Sonya and Sergei. As Masha had not for many years been either to confession or to communion, no one would perform the marriage ceremony. Prince Obolensky suggested bribing a priest. Deeply shocked, Tolstoy said that if Masha was willing to go through the ceremony of marriage in a church, and for the sake of it even to commit bribery, there could be no conceivable reason why she should not go to confession and communion. Weeping at her own apostasy, Masha performed both these rites, and then, with no one but closest relations present, in everyday clothes was drably married to her gentle princeling.

If Tolstoy was left with an intensified sense of spiritual

isolation, Sonya derived a certain cynical satisfaction from the fulfilment of her prediction that Masha would think better of renouncing her money and prove herself no more truly dedicated to the service of mankind than most other Tolstoyans. Moreover, though she greatly disapproved of the marriage, Masha's departure from the family nest was no great personal loss to herself. She had never found her very companionable. But soon she, in her turn, was writhing with parental misery over the engagement of her favourite daughter Tanya, for whose future she had always had such brilliant hopes, and who for years had been surrounded by attractive, eligible suitors, none of whom she could make up her mind to marry. This charming creature had fallen in love with M. S. Sukhotin, a friend of many years' standing, recently become a widower. Tanya, the peacekeeper of the family, was adored by both her parents, and they were horrified by her decision to marry a country squire with six children, described by Sasha as 'an elderly man with a rounded stomach'. To Sonya indeed it was a blow that all the charms of Taneyev and his music were powerless to alleviate.

Stricken to the heart by the news of his daughter's engagement, Tolstoy wrote her a heavy-father letter with a distinct and unpleasant *Kreutzer Sonata* flavour. It cannot have raised her spirits:

'I certainly cannot answer your letter as you would like me to. I understand that a debauched man saves himself by getting married. But it is difficult to understand why a pure girl should go *dans cette galère*. If I were a girl I would not get married for anything in the world. As for falling in love, knowing that it is not a beautiful, poetic, and lofty feeling, but a very bad and morbid one, I would not open the doors to it, but protect myself from it as carefully as we protect ourselves from far less dangerous diseases, such as diphtheria, scarlet fever, typhus. It now seems to you that without this love there is no life for you. Men addicted to drugs have the same feeling, and yet they find real life only when they conquer their addictions.'

Much as Tanya hated to hurt her parents, both of whom she dearly loved, she could not to please them conquer her 'addiction', and on a bleak November day in 1898 she married her 'squire with the rounded stomach'. 'You can't imagine,' wrote Sonya to her sister, 'how sick at heart Leovochka and I were. It was all so gloomy, more like a funeral than a wedding. When Tanya went to say goodbye to Leovochka he wept so much that I couldn't bear to see him.'

A few days later the bereaved father wrote in his diary: 'Tanya has departed with Sukhotin, and *why?* It is sad and offensive. For seventy years I've been lowering and lowering my opinion of women and still it has to be lowered more.'

Time was soon to show that the unwelcome son-in-law had many recommendations. Endowed with good spirits, he was witty and kind, and all the family, particularly Tolstoy who loved playing chess with him, became very fond of him. Nor did marriage in any way sever Tanya from her family. She frequently came back on long visits and her parents stayed with her in her new home. But on the bleak November day of her departure Sonya felt terribly bereft. Of all her thirteen children, only two were now living at home: Misha aged eighteen and Sasha aged fourteen; and though usually the house was only too full of guests, it seemed to have gone cold. No wonder she craved for music and its plump little exponent. She desperately missed her other sons and daughters, or perhaps more truly missed the children they had once been with their as yet unchallenged promise.

Her first-born, Sergei, had married a very pretty, attractive girl. Sonya had been delighted with her daughter-in-law and everything seemed to promise well. But this flash of family happiness was brief. Within a year Manya, no one knew why, left her husband. Endless gossip and speculation arose, but Sergei gave no explanation. More aloof than ever, he withdrew even further into his reserved self and, living alone in his deserted home, composed music and poured out his feelings to his piano. Ilya, who had married in 1888, lived near Yasnaya Polyana, and absorbed in his own family troubles and chronically financially embarrassed, was a source of endless worry to Sonya. His children were continually ill, and soon one of them died of tuberculosis. Leo, the son who adored Sonya, long an acute anxiety because of an undiagnosed nervous illness, had married the daughter of the famous physician under whose care he had lived in Switzerland. Except for the death of their child this proved a happy marriage. But relieved as Sonya was to see him settled, she missed his loving presence and way of making her think better of herself. Andrey, a poor scholar and very extravagant, at the time of Tanya's wedding away serving in the army, made a marriage which seemed in every way desirable, and for some time his wife's influence over him was admirable; but before long he fell in love with another woman and to the horror and shame of both his parents, deserted his wife and their two children.

Like many mothers, Sonya found that she had lost the company of her children without any compensating reduction in worry and expense. None of the anxieties of motherhood seemed to cease with their marriage. On the contrary, she was endlessly troubled by their demands for money and by the illnesses of their children. Life was still a perpetual crisis in which she could never, so to speak, go out of office. The only son and daughter now under her wing—'difficult Misha and naughty Sasha', were both troublesome. Misha was very clever, but idleness, irresponsibility, and precocious dissipation made him a problem. He had, however, charm and glamour for his mother. She was proud of his brilliant violin-playing, singing of gipsy songs, and spectacular figure-skating. Above all, she could never forget that he had been little Vanichka's favourite brother.

Sasha, clever, stubborn, aloof, disobedient, and rude to her mother, was on her own report 'a source of tribulation'. Perhaps she had never been quite forgiven for her unwelcome birth, or for surviving instead of Vanichka. Sonya's diary is full of petulant outbursts against the daughter 'whom God has sent me as a curse. . . . She has never, never brought me anything but annoyance, pity, and unhappiness. There never has been a governess who could manage her'. Sonya had nevertheless to admit that Sasha was clever: 'I like to work with her though her temper (except when she is with me) is unbearable. She even hits her governess and anyone at all.'

No doubt, too, Sonya was uncomfortably aware of Sasha's sulky resentment of 'that sack with sounds', as was the family's irreverent way of referring to Taneyev. All Sasha's love and admiration flowed out to her father, whose principles she seemed instinctively to imbibe long before he imparted them. Hoping her youngest daughter would not break away from the fold, Sonya made a very special effort to bring her up in the orthodox faith; but, at fifteen, Sasha decided she did not wish to go to church any more and one Sunday told her mother so. Assuming this to be the result of paternal influence, Sonya, in tears, rushed to remonstrate with her husband. It turned out, however, that he had never spoken of such matters to Sasha. On the contrary, he at once sent for her and, 'scrutinizing her with his grey, deep, all-understanding eyes', asked: 'Why are you grieving your mother? Before abandoning the accepted, people should be very sure that they have something to replace it. Have you?'

'I don't know,' mumbled Sasha.

'Then why hurt your mother's feelings by refusing to go to church with her?'

Abashed, Sasha hurried off to change her clothes and accompanied her mother to church.

18

'Resurrection'

FAMILY affairs were by no means the Tolstoys' only troubles
in the later half of the 'nineties. In 1895 the fate of the
Dukhobors, an old peasant sect of Christian Communists
exiled to Siberia about a hundred years ago and then resettled
in the Caucasus, became a pressing problem. Their doctrines had
much in common with Tolstoy's teaching. They preached
chastity, teetotalism, vegetarianism, the sharing of everything in
common and, above all, non-resistance even to evil, by force.
Their consequent refusal to serve in the army was bound to in-
volve them in trouble with the Government, become more reactionary since the recent accession of the ill-fated Nicholas II,
an event which had been inauspiciously celebrated by a mis-
managed feast of beer and buns where thousands of the 'children'
of the new 'Father of the Russians' were trampled to death. Whatever hopes of progress had been entertained were shattered by
the new Czar's proclamation, described by Tolstoy as 'indecent':
'I, devoting my whole strength to the national welfare, will
maintain the principle of autocracy as firmly and infallibly as it
was maintained by my late, never-to-be-forgotten father.'
  The people's growing desire for a constitution was declared
to be a senseless dream, and Tolstoy's old enemy, Pobedonostov,
became more powerful than ever. The hapless Dukhobors lost
no time in challenging the Government. They pledged themselves never to serve in the army nor to pay taxes, and, solemnly
chanting psalms, deliberately burned all their weapons. For this
act of public defiance they were attacked by Cossacks and fero-
ciously flogged—some to death. Their leaders were imprisoned
and the systematic persecution that followed was so brutal that
Tolstoy felt compelled to write an introduction to *Give Help!*
an appeal published by Chertkov. In February 1886 the police
raided Chertkov's house and confiscated all the documents he

had collected about the persecution of the Dukhobors, thus destroying all the evidence against Pobedonostov. Tolstoy's great friend, Birukov, and various other Tolstoyans were now banished to small towns in the Baltic, but Chertkov, not yet having lost all influence at Court, was given the choice between accompanying them or going abroad. Deciding to go to England, he was seen off at the station by a vast crowd, headed by Tolstoy, who was not only very sad at the loss of his chief disciple, but miserably embarrassed by his own immunity. It had been agony for him to learn that many Dukhobors had been put in prison merely for reading or distributing his banned books.

Despite Sonya's dislike of Chertkov, she was creditably indignant at his banishment: 'I've wept a great deal,' she wrote to a friend, 'for I believe those who have been exiled to be the best and truest of our friends, and it is very painful for us to be separated from them.'

Tolstoy now launched himself on to a truceless campaign against the Government, giving the plight of the Dukhobors the utmost publicity, and ceaselessly appealing for money to help them to some place of refuge. For some time his family were infected by his zeal, but they thought he was going too far when, in an article translated into Swedish, he declared that the Dukhobors ought to be awarded the Nobel Peace Prize which, rumour had it, was to be offered to himself. For all Sonya's sympathy with the persecuted, the violence of his denunciations of the Government made her frenzied with fear. He would be responsible, she warned him, for her and their children being deported. 'For God's sake, dear Sonya, be reasonable,' he abjured her in a letter. 'Drive away your groundless fears or, if you can't do that, at least endure them calmly so as not to endanger the relationship so dear to both of us because we love each other.'

For years Tolstoy was to keep Sonya on a rack of tension by continuing to wage his hand-to-hand war with the Government until, at last, not only Russian Society, but the entire European Press, were roused to such indignation that the Government gave way, and more than 4,000 Dukhobors were allowed to emigrate and accept the asylum and hospitality offered them by Canada.

Sonya's nerves, later to improve, were at this time in a very bad way, as is shown by her current diary, which, sadly different, is much less subtle than her early one. Grief tends to deteriorate into grievance. Her former only occasional resentment against her husband is much more sustained, indeed almost chronic, and the once intermittent bad weather of her moods is more or less 'settled'. But as she is still consciously, almost deliberately, using her diary as a safety-valve, the impression it gives is probably far worse than the reality. A significant change is that whereas in youth, when things went wrong, she usually blamed her own shortcomings, which she pointed out with a charming candour as well as insight, in later life she nearly always blamed others. There are, however, occasional outbursts of self-reproach: 'If only I could choke the volcano of my uncontrollable nature!'

A recurrent complaint, one made by the wives of many authors, is of the disappointing discrepancy between the writer and the man: 'What a wonderful understanding there is in his books and what extraordinary lack of understanding in his home life! . . . He has never taken the trouble to understand me and does not know me at all.'

Tolstoy's undeniable occasional want of perception probably first struck her when, just after their wedding, he resented her grief at leaving her mother, and for nearly fifty years it was to go on surprising and wounding her: 'If only he had a fragment of that deep psychological understanding which is shown in his books, he must have understood the depth of my pain.' . . . 'He neither knows nor understands me, nor his children, nor any of his friends.' The inconsistency of Sonya's diary is as striking in age as in youth. So many entries flatly contradict others. After repeatedly railing against his neglect of herself and her family—'my children have no father'—she suddenly rejoices in his 'constant care and affection', and declares that 'no matter where he is or what he is doing', he always comes to look for her and she always rejoices to see him. 'I could hardly live without his constant sympathy.' She is shortly bewailing the fact that he has never once allowed her a rest, or given a sick child a drink of water, or spent five minutes by its bedside to give her a chance to go out for a breath of air. 'How very little kindness his family gets from him! And his biographers will tell how he helped the labourers to carry buckets of water!' Complaints of not being needed alternate with complaints of being a drudge: 'A woman likes nothing more than to feel her help and her company are necessary to the man she loves.' . . . 'In the past I had a busy, interesting time with the children, but to be a *slave*, and a slave whom Lev Nikolaevich does not even love! (does he love anybody?)' 'A wonderful moonlight night. It's just my luck that, instead of enjoying a walk, I've got to mess about with poultices and enemas.'

The old dissatisfaction, still gnawing at her heart—the belief that he needs her only physically, or as a household drudge and sick nurse—finds increasingly bitter expression: 'I am a source of satisfaction to him, a nurse, a piece of furniture, a *woman*—nothing more.' This note is struck again and again: 'He has lived with me only with his body, and his love has been only physical love. This side of life is dying and with it the need of being together.' . . . 'I've had both a passionate lover and a stern judge in my husband, but I've never had a friend in him.' . . . 'The time will come when he will no longer be amorous, and then he will cast me out of his life cynically, coldly, and cruelly.'

Craving, as she ages, more and more for affection, she laments that, longing for a poetic, spiritual, even a sentimental relationship—anything to have a rest from this 'eternal sex'—she gets only 'that mad jealous passion'.

Reading Tolstoy's diary deepened her depression: 'There is no love. There is only the craving for intercourse, and the need of a life companion.'

Many of Sonya's charges against Tolstoy are utterly preposterous; for instance: 'The sole cause of his activity is ambition, his feverish, insatiable, boundless ambition.' That, and that only, she declares, is what he has worked for all his life. But for all her diatribes, love for her Leova keeps on breaking through. Like many women far wiser, she tended to spoil the present by comparing it with the past: 'There was a time when he loved me so much that I saw in him my whole world and looked for *him* in every child we had.' But her delight in him still bubbles up: 'It is always such a joy to see him, especially unexpectedly.' . . . 'I love his eyes, his smile, his talk, and his continual desire for self-perfection.' And, for ever crouching in her heart, ready to spring out, was the terror of losing him: 'Everything seemed so unimportant compared to the fear that he might catch a chill, fall ill, and die!'

Tolstoy was not the only one to hurt her in these years. Her sons, too, were tearing her disappointed heart: 1897. 'Everything wears out, even the passionate love for one's own family. I don't want to make myself suffer any more by watching their faults, mistakes, and useless lives. I prefer strangers. I'm weary of family relationships. . . . No, I can't bear the weight of bringing up a lot of weaklings and wastrels!' 'My God! Surely my dealings with my elder sons are not to come down to money, and nothing but money!' Disappointment in her own family, realization of the so often misleading promise of children, made her at first chary of giving her heart to another generation to wound: 'My daughter-in-law arrived with her children. I was glad to see them, but, alas! *they* will never fill my life. The love of my own children is running dry—and children are no longer of the same importance to me.' At one time she declared her intention of writing *The History of a Mother*. Wry reading this book would have made.

The one child who scarcely ever disappointed Sonya was Tanya, in whose heart, she said, she could always find an echo of her own. And, indeed, no one seems better than this daughter, also a diarist, to have understood the difficulties of her parents' married life, and their, none the less, abiding love for one another. 'What a strange combination are these two!' she wrote in 1897. 'It would be difficult to find two people so different, and yet at the same time so deeply attached to one another.' Her love for her mother did not blind her to faults and idiosyncrasies, but they were noted with tender amusement: 'Mamma is in a good mood, as always when she has something to worry about', and 'I can forgive her naïve adoration of Taneyev.'

Sonya was again working hard, copying out Tolstoy's increasingly illegible writings, and her lamentations make a sad contrast to her former delight in this work. She wearies at having *ten* times to copy out a 'mere article'. It gives her, she complains, none of the sense of achievement that had thrilled her when, finding some fresh beauty on every page, she had deciphered *War and Peace*. She was now much too tired for the terrible toil. 'Have been copying L. N.'s MS. till 3 a.m.' is a frequent entry. There were, she wrote, moments when it made her feel like 'weeping, laughing, or screaming from sheer exhaustion'. Again and again she would find all she had written scratched out and minute writing, impossible to read, or put into sequence, scrabbled all over the pages, without any punctuation whatever, and with countless cross-references and footnotes. No wonder her eyesight failed.

Sonya's grievance, or, to do her justice, her genuine grief that Tolstoy now wrote only articles, was temporarily removed. The hapless Dukhobors did at least serve one good purpose. But for the incentive of their need Tolstoy might never have finished his last great novel, Resurrection. This book, begun in 1895, had, to Sonya's chagrin, been worked on only in a very desultory fashion. Two years after starting it, Tolstoy had complained: 'This is all untrue, inventive, weak. It is very hard to put a spoiled thing right.' The desperate financial needs of the Dukhobors now spurred him on to finish the book, in order, by selling it on the highest possible terms to English and American newspapers, to provide funds for their migration. His old dictum that to write for money was prostitution was now glibly quoted against him, the more pedantic of his followers maintaining that even to take money to transmit to others was a 'betrayal of principle'.

In theory Tolstoy agreed with his accusers, but again, as at the time of his famine work, he felt compelled to 'sin':

'What to do when you know there are children, old men, weak, pregnant and nursing women who suffer from want, and you can help them by word and deed, if you will do it? . . . To agree is to find oneself in conflict with one's own convictions. Not to agree means refusing help which can immediately relieve actual sufferings. Through weakness of character I always choose the second path, and that always tortures me.'

Many had occasion to bless Tolstoy's 'weakness of character'.

Once Tolstoy had decided to finish the book he was, he told Sonya, more gripped by the creative urge than he had ever been since writing War and Peace. 'As a bombshell falls to the ground with ever-increasing speed, so it is with me now I near the end. I can't think of anything—no I can't—I can't, and I even believe I don't want to think of anything else!' At the end of 1899, at the age of seventy-one, with a final spurt of energy he finished the book.

Wife, daughters, friends—all were enlisted to copy the manuscript and correct the proofs. The labour was immense. Once again Sonya strained her eyes and overtaxed her nervous system, but she did not work with her old joy. She recognized the excellence of Tolstoy's last great self-portrait, Nekhludov, and appreciated the poetry of much of the writing, especially in the early scenes, but she found the central theme too strenuously didactic. Surely the whole book was really a slenderly disguised tract? (While writing it Tolstoy had himself complained that he was sacrificing the aesthetic side of his novel to the moral theme.) Nor did Katerina Maslov, the innocent girl turned prostitute, seem to Sonya a fully realized character. In the portrayal of this almost entirely fictitious character she felt that Leo had worked without a living model, and she knew his genius lay, not in invention, but in the transmutation of actual persons. She found the indeterminate end of the book unsatisfactory too. Furthermore, was not the whole theme and trend of the book a renewed attack on her own way of life?

Sonya's reactions to *Resurrection* were no doubt affected by her indignation over its disposal, which caused a violent flare-up of the chronic copyright dispute. Her first zeal for the Dukhobors had long since cooled: 'What were they, after all, but headstrong revolutionists, who by refusing to serve in the army obliged others to take their place?' Not one penny of the royalties on *Resurrection*, which, at first boycotted both by Mudie's Library and W. H. Smith's bookstalls, had a larger sale in England than any other of Tolstoy's works, went into the family exchequer. Tolstoy would accept payment only for the newspaper rights. Not even for the Dukhobors would he take money for the novel in book form.

The profits on Sonya's own publishing business, which provided the bulk of the family income, came from the books written before 1881. The copyright in the later ones having long since been renounced, she had, in their case, no legal priority, but having first access to them did give her a valuable start over other publishers. And now, without even consulting her, Leo had sold the serial rights of this eagerly awaited full-length novel, from which, had she been able to bring it out as a book, she would have reaped a small fortune. In answer to her protests, Tolstoy for the thousandth time expressed his grief that he and she could not completely agree. Self-pity and self-justification spurted out in her diary:

'I wore myself out over this new disharmony, but the whole of L.N.'s life has been given over to people and aims alien to myself, while all my life has been given to my family. Neither my heart nor my head can accept the fact that, after printing in all the newspapers his renouncement of all his author's rights, he now finds it necessary to sell this novel for an enormous price and give the money, not to his own poverty-stricken children and grandchildren, but to the Dukhobors.'

Tolstoy had to admit that before long the Dukhobors afforded Sonya ample scope to say 'I told you so'. In so far as they would not go to war, their principle of non-resistance to evil stood admirably firm, but shedding their other ideals they abandoned vegetarianism, took to alcohol, and to smoking, and gave the Canadian Government endless trouble. Organizing public demonstrations, some of them practised nudism in the streets, refused to send their children to be educated, and even burned down schools. In time, infected by Soviet propaganda, they clamoured to go back to Russia, where, they claimed, freedom was at last to be found.

In the last year or so of the 1890s Sonya's diary reflects a marked improvement in her relationship with Tolstoy. There are far fewer outbursts against him. Writing of the 'spiritual tenderness' she feels for him, she in one entry complains that '*he* is affectionate only when tenderness awakes in him'; and then, alas, it is not the 'same kind of tenderness' as hers. Nevertheless, there is not nearly as much misgiving about the nature of the love he feels for her. Growing old together, they seem now tacitly agreeing to respect one another's differences of opinion. Various family troubles held them in sympathy; the death of a grandchild, the shortcomings of Andrey and Michael, and—most painful of all—the tragic succession of Tanya's and Masha's stillborn babies. Not until 1905 did Tanya bring into the world one that lived—a daughter called Tanichka, and Masha was to die childless.

From morning to night Sonya worried over Tolstoy's physical condition—what he wore, what he ate; and he, now growing anxious about her health, urged her not to do so much and to be careful of her failing eyesight. On their wedding anniversary in 1900, Sonya wrote from Moscow to Tolstoy at Yasnaya:

> 'I've just got up and the first thing I want to do is to write to you, dear Leovochka, and to remember the day that united us. I felt sad that we are not together, but then I turned my heart to you and to the infinitely deeper tenderness and better memories of our life, and then I wanted to thank you for the happiness you gave me, and to regret that it could not continue so strongly, calmly, and fully throughout our whole life.'

She intended, she told him, to sit for a few moments in the church where they had been married thirty-eight years ago.

The year 1901 began excruciatingly for Sonya. Tolstoy was excommunicated. The sudden decision of the Holy Synod to excommunicate a man for beliefs—or unbeliefs—he had been proclaiming for years, astounded the world. This step, debated ever since 1883, had always been dismissed as injudicious, but, at last, Tolstoy's implacable foe Pobedonostov was precipitated into action by the description of the Mass in *Resurrection*. His understandable resentment of what he thought hideous blasphemy was surpassed by his fury at recognizing in the book a portrait of himself as the 'dull and morally obtuse Toparov', with whom the hero of the book will not shake hands.

Events promptly showed that even in the interests of the Church the outraged Pobedonostov would have done better, like Alexander III, to refuse 'to make a martyr out of Tolstoy'. The immediate consequences of the edict were a public attempt to assassinate the excommunicator and a spectacular rise in the already immense fame and popularity of the excommunicated. On the very morning of the proclamation thousands congregated in the streets of Moscow, and Tolstoy, out for a walk, was mobbed and acclaimed. 'Look, there's the devil in the shape of a man!' yelled one dissentient. Otherwise all protested against the edict and gave Tolstoy a frenzied ovation. Indeed, such tumult arose that before the popular hero could make his escape in a cab, mounted police had to be summoned to disperse the surging crowd. Exploiting the chance to protest against the régime they detested, enthusiastic students congregated daily in front of the

Tolstoys' house; and festooned with ropes of flowers, Repin's portrait of him, then on exhibition in Petersburg, became such a rallying point of disturbance that it had to be withdrawn from the gallery.

Sonya was shocked and deeply hurt by the excommunication; and agreeing with Tolstoy's sister Marya, now a nun, that whatever Tolstoy might say or do he yet 'had God in his heart', felt impelled to protest. Snatching up her swift pen she wrote letters, more eloquent than judicious, to Pobedonostov and the three Metropolitans who had signed the edict. Exultantly telling of the countless messages of sympathy and love coming to Tolstoy from all over the world, she declared that 'there were many outside the Church who led a far more truly Christian life than certain high ecclesiastics wearing diamonded mitres. . . .'

Elated by her own eloquence, Sonya saw to it that copies of her outburst were published abroad. 'No manuscript of Leo's,' she congratulated herself in her diary, 'ever had such swift and wide circulation as this letter. It has been translated into all the foreign languages. This rejoices me, but does not make me proud. God commanded me to write it, not my will.'

Tolstoy was surprised, embarrassed, and touched by his ostensibly orthodox wife's impassioned defence. He noticed, too, what a tonic to herself it had proved. 'Your mother,' he wrote to Masha, 'has had a very good effect on herself. With men, thought influences action, but with women, especially very feminine women, action influences thought.'

Good-humoured amusement was Tolstoy's immediate reaction to his excommunication; callers were laughingly told at the door that he must positively refuse to accept any more congratulations.

Sanctioned as it had been by the Government, his excommunication had been an attempt to fight his influence over the people. As such it was a signal failure. Become a living symbol, Tolstoy now reached the pinnacle of his fame. Letters and telegrams, only very few of them hostile, came in thousands, and before long consciousness of his immense influence over the people gave him such an oppressive sense of responsibility that it told upon his health. He could go nowhere without being recognized and large crowds assembling to acclaim him. Before long he published a reply to the Holy Synod. Admitting his in-

ability to believe all the Church professed to believe, he maintained that he did believe much that the Church was telling the
people he did not believe:

> 'I believe in God, who, for me, is Spirit, Love, the Prin-
> ciple of all things. I believe that He is in me and I in Him. I
> believe that the will of God is most clearly and intelligibly
> expressed in the teaching of the man Jesus, whom to consider
> as God and pray to, I esteem the greatest blasphemy.'

Near the end of the nineteenth century it became clear to
Sonya that Tolstoy's magnificent bodily strength was at last beginning to decline. He still loved the bicycling he had taken to
at sixty, could play a vigorous game of tennis, race young men
in the river, and outdo his sons in acrobatic feats; but before his
seventieth birthday he wrote: 'Thanks to my gymnasium exer-
cises I have for the first time realized that I am growing old and
weak.' Any agitation, such as public ovations, now exhausted
and confused him. If he worked through the morning he could
no longer write later in the day. The digestive weakness, never
definitely diagnosed, that had troubled him all his life—at times
he would lie on the floor groaning aloud with pain—steadily
worsened.

This summer a new trouble began—the first pitched battle in
the long war over Tolstoy's will. One of the younger sons told
Sonya of the existence of an informal one written in his diary for
1905, in which he had entreated his heirs to renounce the copyrights in his writings. Three copies of this document existed: one
kept by Masha, one by Sergei, and one by Chertkov. Afraid that
her father might die and his wishes be ignored, Masha took him
her copy to sign, on which Sonya furiously intervened, and in
one of her most regrettable losses of self-control taunted her
daughter with being a Pharisee eager enough to accept her own
heritage to 'support a beggar husband'! She then besought
Tolstoy to give her the document to destroy. He refused, but
according to some biographers, when her entreaties agitated him
into palpitations, he gave it to her; according to others, Masha,
alarmed by the effect on his health, handed it over to Sonya, who
at once destroyed it. The last sentence of Sonya's own version of
the incident, 'I asked Lev to give it to me, which he willingly did,'

cannot therefore have been strictly true; but self-justification had by this time become an obsession with her.

In June 1901 Tolstoy fell dangerously ill with malaria. Doctors came from Moscow, and the whole family assembled at Yasnaya Polyana. It seemed unlikely that he would survive. Illness, restoring scope to Sonya, reunited husband and wife. Gazing one day at his tireless sick nurse, Tolstoy said: 'Thank you, Sonya. And please don't think I'm ungrateful, and do not love you.'

Weeping, they tenderly embraced. 'Now my Leovochka sleeps,' Sonya thankfully wrote. 'He's still alive. I can see and hear him, and *care* for him. My God, how unbearable my grief would be, how terrible my life without him!'

So imminent did Tolstoy's death appear that the frightened Government sent secret telegrams instructing various authorities to prevent public demonstrations. With his still remarkable resilience he made an astonishing recovery.

One day, as some of the countless telegrams and letters of sympathy were being read aloud, Tolstoy, indulging in the kind of humour Sonya could not share, laughingly interrupted: 'Now suppose I should again begin to die, I really *must* bring it off. There can't be another farce like this one. All these letters and telegrams, and suddenly it turns out not to be true that I'm dying. No, it's impossible. It's simply indecent!'

At the end of July another severe illness convinced the doctors that their seventy-three-year-old patient would not be able to stand the winter either at Yasnaya or in Moscow, and it was decreed that he must go south. Hearing of this decision, a Moscow friend, Countess S. V. Panim, one of the richest women in Russia, placed at his disposal her house at Gaspra on the southern shore of the Crimea, and at a family conference it was agreed to accept this offer.

19

The Crimea

THE decision to go to the Crimea meant a turmoil of planning and packing for Sonya, followed by considerable trepidation, when on a wet, dark night in September she, the invalid, still so weak that he could scarcely stand, Masha, her husband, and Sasha, set off in two carriages for the station. With the family party travelled Tolstoy's devoted friend, P. A. Boulanger, a Tolstoyan liked and respected even by Sonya. Being a railway official, he had been able to arrange for a private railway coach with kitchen, dining-room, and several sleeping berths to take the party from Tula to Sebastopol. Tolstoy looked alarmingly ill, and it was discovered that his temperature had gone up. It was, however, considered safer to travel in such comfort the 600 miles towards sunshine and sea air than to drive back over the shocking roads into the damp and cold. The next morning Tolstoy's temperature was down and to the general amazement he was placidly dictating to Masha. Another crisis arose when towards evening the train drew into Kharkov for a twenty minutes' stop, and it was seen that a great ovation had been prepared. The station platform was black with a clamouring crowd who surged up to the door of their compartment. Sonya, knowing Tolstoy to be in no condition to stand emotional excitement, was terrified, but he felt obliged to receive two separate delegations of students. After the second had left Sonya congratulated herself that the train was about to leave, but the unappeased crowd on the platform was determined not be baulked of a sight of its hero.

'Ask Lev Nikolaevich to come to the window. Just for one second. We implore you!' they shouted.

'He can't. He's ill,' replied the travellers.

'For the Lord's sake—for one moment—let him just show himself!'

Supported by his son-in-law and Boulanger, Tolstoy, white and quivering, swayed to the window. At sight of him caps were flung up into the air. 'Hurrah!' yelled the throng. 'Good health to you, Lev Nikolaevich!' The engine slowly chuffed out of the station; a mob of students raced after the train. Blowing his nose with emotion, Tolstoy sank back into his seat. Despite the anxiety, everyone was deeply touched, but the inevitable conse-quences followed. Tolstoy's temperature soared, his palpitations returned. Fortunately, as the time of arrival at Sebastopol was not known, the ovation awaiting him there was not so over-whelming as at Kharkov.

After a night at a hotel the party drove on to Gaspra and, late in the evening, reached the large courtyard of a veritable palace. Drawn up at the door, Countess Panim's servants awaited them, headed by the estate manager carrying the traditional bread and salt of welcome. The impression of lavish expenditure, unguided by taste, was almost oppressive. The marble staircase and formal, gilded rooms, overcrowded with ornate, impersonal furniture, redolent of cost rather than of value, jarred upon a family accustomed to simplicity. But, shown on to the upper verandah looking straight on to the sparkling blue of the open Black Sea, they gasped with delight. The lower marble verandah, roofed over by vines with great bunches of ripe grapes, was en-chanting too. Wide, flawlessly mown grass terraces surrounded the house; there were cypresses, walnut trees, and oleanders, and beyond the terraces stretched a magnificent park. The beauty of the place was startling; and more than reconciled the travellers settled in, little thinking that—cuckoos in a most incongruous nest—they were to stay there for over ten months.

To begin with, Tolstoy's health rapidly improved and, stimulated by the change of air and surroundings, he once again set vigorously to work. Sonya, on the other hand, did not take to the Crimean coast. Disliking the strange house, the climate, the food, she craved for familiar scenes and faces. She did try very hard to interest herself in her latest hobby, photography, but could not help pining for music and its little exponent. Advertise-ments of Taneyev's concerts, eulogies of his performances, agitated what her diary disarmingly termed her 'tiny soul': 'Just as a famished person needs food, I suddenly passionately need music, and the music of Taneyev, which with its depth has so great an effect upon me.'

The three servants come with the family from Yasnaya—a cook, a footman, and a seamstress—sympathized with their mistress's homesickness. 'Wherever have we been brought?' they wailed. 'On one side is the sea, on the other the mountains. Nowhere to go!'

Absence from home gave Sonya no holiday from the harassments of housekeeping. Nor from her watchdog rôle. From the moment of their arrival the place was infested with spies who, sneaking about in the park, lurked behind trees to pry on the family. Nor did she ever cease to have to play the hostess. A cousin of the Czar, the Grand Duke Alexander Mikhailovich, soon presented himself, and writers of distinction flocked to see Tolstoy. The most frequent and welcome visitor was Anton Chekov, who years before had visited the Tolstoys and still loved laughingly to tell how on that occasion his host, recently deeply distressed by a performance of *Uncle Vanya*, had pointed out to him his inability to write plays. 'Anton Pavlovich,' Tolstoy had said in his most friendly fashion, 'you are a fine man and I'm very fond of you. But your plays are altogether vile. There is no real action. No movement, only endless conversations between neurasthenic intellectuals. And anyhow, it is incomprehensible what you wanted to say.'

Far from being offended by his host's missionary zeal, Chekov, when he heard of Tolstoy's illness, wrote: 'I never loved a man as I do him,' and now, in their shared exile, they became devoted friends. Chekov, visibly and audibly ill—he had a continuous cough—was living at Yalta in the vain hope that its climate might help to fight the consumption of which he was soon to die. Just in case Chekov should have forgotten, Tolstoy, warmly embracing him, again advised him to give up play-writing. 'You know I don't much care for Shakespeare, but it must be admitted that he wrote better plays than you.' At which Chekov laughed so much that the spectacles fell off his nose. To Sonya's embarrassment, Tolstoy one day went so far as gravely to ask Chekov: 'Is it really worth writing if you have no serious ideas of your own?' But blind as Tolstoy was to the merits of Chekov's plays, he did

appreciate his artistry as a story-teller. 'Pushkin in prose,' he declared, and averred that in his story *Darling* Chekov had drawn
the ideal woman. This annoyed Sonya. 'Yes, Leo, *that's* what
you like!' she exclaimed. 'A she-animal, a slave devoid of all
interest and initiative. Wait on your husband, serve him, bear
and feed children!'

Even more than Chekov's stories Tolstoy valued the beauty
and gentleness of his nature. In many ways so unlike, the two
writers had much in common, in particular the veneration for
life that incidentally exposed both their wives to the same inconvenience. Neither would allow a mouse or even a rat to be killed,
but had ingenious traps made to catch without injuring the
animals, who would then be carried out of doors and released—
Tolstoy's captives into the woods, Chekov's over the fence of
his back garden. Remembering the good living quarters from
which they had been evicted, the creatures scurried back with all
possible speed, and the houses became positively infested. At
Yasnaya, holes were gnawed in the floors, books ruined, candles
eaten and, jumping up on to bedside-tables, rats even ran over
the faces of sleepers. This housewife's plague was bewailed in one
of the most poignant of Sonya's jeremiads:

> 'Oct. 1881. Mouse-traps clicked mercilessly all the time
> with the mice they were catching. Mice, mice without end.
> ... As I was tidying the room I tried to adjust one of the in-
> numerable traps; and suddenly it snapped and struck me in
> the eye, so that I fell backwards, and thought I was blinded.
> I had to wear a poultice on my eyes.'

The other most memorable visitor, also in the Crimea for his
lungs, was Maxim Gorky, recently imprisoned for political
activities, and still under police surveillance. He too had visited
the Tolstoys both in Moscow and at Yasnaya. His description of
the unquelled aristocrat still alive in Tolstoy has already been
quoted. Their meetings in the Crimea inspired other eloquent
passages. No one indeed has better conveyed the immensity of
Tolstoy's presence. Before Gorky knew him personally he had
hated what he described as Tolstoy's 'misty preaching of non-
resistance', condemned by him as the 'negation of all affirmation';
but, after meeting him, he wrote:

'I realize that no man is more worthy of the name of genius; more complex, contradictory, and great in everything; great in some strange sense, not definable by words. There is something in him which makes me want to cry aloud: "Look what a wonderful man is living on this earth!"'

Gorky pronounced Tolstoy's relationship with God to be extremely ambiguous. It reminded him, he said, of the relationship between two bears in one den. But then Gorky saw Tolstoy, himself, as a god, 'not in the least a Jehovah or an Olympian, but a 'Russian folk god, who is perhaps more cunning than any of the other gods!'

'Each time I saw Tolstoy,' said Gorky, 'he appeared to me to be a different man,' and, now irresistibly attracted, now repelled, he could never finally make up his mind whether he loved or hated him: 'I saw what a vast amount of life was embodied in him, how inhumanly clever he was, how terrifying. I, who do not believe in God, looked at him and thought: "This man is godlike!"' Later he wrote: 'So long as this man lives on the earth I am not an orphan on it.' And when he heard of Tolstoy's death he cried with pain and rage.

When Gorky had called in Moscow, Sonya had not been prepossessed by his unkempt, unhealthy appearance, and she had liked his coarse black blouse no better than his long hair, snub nose, and small, deeply sunken eyes. Nor when he had come to Yasnaya did his manner counteract this first impression. At the evening meal he sprawled in silence with his elbows on the table and, later, while Tolstoy read aloud a newly written article, noisily turned the pages of a book he was reading to himself. At Gaspra, however, she consented to honour him as a writer by photographing him and her husband together.

It is interesting to read what, in an article hitherto not printed in English, Gorky wrote of Sonya. As he had not met her until after her glow and charm had faded, and was not under her personal sway, his defence of her, for defence it is, deserves quoting:

'I think I can write of Countess Tolstoy with the utmost impartiality, for I never liked her. She, in her turn, had no friendly feelings for me, for, as I could well see, she had come to consider most people who approached her husband as one

regards flies, mosquitoes, parasites. And it must be remembered how dense was the cloud of flies surrounding the great
writer, and how pestering the parasites who fed on his mind.
His wife's hostility to them was natural, and she was a quick-
tempered woman. Her sharp distrust of the disciples of her
husband is easily understandable, and her desire to keep them
off. There can be no doubt that, thanks to her, Tolstoy was
spared many a blow dealt by brutes in the shape of men. She
kept away from her husband many grimy covetous hands,
averted many curious callous fingers brutally anxious to probe
the depths of the wound of this rebellious man who was so
dear to her.'

Gorky thought the hardest time in Sonya's life must have been
in the 1880s when Tolstoy's 'mutinous conscience' was stirring up
so much resentment:

'I consider,' he wrote, 'that she played a truly heroic part.
She must have had a tremendous power of inner resistance
and great sagacity to keep from Tolstoy so many mean and
crude attacks which might have affected his attitude towards
mankind in general. Calumny and evil are best killed by
silence. . . . One should remember that his wife was the only
woman in his life during half a century. She was his true,
intimate, and apparently only friend. For though Tolstoy considered many people as his friends, they were all really no
more than disciples.'

The Crimea gave Sonya very little respite as a hospital nurse.
It was not long before Tolstoy again fell ill. Local doctors were
called in, then a celebrated one from Moscow, and soon the
Emperor's physician came from Petersburg. None would accept
any payment. Pleurisy and then pneumonia were diagnosed; the
patient's condition pronounced hopeless. The Government sent
a lawyer to Yalta to be ready in the event of Tolstoy's death to
confiscate his papers. All the family assembled. Performing
prodigies of nursing, Sonya was at his bedside every night until
four in the morning, when Tanya and Sasha took her place.
Masha, ill herself, but an inspired sick nurse, was on duty in the
daytime. One focal point of infection would clear only to flare

up in another. For weeks and months the illness dragged on, and Tolstoy, often scarcely able to breathe, suffered terribly. A rumour that he was dying reached the Holy Synod. Anxious to be able to announce that, recanting on his deathbed, Russia's greatest writer had died in the arms of the Church, the Synod sent ecclesiastical dignitaries to the neighbourhood. Told of their presence and appeals to be admitted, Tolstoy merely gasped: 'Cannot these gentlemen understand that even in the presence of death two and two still make four?' Later he said: 'A quiet death under the influence of the Church is like death under morphia.'

A terrible evening came when the doctors said there was no hope. Tolstoy was in great pain, and his pulse had all but ceased. No one slept that night. But in the morning he at last dozed off. The crisis was over, and from that moment he began very slowly to improve, but his heart was so much weakened that he had to stay in bed for four months.

'My Leovochka is dying. And I realize now that my life cannot go on without him,' Sonya had written in her diary. 'For everyone else he is a celebrity, for me he is all my being. Our lives were lived for each other, but, my God, how much blame and remorse have accumulated! How much love and tenderness I gave him, but how much have my frailties grieved him! Lord, forgive me! My dear, dear, sweet husband, forgive me!'

Besides the strain of desperate anxiety there had been many subsidiary trials for her. Again that sharp-eyed onlooker, Gorky, deserves to be quoted:

'I could well see in what a storm of poisonous trifles of life she had to whirl—trying to protect the manuscripts, and the peace of the sick man; make all the children comfortable, suppress the intrusiveness of "sincere condolers", visitors, inspectors, and give them all enough to eat and drink. She was obliged as well to reconcile the mutual jealousies of the doctors, for each was convinced that to him belonged the great merit of attending the patient. She had to worry about household expenses too, for there was not nearly as much money as others supposed, and it seemed that none of the sons was able to support themselves. In this whirlwind Sonya was swept from morning to night, her teeth nervously clenched, her clever, vigilant eyes half-closed, astounding everyone by her indefatigability, her capacity of being on time everywhere, of comforting everyone, and suppressing the mosquito-like buzzing of shallow mutually hostile human beings.'

All through Tolstoy's long illness his daughters and elder sons had done their admirable best, but the background of the family atmosphere was not easy. Tanya's husband was gasping for breath from heart disease; Andrey's wife, who had had a fall, crept about the house in momentary expectation of a miscarriage, and while Tolstoy was at his worst, gave birth to a dead child. Of the sons, shy, ungainly Sergei was the most helpful. Large and strong, he could lift and carry the shrunken body of his father as though it were a child's, and always able to divine his wants, attend to them with clumsy solicitude. Ilya was helpful too. Remembering the unregenerated father of their happy boyhood, unlike their younger brothers, these sons remained devoted to him until the end. Sonya's favourite, Leo, was as usual giving trouble. He had recently published a feeble story flouting his father's doctrines and ridiculing his followers. Sonya tried in vain to keep it from Tolstoy's eyes. The invalid, far more pained by the badness of the story than by its import, believing himself to be dying, wrote a touchingly conciliatory letter to his hostile son, to which the young man's only reaction was, before the whole family, to tear the letter into tiny fragments.

The spring came. Almond and magnolia blossomed. Once again Tolstoy started to write. Sonya began to count the days until they would be able to travel home. But yet again Tolstoy fell dangerously ill, this time with typhoid. Another fortnight of breathless suspense. Once more he recovered and, pining for air and sunshine, insisted on being taken out for drives.

To add to Sonya's cares, Sasha now fell very ill with dysentery. But at last, to her infinite relief, though still too weak to stand— Sasha had to be carried downstairs by Sergei—in June 1907 they left Gaspra to return to Yasnaya.

As a health resort the Crimea had not been a success.

20

The Nurse Falls Ill

To a surprising degree Tolstoy regained his strength, and in time was able even to resume riding and gymnastics. But Sonya's nerve was shattered and a sense of inner estrangement made her concentrate too much on his physical condition. She was always snatching at his wrist to count his pulse and, convinced that he could not survive without the meat juice she poured into his vegetable soup, lavished ceaseless thought on his diet. On his clothing too. She knitted his caps, cut out and sewed his blouses, and whenever he seemed ill sat all night by his bedside.

To Tolstoy's infinite relief the doctors decreed that another winter in Moscow must not be risked. Sonya, for whom, tired as she was, the 'toys of life' had lost their glitter, made no objection to staying on at Yasnaya; nor did she contest the decision about separate bedrooms. After having for forty years shared a ground-floor room, Tolstoy moved upstairs into sunnier and airier quarters. His new study opened on to that balcony upon which Sonya, forty-five years ago, on her first visit to Yasnaya Polyana, had sat alone gazing into the future. Another door led into his small bare bedroom that contained only a narrow bed, a footstool, a wooden washstand with basin and pitcher, and a slop-pail which, when well enough, he would himself still carry out of doors to empty.

Having stopped writing only while desperately ill, Tolstoy was now hard at work again· and, briefly returning to fiction, wrote some short stories, including the famous *Hadji Murat*. Sonya, who had hailed these 'artistic' works with delight, was correspondingly disgusted when, reverting to preaching and symbolism, he wrote *The Destruction of Hell and its Restoration*, a legend telling how hell, destroyed by Christ, is restored by the devil's travestying of his teaching. Hearing him read this work to a group of disciples, Sonya flew into a rage.

'Leo wrote a beautiful thing in *Hadji Murat*, and now he is again at that hateful propaganda—devils, hell, all sorts of nastiness—revolting. . . . This piece of writing is saturated with a truly diabolical spirit of negation, with mockery of everything on earth, beginning with the Church. And the children, Sasha still unreasoning, and Masha who is alien to me in feeling, added their fiendish laughter when he finished reading his horrible legend. But *I* wanted to sob. That I should live to see such work! God grant his heart may be softened!'

Nor did Sonya like Tolstoy's cross-grained attempt in an article on the drama to discredit and vilify Shakespeare on the grounds that his writings embodied no moral philosophy. At this time Tolstoy also worked on *The Light Shineth In Darkness*, a play begun long ago, ruthlessly depicting himself and his failure to put his principles into practice.

The multitude of visitors from all parts of the world who would have called in Moscow was this year diverted to Yasnaya Polyana. No foreigners felt they could leave Russia without seeing her greatest writer. Sonya was dazed by their diversity—pilgrims, petitioners, beggars, millionaires, the learned, the illiterate, the insane, and the saintly. 'There is a continual commotion and throng of people here,' she complained to her sister. 'I invite positively no one, but there are guests all the time—guests without end—and sometimes I simply want to cry from weariness.'

Parties of young students often arrived and after the middle-day meal, while Tolstoy had his nap, would be taken in charge by Sonya, who showed them all over the house like a professional guide:

'Here you see the portrait of Tolstoy's grandfather, Prince Volkonsky, depicted by him in *War and Peace* as Prince Bolkonsky. . . . There is Tolstoy's writing-table. . . . There the couch on which several generations of his family have been born. I, too, gave birth to all my children on it. Tolstoy's bedroom. Note the extreme simplicity of everything. He hates luxury. There is his hand-basin. He empties his own slops when he remembers.'

Praised as the 'skilled nurse' of her husband's genius, Sonya had untiringly gloried in her rôle as the wife of a great man; but painfully aware now of being harshly criticized, the part no longer satisfied her.

At times, all clutches of reticence slipping, she flabbergasted strangers by complaints of the hardships of her fate. 'You have probably heard horrible rumours about me,' she said to one deeply embarrassed student. 'I have enemies, and many envy me for being the wife of Leo Tolstoy. They little know the difficulties of my position. If I were not religious I would long ago have killed myself!' Revived by a snatched cup of tea, Sonya then blew pitiful little blasts on her own trumpet, intimating that she was not merely the consort of a world-wide celebrity, but, in her own right, something of a lioness. Expatiating on her love of both music and painting, she said to the gaping student: 'I, too, write. Not long ago I published a prose poem in the style of Turgenev. It's called *Wailing*, and I signed myself "The Weary One".'

In this expansive mood 'The Weary One' tearfully poured out all the family troubles—the death of Vanichka, Andrey's broken marriage, Tanya's and Masha's stillborn babies, dometic dissension, and so forth. Dazed, the student went away a sadder and a wiser man.

The more exhausted was Sonya the more uncontrollable became her now truly terrible energy. Like many overwrought women, just because she had too much to do she piled upon herself unnecessary tasks. As though housekeeping, estate management, publishing, keeping the family archives (her collection of Tolstoy's manuscripts was to prove invaluable), and the writing of innumerable records were not enough, she worked as hard in the garden as if there were no gardeners. She picked up and burned the litter of cigarette-stubs and scraps of paper, cut down the nettles, pruned the lilacs and laburnums, painted the garden seats. Spades, scythes, rakes, saws, cluttered up her bedroom. She learned to type, she painted, copying portraits of her husband or his ancestors, or making Sasha sit to her, and every day she spent hours at the piano.

Now that Tolstoy no longer needed her in the old urgent way she had so often deplored a sense of loneliness saddened her. 'There has come that time which I foresaw. My *passionate* husband is dead. A husband friend there never was. . . . Happy wives live to the end in friendship and sympathy with their husbands, but the unhappy lonely wives of egotists, great men, are the wives of whom posterity makes Xantippes.' Her dread of being misrepresented, called a shrew, had now become obsessive. Doubtless she would be blamed for thwarting her husband's desire to give up all material concerns and lead a wholly spiritual life. But who except herself knew about the state of the family finances? Naturally she was tempted by a publisher's offer of a vast sum for a copyright limited to only two years; but the only result of her efforts to persuade Tolstoy to agree was to determine him never to publish any more literary works.

All through this last decade of Tolstoy's life, public as well as family events conspired to widen the gulf between husband and wife, and to keep Sonya in perpetual alarm as to the consequences of his furious indictments of Church and Government.

At the beginning of 1904 came the terrible blow of the Russo-Japanese War with all its, to Tolstoy's mind, utterly senseless slaughter. In answer to a cable from an American newspaper asking his opinion, Tolstoy replied: 'I am neither for Russia nor Japan, but for the working people of both countries who have been deceived by their governments and forced to go to war against their own good, their conscience, and their religion,' and in a pamphlet called *Bethink Yourselves* he denounced both the Czar and the Commander-in-Chief for condemning thousands of peasants to death in a particularly purposeless and unpopular war. Were not wives and mothers actually laying themselves down on the railway lines to stop the trains from carrying their husbands and sons off to the Far East?

Despite patriotic letters fiercely attacking him as a traitor, Tolstoy continued unflinchingly to oppose the war. But with chagrin and self-disillusionment he soon discovered that his con-demnation of war had not freed himself from the bonds of patriotism. To his shame, and Sonya's amusement, he found his emotions were still hopelessly involved. Unable to wait for the arrival of the newspapers, he would often ride to Tula for the latest news of the campaign, and each Japanese victory agonized him:

'I can't get rid of a feeling of grief when I learn that the Russians are being beaten. . . . The surrender of Port Arthur made me miserable. This is patriotism. I was brought up to it and am not yet free from it, any more than I am free from personal egoism and even from the aristocratic brand. All these egoisms survive in me, but there is also a consciousness in me of divine law, and that consciousness keeps the egoisms in check. And little by little they will become atrophied.'

Sonya had no sympathy with this yearning for atrophy. She wept for the dead and the bereaved; she trembled for the fate of her son Andrey who had gone to the war, and to her mind patriotism was an ennobling, not a debasing, emotion.

The news from the Far East grew yet worse. In 1905 the Japanese sank the Russian Navy. Tolstoy was not only agonized by the war, he was terrified of its consequences: 'This is the destruction, not of the Russian Army and Navy, not of the Russian State. It is the destruction of all pseudo-Christian civilization.'

No prophet was needed to foretell that the war would precipitate the uprising of the Russian people against the anachronism of autocracy. The first wave of the oncoming tide of revolution broke in January 1905 when, under the leadership of a priest, Father Gapon, an unarmed crowd marched with a petition upon the Winter Palace at Petersburg. Not allowed to approach the palace, they were dispersed by the police and soldiers, and hundreds were killed and wounded. The result of this 'Bloody Sunday' was the unification of all the various socialist working-class parties. Frightened into a feeble concession, the Government summoned a National Congress of the Imperial Duma. Its function was merely to deliberate, and the retort to this futility was a general strike. Water and electricity supplies were cut off from all the large cities, railway services suspended; and in December an insurrection broke out in Moscow. But the masses were not yet ready for the extreme measures advocated by the Bolsheviks under their leader Lenin. The strikes were therefore soon broken and the riots suppressed. For the time being the revolution was staved off. To Sonya's alarm, violence had, however, reached districts as remote as Yasnaya. Houses were burnt down and in some cases the landowners murdered by peasants. Before long strikes broke out as near home as Tula. More than ever, too, Sonya trembled for the possible repercussions of her husband's diatribes on political events.

Newspaper correspondents from America, England, France, Sweden, and Hungary rushed to Yasnaya to try to discover the political opinions of Russia's greatest citizen. Tolstoy received them with the utmost civility but gave them little grist for their mills. Instead of dissertating on current events, he tried to engage his questioners in talk about God and immortality; courteously told them how very difficult he found it to understand how anyone could be a journalist and catechized them about their private lives and the political customs of their own countries.

In his own family incessant controversy raged over the new acts of violence, now sickening him as much as had the slaughter in the Far East. Hearing that the Governor-General of Moscow had been killed by a bomb, he buried his face in his hands and, groaning aloud, anathematized terrorism. Apart from his horror of all violence, he maintained that the revolutionary leaders had no ideals. 'Economic ideals,' he maintained, 'are not ideals.' Characteristically and in perfect consistency with his creed of non-violence, Tolstoy would not—indeed, could not—side with any of the contending parties. He was not sitting on the fence, he sympathized with none. Loudly as he had denounced the abuses of autocracy, he fulminated still more fiercely against the revolutionaries. What good was there in exchanging one form of violence for another? If he had to choose he would rather, he declared, have in power those who had already made their pile: 'We may perhaps not be worth very much,' said the aristocrat in Tolstoy, 'but at least we have lasted a thousand years.' Was not the illusion of liberty, which other countries called democracy, worse than despotism? 'There is nothing in it for the people,' he complained of the manifesto wrung from the Czar which promised 'civil liberties' and an elected Duma. His dismissal of the idea that a constitutional government could possibly provide a solution provoked a distressing quarrel between him and his usually devoted son Sergei, who, unlike his violently reactionary brothers, Leo and Andrey, was now a Liberal pinning his hopes on democracy. 'A constitutional subject who imagines himself to be free,' declared Tolstoy, 'is like a man who imagines himself to be free because he has the power to elect his gaoler.' He had always condemned the Russian Liberals for being wholly ignorant of the core of their country—the peasants, and of the religion by which they lived. 'What do Liberals know of the people?' he asked. 'Who *are* the people?'

At this juncture Sonya would probably have welcomed any clear political lead from her husband. His nihilism made her feel lost and bewildered. 'If *you* had been a revolutionist,' he said to her jokingly, 'you would have been a terrific one. For that business a certain narrowness and a terrible energy, usually only directed into motherhood, are necessary.'

Tolstoy's lone stand was, in fact, perfectly consistent with what he had been preaching for twenty years, non-resistance by force—even to evil. All governments, he maintained, owed their very existence to the exercise of physical force. 'Therefore,' he argued, with that over-simplification that so often dismayed Sonya, 'all governments are evil.'

Lenin categorically declared Tolstoyan non-resistance to have been the chief cause of the defeat of the first revolutionary campaign. That may be so. Nevertheless, from the outbreak of violence, Tolstoy's influence over the people began to wane. Challenged by bayonets and rifle-fire, passive resistance demanded more endurance than most Tolstoyans possessed, and, despairing of their leader's patient faith in the moral perfectibility of Man, many of them now joined the ranks of the revolutionaries.

It was during this disturbed time that Tolstoy, while still busily engaged on polemical articles, embarked on the literary task that was to occupy him until the end of his life, *The Circle of Reading*, a compilation from the works of the thinkers of all time, in which passages more or less in agreement with his own philosophy were quoted. Thirty-one themes, Faith, the Soul, Love, and so forth, were chosen, and a number of relevant quotations set down for each day in the year. Family and guests sat at a huge table translating and transcribing the selections, while Tolstoy ransacked his library to re-read all the favourite authors of his youth, of whom, he declared, Charles Dickens gave him the purest enjoyment. Sonya could not consider this garnering of other men's thoughts worth so much of a great creative writer's time, but while political strife was driving Tolstoy to despair this book, to which he rewrote his introduction more than a hundred times, was an invaluable refuge. He was finding it so hard to bear the perpetual wrangling with his two extremist sons, Leo and Andrey, and no one else in the family circle shared his own inability to side with any one particular party. He felt, as Gorky described him, 'alien to all, a solitary traveller through all the deserts of thought in search of an all-embracing truth which he has not found'.

All the misery and executions now going on in the country inflamed his chronic sense of guilt about the luxury he was supposed to enjoy at Yasnaya Polyana: 'We sit indoors and eat ten dishes. Ice-cream, lackeys, silver service, and beggars pass, yet kind people continue calmly to eat ice-cream. Amazing!' An attitude of mind with which Sonya, who knew ice-cream to be both inexpensive and wholesome, had no sympathy whatever. So hypersensitive did Tolstoy now become that he could not even bear the peasants to see his family play lawn tennis, a game he had himself only just given up. The life he was leading no longer seemed endurable, but what, he asked, would be the use of leaving home? Wherever he might go, there the very next day his wife would appear with servants and doctors, and everything would go on exactly as before.

The family rift widened; siding with their mother, the younger sons, both staunch believers in property, insisted on protecting their interest in the estate by defending law and order against their father's 'anarchism'. Worst of all, when Tolstoy decried the Duma's advocacy of the death penalty they made him literally weep by their mockery of his doctrine of non-resistance.

A relatively new inmate of Yasnaya Polyana had become a great solace to Tolstoy. After his illness in the Crimea it had been decreed that there must always be a doctor in residence, a decision to which he consented only on condition that the chosen man should give most of his time to treating the peasants, and keep a dispensary for them. In 1904 this post was filled by Dr. Dushan Makovisky, who stayed until Tolstoy's death. By no means a brilliant doctor, this gentle Tolstoyan was all but a saint. He worked hard for the peasants and acted as informal secretary to

Tolstoy. Never moving without a paper and pencil, almost every time the Master opened his mouth he would, unperceived, jot down his words and then sit up till all hours amplifying his notes and chronicling the events of the day. Not knowing how late Dushan went to bed, Tolstoy would be surprised at his way of falling asleep at any spare moment in his crowded day. 'You don't sin when you sleep,' Dushan used apologetically to say.

The doctor and Sonya frequently fell out over the care of Tolstoy's health. He thought she over-fussed his patient with all her specially prepared dishes and home-made medicaments; but no new watchdog could hope to keep off one of forty-four years' standing, and rather than risk agitating the Master by upsetting his wife Dushan usually gave way. Humble, self-effacing—so gentle that he could not even bear to hear anyone else quarrel— Dushan completely won Tolstoy's heart and became indispensable to him. Once when his doctor had to go away for a month Tolstoy asked how he was to live without him. 'I don't need his medicine, but when I can't see his hat about I somehow feel lost. Holy Dushan!'

This year, 1906, Fate forced a strange reversal of rôles upon Sonya. For so many years she had been as busily engaged in looking after other people as the matron of a ward full of emergency cases that came and went, but with one permanent chronic patient—her husband. But at the end of the summer the nurse herself fell desperately ill. For some time she had been feeling wretchedly unwell, and recently life at Yasnaya had been specially harassing. Pillaging the estate, the peasants had little by little been destroying Tolstoy's favourite grove of birch trees. Having denied the rights of ownership, he could not himself protest. But Sonya felt impelled to prosecute, a step for which she well knew she would be abused, as indeed she was. In this matter once again Maxim Gorky sprang to her defence, maintaining that though everyone was grieving, she alone had the courage to protest, and he could only respect her for it. 'No one,' he wrote, 'would dare say that Tolstoy was insincere in his rejection of property, yet I am convinced that he did deeply sorrow over that grove of trees which had been the work of his own hands.'

Whatever Tolstoy's feelings, he could not endure the intervention of the police, and thanks to this prosecution the atmosphere at Yasnaya Polyana became more and more tense. But when at the beginning of September Sonya's illness took a critical turn, everything was forgotten in acute anxiety. Suddenly fierce pain leapt upon her. A famous gynaecologist diagnosed a tumour of the uterus and advised an operation. The pain abated and there was an illusion of improvement. But Sonya's temperature shot up to 104, violent pain returned, and peritonitis set in. An operation was now urgently imperative and it was too late to move the patient to a hospital. A distinguished surgeon arrived with assistants, nurses, and an operating table; telegrams assembled every absent member of the family, and while husband, sons, and daughters shared the same suspense all disputes were forgotten. With its tireless mistress laid low, the stillness of the house was uncanny. In the weird hush it was as though a dynamo had run down.

'You are ill, Sonya,' said Tolstoy. 'You do not walk about, and do you know that not hearing the sound of your steps I can neither read nor write?'

Convinced that she was about to die, Sonya bore her sufferings heroically, amazing everyone by her fortitude and sweetness. Making no demands, she murmured grateful, tender words to each member of the family and the household, and whenever Tolstoy came into her room made every effort to conceal her pain. 'Leovochka, forgive me, forgive me,' she murmured, seizing his hand to kiss it. Tolstoy, tears streaming down his furrowed face, strode about the house, his hands thrust deep into his broad belt; but he wept with joy as well as with grief, for to him it seemed that, conscious of the approach of death, Sonya had been uplifted high above all in her that he had ever thought worldly or trivial. He was, he felt convinced, beholding 'not an end of something, but its full unfolding'. Even the least loving, least loved, of her children, the critical Sasha, for the first time realized her true love for her mother. 'I looked into her beautiful eyes,' she wrote, 'so helpless and full of suffering, and all the corroding antipathy I had sometimes felt seemed like a far-away nightmare.'

Sonya confessed and took communion. 'She asked to have a priest,' wrote Tolstoy in his diary, 'and I not only agreed but was glad to co-operate. There are people who cannot reach an abstract, purely spiritual relationship with the First Principle of Life. They have to have some crude form.'

Just before the operation Sonya asked forgiveness of her children and of the servants, and took leave of each in turn. All left the room in tears.

While the operation was being performed Tolstoy, who had left instructions that if it was successful the great bell should be rung twice, if not, once, went away into the forest to be alone and pray. His younger sons indignantly declared that they felt sure his prayers were much more for their mother's spiritual rebirth than for her bodily survival.

At last Sasha, Ilya, and Masha ran out into the forest with the news that the operation had been successful. Tolstoy turned back alone into the forest to pray.

After two or three critical days Sonya made a good recovery. Writing to her sister she described her state of mind when she had supposed herself to be dying; how insignificant and trivial had then seemed to her all the concerns and vanities of the world, and how much she had wanted everyone to give them up. She had felt, she said, quite resigned to leaving all that she loved— even her children. 'I grieved only when I said goodnight to Leovochka as I thought for the last time, and he went to the door, his thin shoulders hunched, sobbing, crying, and blowing his nose.'

With the return of her physical strength Sonya's detachment ceased, and to Tolstoy it seemed that as she regained strength so she relapsed from spiritual grace. Once again the hope of perfect harmony faded. Not very many weeks after the operation he wrote in his diary: 'Our life is again very disgusting. They sport, doctor themselves, go hither and yon, take part in this or that, concern themselves with what is not their business, but they have no real life because they have no obligations. It is frightful!!!'

Having reshouldered her load of responsibilities Sonya could scarcely be expected to agree that she had 'no obligations'.

'At times,' wrote Sasha, 'Father remembered with deep feeling how beautifully Mother had borne her pain, how kind and thoughtful she had been to everyone. For the second time in my life, just as after the death of Vanichka, a window had opened, let in a stream of light that brightened our life—only to close again.'

But soon tragedy was again to blow that window open wide. Before 1906 was out father and mother were reunited in sorrow.

'This terrible grief,' wrote Sonya, 'falls heavily upon our old hearts. The mutual reproaches and disagreements have ceased.' This time the grief was for the uncensorious saint, Masha. In November she fell ill with pneumonia and, after nine days, visibly wasting, and for the first time in all her loving life, aloof, she died as gently as she had lived. When the end came her husband was standing at the window trying to suppress his sobs, her father sitting by the bed holding, as for so many hours he had held, the transparent hand, turning cold in his withered grasp. Directly news of Masha's death reached the village, wailing women ran to the house to beg to watch over her body, and men hurried to the priest with coppers for memorial services. The stricken father followed the coffin as far as to the gate of the churchyard, then he turned back and walked all the way home alone.

Sonya's grief was not comparable with that which she had suffered over Vanichka's death. She had never loved Masha as she did Tanya, but she had long since learned to revere her spirituality and determination to live rather than to preach her ideals. 'Of all our family Masha loved Leo most,' she wrote.

Of her thirteen children Sonya had now outlived seven.

21

Re-enter Chertkov

ANY and varied as had been Sonya's troubles in the
last ten years, she had at least enjoyed respite from
the presence of Chertkov who, since his banishment
in 1897, had lived in England, where he had founded The Free
Age Press and printed and published the banned works of
Tolstoy. But his term of exile had now ended, and in the summer
of 1907 he took for a couple of months a house only about three
miles from Yasnaya. His return ushered in a heyday for the
Tolstoyans, several of the more distinguished of whom had
settled in the neighbourhood, notably the pianist, A. B. Goldenweiser, the editor of *The Intermediary*, I. I. Gorbunov, and the
Henry George expert, S. D. Nikolayev. These and others now
assembled almost daily to hear the Master and his 'Heir Apparent'
expound their doctrines. Unfortunately, a swarm of lesser Tolstoyans came too, and this perpetual infestation of her home by
'Dark Ones' made Sonya feel it was under enemy occupation.
As for Chertkov himself, grown bodily much larger—a fact
which seemed to symbolize his increasing importance—he struck
her as more oppressively dominating than ever. She was alarmed,
too, as well as hurt, by the visibly revitalizing effect of his return
on her husband. Evidently Leo had been starving for the company of this intruder, who blatantly basking in the presence, was
once again arrogating to himself so many privileges. The pre-
sumptuous creature would actually burst unannounced into
Tolstoy's study while he was writing, a liberty his family seldom
dared take. She was irritated, too, by *The Vault*, as Chertkov
ponderously called the vast volume where he devoutly entered
all his Master's dictums. Above all, she became alarmedly aware
of how this 'pseudo saint' was focussing his iron will and coercive
power on his relationship with the 'Master'. Might he not acquire

over a failing old man of nearly eighty a real ascendancy? And it was obvious that so domineering a man would quarrel with anyone who tried to oppose his sway.

Sonya had neither forgotten nor forgiven old disputes over publishing rights, and she now suspected Chertkov of calmly appropriating any manuscripts he could lay hands upon. With asperity she wrote to enquire whether he had in his keeping certain of her husband's diaries she was unable to find. For the time being, however, outward peace was kept, and in September Sonya was able to heave a great sigh of relief, for business compelled Chertkov temporarily to return to England. He left behind him his devoted young follower, N. N. Gusev, whom he had persuaded Tolstoy to employ as secretary, but only a month later Gusev, denounced for proselytizing peasants, was arrested and imprisoned. Agonized, Tolstoy felt personally responsible. He visited the young man in prison, supplied him with food, clothes, and books, and directly he was released took him back again.

Disgusted to see how much her husband missed his disciple, Sonya was maddened by Chertkov's letter rhapsodizing to him over their 'joyous communion', and ending with the words 'loving you so much that if I could love everyone in the same way, it would be paradise on earth'.

Apart from the strain on Sonya's nerves of Chertkov's looming presence, the summer had been much too exacting for a woman only lately recovered from a desperate illness. Visitors of every description had ceaselessly overfilled her house, but far worse had been the assembling, evening after evening, of all those oppressively earnest 'Dark People' with long beards and tousled hair, crouching in a rapt circle round Tolstoy and Chertkov. Loyal disciple as Sasha was, she began to think that the Tolstoyans must have taken a vow 'never to joke, laugh or be gay'. Chertkov, it is true, occasionally made a pun, but it was really only Tolstoy's humour, undying love of fun, and at times still uproariously loud laughter that redeemed the atmosphere from gloom.

Before long parental distress again closely united husband and wife. Abandoning his family, Andrey embarrassingly eloped with the wife, a mother of six children, of the Governor of Tula, who, resigning his post, implored the bitterly ashamed Tolstoy to intervene, and, very reluctantly and quite unavailingly, he did.

Young Leo, still suffering from literary aspirations as well as bad health, gave trouble too. This son, of all the family the one most attached to his mother, now positively disliked his father. Tolstoy sadly diagnosed his son's resentment as 'envy of me leading to hatred'. Leo openly attacked his father in an article indicting him as 'a baneful influence largely responsible for the present revolutionary spirit in Russia'.

In the autumn of 1907 local trouble set up fresh friction between husband and wife. Sonya had for some time been alarmed by nearby acts of violence. Farm buildings had been burned down, and a neighbour's coachman shot at by poachers. One day a steward caught several peasants stealing cabbages from her own garden, and in the ensuing scuffle shots were fired, whether by the thieves or by the steward, it was never ascertained. This incident made Sonya, spurred on by Andrey, appeal for protection, and, only too pleased to be asked to defend the property of the great exponent of non-resistance and decrier of ownership, the authorities at once arrested several peasants and installed an armed guard on the estate. Needless to say the Press jubilantly proclaimed the news that the great reformer, who denounced property as the root of nearly all evil, had appealed for protection the instant his own estate was threatened. Bitterly distressed by the arrest of the peasants, Tolstoy became more painfully than ever conscious of the anomaly of his position. How many people knew or cared that Yasnaya Polyana no longer belonged to him? 'I ought to have gone into a monastery,' he groaned to Gusev. 'And so I would have done had I not had a wife!'

Tolstoy at once wrote to the authorities to beg for the release of the peasants, but his appeal was refused. Sonya, at this time mourning the recent murder by terrorists of one of her brothers, welcomed the protection of the law, and so, with the exception of Sasha, did all her children; but the sight of armed men around his home tormented Tolstoy. 'I suffer *physically*,' he wrote, and his distress drove him to give the Press an explanation of his peculiar position as a supposed owner of property. His motive was not only self-justification but also an endeavour to reduce the appeals for money with which he was now pelted from every part of the world. Just as though he had died, all his property had been transferred to his heirs. How, then, could he help others with money? Sonya's fears that this explanation would provoke ridicule were fully realized. Derisive letters poured in, and no scurrilous newspaper missed its cue. One caricature depicted Tolstoy in a room full of valuables, labelled 'Property of my wife'. He was guzzling rich foods and quaffing wine, while famished onlookers, staggering round the loaded table, held out beseeching hands in vain.

More and more painfully Sonya was now realizing the irony of her own position. All her struggles to cope with the responsibilities shifted on to her by her husband now served only to widen the breach between them. But what could she do—she who felt responsible for the financial future of the whole family? She had not, as had her husband, changed into a different person, but remained faithful to the man she had married and, for that reason, she now seemed doomed to make him miserable and to bear all the odium.

In January 1908 the celebration, on August 28th, of Tolstoy's eightieth birthday began to be discussed. A celebration committee was set up in Petersburg and a national holiday planned. Sonya, delighted, started to write the little speech she intended on the great day to make to the committee. What kind of a life, it was now being widely asked, did the 'Prophet of the Century' lead at the age of seventy-nine? In as far as was possible Tolstoy still kept to a daily routine. Every morning a throng of petitioners awaited him in front of the house under the great elm, called the 'tree of the poor'. He would attend to every one and then disentangling himself, walk to his favourite grove of firs where, seated on a bench, he jotted down thoughts. After his return he would work for several hours, at this time mostly on *The Circle of Reading*. In the afternoon he often went for a ride, accompanied, for it was no longer thought safe for him to be alone, by Sasha, Chertkov, or Dushan. After tea he would again write; in the evenings play chess, or cards, or—for mercifully the absurd battle against music had long been given up—joyfully listen to Goldenweiser's piano-playing.

The strong, erect, striding man Sonya had married was now shrunken, bowed, and shuffling in his gait. But if his body had dwindled, his bearded face, furrowed and gaunt, had become magnificent in old age, and the sorrowing eyes were as piercing as ever. Wistfully as Sonya might pine for the unregenerated Leo Tolstoy of her youth, she had to admit that the long transitional phase had ended and his spiritual side now really predominated. He still, noted her diary, enjoyed good food, riding, cards, chess, song, and talk, and believed in the sacredness of gaiety—'gaiety is one of the fulfilments of God's will'.

'Yet,' mourned the widow of all the other Leo Tolstoys, 'his body now lives a separate existence and his spirit remains indifferent to earthly life, somewhere aloof, independent of the body. . . . Something new, strange, and far away is being experienced by him, and I'm often unbearably saddened by his remoteness, and the loss of *something* in him, and in his relationship to me, and to everything around him.'

Tolstoy had acquired another virtue. He had taught himself —no easy lesson for a man of his temperament—humility. Vituperative letters would now be answered meekly, and violent abuse, occasionally screamed at him by passers-by, gently reasoned with. An old friend wrote a hostile article accusing him of hypocrisy. Sonya sent a scathing protest; Tolstoy a conciliatory and loving letter.

In March came another severe shock for Sonya's overtaxed nervous system. Rising from his writing-table after putting the last words to a short story, Tolstoy fell unconscious to the floor and, when he came round, his jumbled words betrayed that for the time being his mind was completely clouded. He could not even recognize his own grandson. This condition soon cleared, but fainting fits, usually brought on by emotional stress, now became recurrent, and his prodigious memory began to show signs of deterioration. His pen, however, still drove on. And there was plenty to impel it. The imprisonment of Tolstoyans, caught publishing or even merely possessing and distributing copies of his banned books, kept him in perpetual anguish. Still afraid to prosecute a writer of world-wide fame, the Government could, for him, have devised no severer penalty than this systematic victimization of his disciples. Nor was it only Tolstoyans for whom he wept. Having regained its illusion of security, the Government was now reverting to all the old repressive measures. The ferocity of its sentences drove Tolstoy distraught and, when twenty peasants were hanged for robbing a landowner's estate, in a fury of indignation he wrote *I Cannot Be Silent*, his most famous protest against man's inhumanity to man. Translated into scores of foreign newspapers, this indictment made an immense sensation. Proprietors of Russian newspapers who dared to print passages from it were fined or imprisoned, but thousands of letters acclaimed Tolstoy's courage and eloquence, and the few exceptions were nearly all anonymous. *I Cannot Be Silent* contained the celebrated passage:

'It is impossible to live like this! I, at any rate, cannot and will not. That is why I write this and will circulate it by all means in my power both in Russia and abroad, so that one of two things may happen: either that these inhuman deeds may be stopped, or that my connection with them may be snapped and I put in prison, where at least I may be clearly conscious that these horrors are not perpetrated on my behalf; or better still (so good that I dare not dream of such happiness) that they may put on me, as on those twenty peasants, a shroud and a cap, and may push me, too, off a bench, so that by my own weight I may tighten the well-soaped noose around my old throat.'

This spirited sally led to an ugly shock for Sonya. Unpacking a neat parcel addressed to her husband she was surprised to find inside it a coil of thick rope. Not till she read the enclosed letter did she understand the significance of the rope: 'Count. In answer to your article. Without troubling the Government, you can do it for yourself. It is not difficult. In this way you will benefit our country and its youth. A Russian mother.'

Meanwhile Tolstoy was becoming more and more embarrassed by the publicity of the birthday preparations. Celebration Committees had now been formed in America, Russia, Japan, as well as in nearly all the European capitals. In a letter to the Press a leading disciple declared that 'nothing would give Tolstoy more pleasure on his birthday than to be put in prison according to what in Russia is accepted as justice'. Sonya was disgusted, Tolstoy delighted, by such discernment. 'In truth,' he wrote, 'nothing *would* give me such complete satisfaction and such joy as to be put into prison—into a real good stinking prison

—cold and hungry.' But this was a birthday honour he was never to be awarded.

The world-wide impulse to honour Tolstoy was, of course, not unanimous. Bitter letters of protest appeared in newspapers and, exhorting the 'faithful' not to celebrate the birthday of an anathematized atheist and anarchist, the Bishop of Saratov denounced him as an 'accursed and most disdained Russian Judas, a damned blasphemer, and a mental debaucher of youth'. Finally Tolstoy himself published a letter stating his own objections to the proposed jubilee. Apart from his personal distaste for publicity, the plan, he contended, was stirring up hostility against himself. To the bitter disappointment of Sonya the Celebration Committee was reluctantly compelled to give up all its elaborate plans. The world-wide veneration for Tolstoy was, however, widely expressed. Hayberg Wright brought to Yasnaya Polyana a testimonial signed by hundreds of distinguished English and Americans, including George Meredith, Thomas Hardy, H. G. Wells, Edward Carpenter, and Bernard Shaw. Over seventeen hundred telegrams came. Even Tolstoy's Sebastopol battery sent congratulations to their old comrade-in-arms, now the most famed denouncer of all things military, and so did the University of Kazan, at which he had been so undistinguished a student. Greetings from countless peasants moved him to tears: 'Do not be silent, old man inspired by God. Live and write for multitudes.' Gifts poured in; not a few of them as unintentionally ludicrous as the huge case of cigarettes with a portrait of the eschewer of tobacco on each packet. Wine, too, was sent in large quantities to the total abstainer.

The birthday party was limited to the family and closest friends. Even so, the emotional strain exhausted Tolstoy, who recently had again been seriously ill, this time with thrombosis in his leg, and while champagne sparkled, laughter rang out, and his health was repeatedly drunk, he looked exhausted and deeply depressed. After dinner the 'Dark Ones' swarmed around, hungry for some memorable birthday announcement, but, too tired to play the great man, the 'Master' firmly withdrew, first to enjoy a game of chess and then to the delight of listening to Goldenweiser playing Chopin. After he had gone to bed Sonya, according to habit, came in to wish him good night and wrapped him up in a large shawl she had knitted. He looked ineffably weary, and with a pang she saw that his sunken eyes were full of tears. The hunted look in them alarmed her. Did he again, she wondered, want to go away from his home? Or was it the whole world that he now longed to leave?

Meanwhile Chertkov, his business in England finally wound up, was building only two miles from Yasnaya a house he hoped to make his permanent abode. The amount of money being spent distressed Tolstoy, but to accommodate the family and Court of the Heir Apparent plentiful space was needed. There had to be a large lecture hall, and what with the secretaries, the typists employed on Tolstoy's manuscripts, and all the helpers (the term 'servant' was, of course, never used), over forty people had to be housed. The whole community ate together, at a huge table, the food served in the large cauldrons in which it had been cooked. Ostensibly equality prevailed, but according to Sasha and others the categories of first, second, and third class were as plainly distinguishable as in any railway train. 'Above the salt' at the upper end of the table presided the 'Czar of the Tolstoyans'. Propped up on pillows, his invalid wife reclined at his side in a large armchair, their children around them. In the middle of the table sat the clerical staff, and at the lower end the 'helpers'. 'Look, look,' Sasha overheard a stable-boy whisper, 'Aloysha is trying to squeeze himself up into the second class!' 'Well,' tolerantly replied another lad, 'no doubt he likes rice cakes, jam, and stewed fruit! He may well be tired of boiled potatoes and sunflower oil.'

Sonya's worst fears were realized. As unfailingly as darkness fell, Chertkov appeared at Yasnaya. 'He is practically living in our house, and hardly ever leaves Leo alone,' protested her diary. More than his oppressive presence she minded the fact that, reading every line Tolstoy wrote, he now often dictatorially suggested alterations and, to Sonya's consternation, her husband usually complied. Nor could she bear to see how perpetually Tolstoy's 'Black Shadow' dogged him about the house, jotting down nearly all he said. Worst of all, she suspected that he took a copy of whatever her husband wrote in his diaries.

Appointing himself a kind of Court Chamberlain, Chertkov began annoyingly to lay down the law as to what was proper in the home of Tolstoy, and any visitor who offended his sensibilities fell under his ban. Scared by recent local disturbances, a friend of Sonya's arrived carrying a small revolver which she left

in the hall. 'What effrontery to visit Tolstoy with a firearm!'
exclaimed Chertkov, and wrapping up the weapon in a copy of
Do Not Kill, he stuffed various other banned works into the
visitor's coat pockets. This was sufficiently annoying to the
mistress of the house. It was worse to overhear the despot warn
her husband that his habit of occasionally making the sign of the
Cross might mislead people into supposing he had returned to
the Orthodox Church. 'What a limited creature Chertkov is!
How narrow his point of view in everything,' wailed Sonya's
diary. If only he would keep to what she considered his 'place'
she might have put up with his presence. 'All he has to do is to
take notes, collect and photograph, and that *only!*' As a matter
of fact, Chertkov's photography was in itself bad enough. Sonya
grew sick of the very sight and click of his inevitable camera.
Why must he come so often; loom so large! The house no longer
seemed her own, and as though, silently, he were willing her to
leave the room, his portentous presence made her feel her own
unwanted. Thanks to rapidly deteriorating health, self-confidence
had deserted her—conviction too. Hitherto she had seldom felt
much real doubt as to where her duty lay. But now she wondered
whether perhaps she should not throw off her load of responsibility and try, like her husband, to lead a life of self-fulfilment.
Yet she could not believe that this would be anything but a
selfish betrayal of her children. Looking after the family had been
her life's job; in pursuance of it—a Mary distorted into Martha-
hood—she had, so she now told herself, stifled all longings for
some achievement of her own—in writing, painting, or music.
But now, complained her diary, 'all artistic ferment as well as
passion is dying down. . . . Only prayer remains, and even that
grows cold in this weary material life. Get rid of the weight of
responsibility? Throw it off? But upon *whom?*'

Persuaded that she had no right to turn from practical matters
to that life of contemplation of which, at moments—moments
doubtless of delusion—she believed herself to be capable, Sonya
became more than ever absorbed in the material welfare of the
family. Overstrained, fretted with worries, with self-pity verging
on persecution mania, she grew resentful, even acrimonious. '*He*
always worked,' she complained, 'according to his whim, and not
from necessity. He wanted to write and he wrote. He wanted to
plough and he ploughed. He took it into his head to make boots,

and stubbornly made them. He planned to teach the children, and taught them. He grew bored and threw it up.'

Increasing loss of self-restraint betrayed itself in sudden outbursts. One day Tolstoy read a love-story to the company. 'In this tale,' he observed, 'the very lowest feeling is represented as an elevated one.' 'There he goes again!' bitterly exclaimed Sonya. 'I always say he doesn't understand love and has never really loved anyone!' No one rose to the bait. 'No, really!' she went on. 'How have I managed to live with him for forty-six years if he really believes love is a low feeling? Love is the best feeling. Had there been no love as I understand the word, I would long ago have hanged myself from grief!'

Tolstoy tried to ignore this embarrassing outburst, then finally protested: 'But really, I didn't say anything. There is nothing bad in love. It is only bad when people exalt it.'

The constant irritant of Chertkov's presence was enough in itself, but before long Sonya's suspicion that he intended to filch from her all publishing rights was confirmed. Day after day he carried off, in the large carpet bag he invariably brought to Yasnaya, folders full of manuscripts. She knew, too, that he had in his keeping copies of practically everything her husband had written in the last ten years, including fiction as potentially profitable as that story she had never been allowed to publish, *Hadji Murad*. And all the while he was sending manuscripts off to his own archives in England! These, no doubt, he would himself publish after Tolstoy's death, and so do her children out of their literary inheritance. Whatever writings she could herself lay hands on she now deposited in the Historical Museum at Moscow. No wonder quarrels repeatedly flared up, unfortunately often before goggling witnesses, and, worst of all, with Chertkov jotting down in his accursed notebook things said in the heat of the moment. His reporting was invariably unsympathetic to Sonya. Here, in the historic present, he records a particularly bitter quarrel at the end of the exhausting Jubilee year of 1908:

'Sofya Andreyevna, turning to Leo Nikolayevich, irately asserts that the copyright of all his published works belong to the family. He demurs. She runs to her room, fetches her diary and reads a passage to the effect that he had made public property only those writings which had appeared after 1881, not any that were unprinted. Leo Nikolayevich protests. She shouts him down. Finally in an authoritative tone he obliges her to hear him.

Leo Nikolayevich: "You suppose our children then to be rogues who want me to do something opposed to that which is most sacred to me?"

Sofya Andreyevna: "To wish for money with which to support your children is no proof of being a rogue, . . . but——"

Leo Nikolayevich (resolutely): "No, let me finish speaking. According to you, our children will play on me the lowest possible trick. You know the principles that made me renounce my copyrights—the principles of my faith, and what do you want? I gave you my fortune—my early writings, and now it seems that you expect me to give you that for which I live. Daily I receive abusive letters, accusing me of hypocrisy. And now you ask me in very fact to become a hypocrite and a scoundrel!" And finally closing the door behind him he leaves the room.'

Sonya did not like Chertkov any the better for having overheard and chronicled this public rebuke.

Disputes over copyrights, further arrests of peasants, the presence in the very grounds of his house of an armed guard, and Sonya's continual complaints of the 'Dark Ones' all conduced to Tolstoy's mounting misery. It irked him, too, that Chertkov had extracted his permission to read whatever he wrote, even his diaries. Craving for some privacy he now began his 'Secret Diary', a safety-valve intended to be wholly private. He was right to wish to keep this from Sonya's eyes. It contained plenty to bring tears into them. Alas—striking proof of the disciple's growing ascendancy over the Master's weakening will—only a few months later, when Tolstoy supposed himself to be about to die, he sent his 'Secret Diary' to Chertkov with instructions to copy only those passages which he knew could *hurt no one's feelings,* and then to destroy the manuscript. And what did Chertkov do? He took a complete copy of all the entries he fancied, and then destroyed the original manuscript with its many affectionate passages about Sonya.

Tolstoy's 'Secret Diary' reveals his intense unhappiness at this time when, tired and bewildered, he could no longer be certain of his own motives. Did he want to go away, but feel that he ought not to leave his wife? Or was it the other way round? Did he really want to stay, but feel that he ought to go? Go away from all this? Where? To God, to die.

'I criminally desire death, . . . I thought of writing her a letter. Thank God there is no unkind feeling. One thing is always more and more distressing: the falsehood of senseless luxury in the midst of all the undeserved poverty around me. It all grows more and more grievous. I cannot fail to see it, nor forget it.'

What cannot be too clearly stated is that the 'luxury' for which Tolstoy was reproached by others and by himself was purely relative. Still without either running water or electricity, Yasnaya was simple in the extreme, and references to staff and horses give a misleading impression. Men servants in Russia were at the time far cheaper than maids in England. Horses, too, cost little, and on an estate ten miles from the nearest town were indispensable.

Meanwhie Sonya was suffering from oppression, spells of dizziness, and headaches, physical symptoms soon to become excruciating, and the depressing fact that her head had begun to shake made her feel her age. Her very exhaustion forbade her ever to relax. Impelled by a demonic restlessness, she could no longer sit still, concentrate on a book, or listen to conversation, but incessantly darted from room to room, leaving a wake of harassment behind her. Despite the devotion of her sons, like most ageing women who are ill and unhappy, she suffered from the feeling that no one loved her. Why did so many people now seem to try to avoid her—her of whom her family had said: 'We all love Sonya so much that we feel we *must* see her every day.' She remembered, too, her father writing: 'What peace'—peace! 'and happiness are in store for me when I see you again!' and a famous poet had likened her to a 'beautiful bird that had come flying into the house and brightened everything by her presence'. Irony of ironies! What had her husband himself so often called her? 'Harmonious!' Tearfully she thought of that young self who had leapt over fences and made the woods echo with her laughter. What had become of that cherished 'Sonichka?' Alas, too, for the time, not so long ago, when a quick glance at her reflection could raise her spirits. Brilliancy of complexion, brightness of eye had been slow to fade, but both were now dulled, and her willowy figure had thickened. Bereaved of her beauty she could not, like other women, have recourse to artifice. Had she used rouge Tolstoy would at once and for ever have left the house. A happily married man, she knew, can remember his wife's youthful beauty so clearly that he is still able to see it in her faded face. But a husband for whom marriage has ceased to be happy wonders what it was he ever saw in his wife. Much as Sonya's looks had been admired, her photographs do not convey that lasting beauty of bone-structure that, surviving the loss of bloom, can in a measure defy the outrages of time. As for that 'throughshine' of which Donne wrote, the 'beauty wrought out from within', its deadliest enemy is perpetual harassment.

Yet even now spells of relief—breaks in the darkness—came. Sonya's natural high spirits would revive and, taking her grand-children into the woods for a mushroom hunt, she could again be almost as happy as she had been with their parents.

And there were still lucid intervals in which the widening gulf between husband and wife would be spanned. But, as is often the case, so-called friends tended to blow up the bridges. Unfortunately the domestic dissension was now common know-ledge. Reticence had never been a fault of either husband or wife, and now that both were ill, mutual loyalty was a total casualty. In this respect they were equally culpable. Obsessed by the urge for self-justification, Sonya would break out to anyone in abuse of the man she still so much loved, and Tolstoy once went so far as to say to Goldenweiser, who was enquiring about his health: 'My illness is Sofya Andreyevna.' In his considered utterances he would, however, still defend Sonya against others and, asked why he did not practise what he preached, would declare that his reason for staying at home was not love of comfort but inability to hurt a woman he loved.

Meanwhile the Tolstoyans were suffering severer persecutions than ever, and in March 1909 the Government again struck at Chertkov. On the charge of 'pernicious activities' he was given only three days to clear out of the province of Tula. Despite her now unconcealed detestation of him, Sonya wrote a letter of protest to the Press. Though Chertkov's enforced absence was a great relief, the spring and summer were none the less an extremely difficult time. There was perpetual bickering between Sonya and Sasha, and the two-year-old vexed question of the armed guard at last burst into blaze. Seeing one of them on the point of striking a peasant he had collared, Sasha called him a villain and ordered him instantly to release his captive. The guard told his superior officer that he had been insulted, and a complaint was lodged against Sasha. Maintaining that the man had merely been doing his duty Sonya defended him, and when the district officer came to the house to charge Sasha she screamed at her mother: 'If a daughter of mine had treated me like this I would have turned the officer out of my house! I'll pack up my things and leave.' To which Sonya snapped back: 'And good riddance too!'

Sasha then went straight to the Vice-Governor of Tula and implored him to withdraw the armed guard, whose presence was making her father so unhappy. Her mission succeeded, whereupon, genuinely afraid of violence, Sonya on her own initiative hired a mounted Circassian to defend the property.

More than ever Sonya was now feeling the strain and expense of running a perpetually full house. Many distinguished guests came this year, among them I. I. Mechnikov, the Director of the Pasteur Institute. Pleased to welcome him, Tolstoy was as delighted, as Sonya was disgusted, to find this famous scientist to be one of the many readers who honoured him far more as a writer of immortal fiction than as a moral thinker. Disparaging his own novels, Tolstoy would explain that, just as a clown might cut capers *outside* the theatre where the real play was to be performed, so the only point of his fiction was to direct attention to his serious works. 'No, no,' he said to a eulogist of his fiction. 'You must not be like a former admirer of an ancient courtesan who says "How prettily you used to dance!"' He, however, consoled himself for Mechnikov's misjudgment by remembering that all scientists suffered from over-preoccupation with non-essentials. 'How many varieties of flies do you suppose they have already classified?' he asked. 'Seven thousand! How then can they find time for spiritual problems?'

To add to Sonya's troubles she now underwent an attack of

jealousy in its crudest form. Nowadays she seldom copied out her husband's writings, but discovering that he had at last finished another work of fiction she eagerly fell upon it, only to receive a horrid shock. In its heroine she instantaneously recognized that bane of her early married life, her husband's last mistress, the peasant girl Aksenya. Disgusted, she read of his delight in the 'strong peasant's body of a woman with tanned legs'. 'Yes,' she tremblingly wrote in her diary, 'it *is* that same Aksenya with the shining eyes, who in his old age now rises up from the depths of his memory!' At sixty-four Sonya writhed with the jealousy that had tormented her at eighteen.

In June, partly to escape the jangled home atmosphere, partly to meet Chertkov, who was living nearby, Tolstoy journeyed the hundred miles to Kotchety, the home of his daughter Tanya. He stayed there for a whole month, more than long enough to give Sonya a terrifying foretaste of what her desolation would be were he really to go away for good. 'We live without you at Yasnaya Polyana,' she wrote, 'like a body without a soul.'

But soon after her enraptured welcome of her husband's return new perturbation arose. Tolstoy was invited to take part in the International Congress of Peace, that year to be held in Stockholm. Feeling it his duty to seize such an opportunity to tell the world of his conviction that there was only one way to get rid of war, and that was to abolish all armies, he at once excitedly set to work on his speech. Sonya frantically opposed his going to Stockholm. He was too old, she pleaded, too frail. Besides, he would have to pass through Petersburg where there was cholera. His refusal to give up the project brought on an-other violent attack of hysteria; locking the door of her room, Sonya declared she was about to poison herself. Scene followed scene, until at last Tolstoy decided not to go: 'I went and told her. She was a sorry sight and I deeply pitied her.'

Sonya then proposed accompanying him to Stockholm and, when he declined, even suggested going in his stead and reading his address. The matter only ended when a strike caused the Congress to be postponed.

This summer saw yet another flare-up of the copyrights strife. Incensed by the unsanctioned publication in an anthology of some of Tolstoy's early writings, Sonya threatened to sue the publisher. Tolstoy's diary tells how this horrified him: 'Distressing talk with Sonya over the proposed prosecution. If she only knew how she alone is poisoning the last hours, days, and months of my life!' Sonya showed a lawyer the Power of Attorney, given her in 1883, and asked whether this document authorized her to prosecute infringements of her publishing rights. To her dismay he told her that this Power of Attorney did not really even convey—as the public, as well as herself, had always believed it to do—a legal title to the works published before 1881. Demented by the thought that after his death she would lose all control over her husband's works, she now implored him legally to secure her copyright in them and empower her to sue publishers for unauthorized publication. His refusal brought on another outbreak of hysteria and threats of suicide. Exhausted, and unable to face any more scenes, Tolstoy reluctantly recognized the necessity to make a legal will—a course though long urged upon him by Chertkov, the Law being an arm of the Government he repudiated, he had hitherto found too repugnant. But as he could not trust his natural heirs to carry out his wishes, there seemed no other way of ensuring his works becoming public property. He must have recourse to the Law, not to safeguard, but to renounce his property. He therefore gloomily instructed a lawyer to make a draft of a Will leaving his writings to the public and—forgetting that it had long since been made over to the family—his land to the peasants. Needless to say, the evidence of failing memory made this particular Will invalid. The long secretive campaign of litigation that was to poison the remaining sixteen months of his life had, however, begun.

Before the end of this troubled summer there came yet another heavy blow from the Government—the rebanishment of Tolstoy's invaluable secretary, Gusev. Arrested without any notice, he was given only a few minutes to collect his belongings before he was taken away. Pale, with tears in his eyes, Tolstoy, who was never again to see his devoted disciple, watched his departure in silence. His sister Marya, then at Yasnaya on a visit from her convent, was less restrained. Uninhibited by her nun's habit, she spat with good aim at the two officials who were carrying off Gusev.

In September Sonya was again left alone. Tolstoy and Sasha went to stay with Chertkov in his new temporary home, Kryokshino. As before, the clerical staff, farm labourers and 'domestic helpers', all ate with the family—a custom painfully distressing to Tolstoy's manservant, who, purple with embarrassment, leapt to his feet whenever any of the 'quality' approached the chair he had, loudly protesting, been forced to occupy.

The distasteful purpose of Tolstoy's visit to Kryokshino was to make the valid Will which his disciples were urging upon him. The main discrepancy between the Will now drawn up and the unbinding one, made in 1895, was that whereas in the informal one he had merely requested his heirs to give up the copyrights in his works, he now legally—at least, so he erroneously supposed —bequeathed to the public all his books written after 1881, whether as yet published or not. In 1895 he had appointed as literary executors Sonya, his old friend Strakov, and Chertkov. Sonya's name was now pointedly taken out. This, Strakov now being dead, left Chertkov the sole executor.

Except for all the worry over his Will, the concealment of which gave him an ugly sense of conspiracy against Sonya from whom for nearly fifty years he had had no secrets, Tolstoy enjoyed being at Kryokshino, where he was reverentially surrounded by whole-hearted adherents, and in the evenings royally entertained by distinguished musicians, come all the way from Moscow to play to him.

But after some days of this halcyon existence the atmosphere was shattered by the advent of Sonya, bringing with her that nervous tension now inseparable from her presence. The legal business had not yet been completed, but shortly after Sonya's arrival Tolstoy signed what he believed to be a legal document. He hoped the wretched business was now done with.

The journey back to Yasnaya via Moscow nearly proved fatal. Thousands had assembled at the railway station, the Tolstoys' carriage was surrounded and, struggling out of it, they were all but crushed. It only became possible for them to reach their train when two long lines of students, their arms linked, made a living avenue for their passage. The train began to move out of the station. As years ago on his way to the Crimea, Tolstoy appeared, his eyes full of tears, at the window. 'Keep on helping us,' roared the crowd. 'Live to be a hundred!' Far from living to be a hundred, Tolstoy, overcome by the emotional strain, scarcely survived this enjoinder. As the train gathered speed he fell into such a deep faint that Dushan declared him to be dying. But his remarkable recuperative power was not yet exhausted, and as soon as he got home he again seized his pen. In this phase of his life he wrote an immense number of letters, and this summer corresponded with an unknown Hindu who, addressing him as the 'Russian Titan' and the 'highest living moral authority', signed himself 'a humble follower of yours'. This 'humble follower' was Mahatma Gandhi.

Before long the accursed question of inheritance again reared its head. To assure herself of the legality of the new Will, Sasha showed it to a lawyer. He pronounced it utterly worthless. According to Russian law, property could not be left to the public. Tolstoy, his lawyer explained, must appoint as an intermediary some individual legatee upon whom he could rely to transmit the inheritance according to instructions. Chertkov and his friend F. A. Strakhov now conferred with the lawyer, who drew up various drafts of a new Will to be submitted to Tolstoy. These Strakhov brought to Yasnaya on a day specially chosen because he believed Sonya was to be away in Moscow, but to his embarrassment he found her returning home in the same train, her face sharp, her eyes bright with suspicion. Tolstoy chose a draft, then suffered a violent reaction against making a Will at all. But Strakhov would not let him off. Reminding him how painful it had been to Tolstoyans to hear their Master criticized for condemning property and yet making over his estate to his family, he told him how far worse it would be to hear him accused of failing to ensure that his copyrights did not become private property after his death. Tolstoy withdrew to think the wretched matter over, and several hours later announced his decision. Confident that he could rely on Sasha to make them public property, he would leave all his copyrights to her. Strakhov was astounded. Did this mean, he asked, that Countess Tolstoy would lose the income even from those works, published before 1881, she had so long believed to be hers? Tolstoy said he knew that he could trust Sasha amply to provide for her mother.

A new Will was now drafted and brought by Strakhov and Goldenweiser to Yasnaya, and—again behind locked doors—uneasily signed by Tolstoy, still tormented by a sense of guilt about the unsuspecting—or had she guessed?—Sonya. Perpetual whispering in corners, and embarrassed looks, gave the house an atmosphere of plotting, and even if Sonya did not know exactly what was going on she realized that some kind of conspiracy was afoot and that an important matter, from which she was excluded, preoccupied her husband. A sense of isolation made her feel miserably lonely in her own home, where her husband was surrounded by devoted disciples who, she felt sure, were all accusing her of 'poisoning the last days of a sainted man'. That was the verdict she read in their reproachful eyes. But when she complained to him of his disciples' hostility towards her, Tolstoy, his nerves in tatters, threatened to shoot himself unless she left him in peace. At times he would make fumbling efforts to be kind, but consciousness of concealment paralysed them, and Sonya felt desolately alone. It was not surprising that her nerves, and with them her behaviour, became more and more uncontrolled.

22

'Where Do So Many Tears Come From?'

THE deepening tragedy of the Tolstoys' marriage now took on a nightmare quality as, week after week, Sonya's hysteria, soon to be diagnosed by doctors as 'uncontrollable', turned Yasnaya into a veritable hell. Unhappily for her reputation, of all Tolstoy's life this last phase was the most documented. No fewer than seven onlookers were writing daily detailed reports on her relations with her husband, and to add to the confusion the two protagonists were themselves each keeping two records of their shared misery: Sonya her relatively reticent 'Day Book', largely a chart of the weather, her own and her husband's health and, unfortunately, also a wholly uninhibited diary; while Tolstoy at first writing only his usual diary, in July began a second one, intended to be stictly private, called 'For Myself Alone'.

The consequent jungle of material makes drastic compression as necessary as it is difficult.

The year of 1910, the last of Tolstoy's life, started well enough. Despite her ever-worsening health, Sonya gave several grandchildren a very happy New Year. There was a Christmas tree, a cinematograph performance, and a masquerade, in which, dressed up as an old witch, Sonya herself took part; and for the last recorded time the eighty-two-year-old grandfather led his traditional 'Charge of the Numidian Cavalry', with which he had so often convulsed the parents of these children.

Frequent bulletins make it clear that all through January and February Sonya was very seldom not feeling ill: 'Neuralgia in my temples and eyes. I'm afraid of going blind. . . . I've been feverish for three days,' is a mild lament. Ill-health only drove her to yet more fevered activity. She was extremely busy with her new twenty-eight-volume edition of Tolstoy's works, but this never kept her from mowing the grass or writing her own book, *The Story of My Life*, which she had begun in 1904. Meanwhile visitors were exhausting her:

> 'Guests are always preventing me from working. I dream of solitude in which to get on with my work. . . . Frittered my day away with trivial cares about everybody and everything. . . . In a terrible state of nerves. I'm short of breath and keep wanting to cry. I have too many *different* things to do!'

However too many things Sonya had to do, she never did any less needlework. One day she made her husband a 'new nightshirt out of an old one', another a waistcoat and two pairs of trousers (can these thrifty gifts have been really welcome?), the next, three caps. One barren day, 'illness and weariness' preventing her from doing anything of importance, she merely re-upholstered some chairs and a sofa. Meanwhile Tolstoy's ill-health was all the time distressing her. Besides coughing badly, he constantly complained of heartburn and hiccoughs and, before the end of January, again suffered from temporary loss of memory. As his, as well as her, diary tells, he awoke in the morning unable to remember anything—not even his name, nor where he was.

On the top of everything else Sonya was battling with financial worries. Most of her sons had spent all they had been given when their father's estate was divided up, and she was always having to scrape together doles of money to send them. Grief died with worry. Within six months Sonya had lost two of her brothers. Despite everything, her natural capacity for enjoyment survived: fine weather could still delight her, and as though consciously counting her blessings, her diary pays frequent homage to the beauty of this spring—the last of Tolstoy's life:

> 'The roads are drying, the grass growing green, the crocuses peeping, yellow flowers are breaking into bud. . . . They are ploughing everywhere . . . fragrant violets are in bloom . . . strawberry leaves have begun to show themselves. The birch trees are lovely in their fresh tender foliage. The

bees hum merrily and the birds are singing. . . . The oats are budding and the cowslips out. . . . Abundance of apple-blossom with all its magic beauty.'

Carrying the cherished little basket that had once been Vanichka's, Sonya took her grandchildren into the woods mush-room-gathering, and on wet days kept them blissfully busy painting Easter eggs, or watching her give a puppet show in the toy theatre she had herself built. She had forgotten her reluctance to give her heart to another generation and had grown especially fond of Tanya's precious only child, little Tanichka, whom she quoted as exclaiming: 'Granny is an angel, and I love her more than anyone in the world.'

For the first four months of this fatal year husband and wife were on peaceful, even amicable, terms: 'Every day Leo gets up early and brings me a bouquet of flowers.' Though Tolstoy's diary does sometimes use the formal name 'Sofya Andreyevna', it makes no complaints of her. On the contrary: 'Sonya has gone to Moscow. Thank God we parted well. Sofya Andreyevna has returned. It is pleasant. . . . A very kindly agreeable feeling for Sonya, spiritually affectionate.' Occasionally Tolstoy even blames for their frequent disputes his beloved daughter instead of his wife: 'Sasha behaved badly to Sonya.' His social conscience has not ceased to harrow him:

> 'Tormenting pangs from awareness of the vileness of my life in the midst of working people scarcely able to keep their families from starvation. Yesterday fifteen people gorged themselves on pancakes, while our servants with families of their own ran about scarcely able to prepare and serve what we devoured. I'm miserably ashamed. When I rode past some stone-breakers I felt as if I were running the gauntlet.'

But if Tolstoy's conscience gave him no peace he was not at this time specifically blaming Sonya for its pangs, and the apparent harmony between husband and wife made a very favourable impression on a new visitor, the writer Leonid Andreev:

> 'They seemed to me excellent people,' he wrote, 'and they always will. Only six months divided Tolstoy from death,

which means that whatever brought him to the terrible decision of leaving home must already have existed, but I
noticed nothing of it. On the contrary there was much in
Countess Tolstoy's treatment of her husband and in her words
that greatly touched me, and gave me confidence that his
last days would be passed in peace and joy. And I cannot
believe that there was on either side any conscious or unconscious deception such as often occurs in the presence of
strangers.'

Once again parental anxiety drew the Tolstoys close together.
The usually robust Sasha fell ill, and symptoms of tuberculosis
were detected. Sonya, whose maternal instinct was far too strong
not to make her at once forgive and cherish any child of hers who
fell ill, was as distressed as Tolstoy, and when it was decreed that
for a time their daughter must go to the Crimea, father and
mother wept together.

Not until Chertkov again cast his black shadow over Sonya's
life did calamity set in. At the beginning of May Tolstoy went
to stay with his daughter Tanya at Kotchety, and Chertkov,
whom Tolstoy had not seen since he had been exiled in the
winter, came there at the same time. Tolstoy was annoyed by
his disciple's having brought with him his private photographer
who, without even giving warning, perpetually took snapshots
of him. Otherwise he was delighted to resume long secluded
talks with Chertkov. But the arrival, one week later, of Sonya
and Andrey brought thunder into the air. A curt entry in Sonya's
diary tells volumes: 'May 9th: Leo Nikolayevich' (note use of
formal name) 'looks well. Chertkov is here. That must be why
Leo Nikolayevich was in such a hurry to leave home.' Tolstoy's
diary recognized the need for appeasement: 'To Sonya for the
first time I expressed part of what weighs upon me. And then in
order to soften what I had said, I silently kissed her. She quite
understands that language.'

The mere sight of Chertkov had acted like an east wind
on Sonya; from this meeting onwards her condition rapidly
worsened, and under the strain of far too many summer visitors
nervous exhaustion rose to danger point. 'A multitude of people,'
she complains, giving a long list of names, ending up with: 'and
a Dark One!' Tolstoy, too, found so many guests exhausting,

but he enjoyed the bracing company of one of them, the sculptor, Paul Trubetskoy, who came to make an equestrian statue of him. The host wished that this congenial fellow-vegetarian would not with his wife bathe stark naked in the river Veronka, but apart from that he delighted in Trubetskoy and roared with laughter when, asked by Sonya whether he had read *War and Peace*, the sculptor indignantly answered: 'I? I never read anything!' He was delighted too to learn that Trubetskoy housed in his studio a bear, a fox, a horse, and a *vegetarian* wolf.

At the end of May Sonya's diary complains that, grown 'wooden', Leo 'neither talks to her nor caresses her', and no longer seems to interest himself in anything. She therefore—curious prescription—makes him yet another pair of trousers and a waistcoat.

Meanwhile Sonya's diary was bemoaning the 'torments of estate management'. The flower garden had been attacked by weevils; the rye was thin because the soil hadn't been manured, the cattle were ruining the lawns. It had all become too much for her. Then fresh trouble broke out over the Circassian she had engaged to guard the garden who, whip in hand, was now exceeding his duties. Peasants protested to Tolstoy and he told Sonya that she must put things right—no easy matter. She told him how difficult it all was, but was bitterly offended when he advised her to give up trying to run the estate. Still more so when, well-meaningly, he added that if she found life at Yasnaya too tiring she was not compelled to stay there. Misunderstanding him, Sonya screamed: 'You want to drive me away!' and tore out of the house. 'I went into the garden,' reports her diary. 'It was very hot. My leg hurt and my pulse beat terribly. Lay down in a ditch till they sent a horse for me.'

A horse seemed an odd emissary, and a ditch a curious refuge to choose, but then Sonya's own diary had just described herself as quite 'crazy' from overtiredness.

A few peaceful days followed. 'An unkindly feeling towards Sergei,' confessed Tolstoy's conscience chart. 'But on the other hand a very *good* one for Sonya.'

Further agitations over the Circassian brought on yet another of Tolstoy's bad fainting fits, followed by extreme weakness and loss of memory. Once the anxiety was over Sonya, imputing his disorder to a distended liver, wrote acidly to her daughter Tanya: 'It is a long time since I have seen Papa in such an unkindly (not to put it more strongly) state as he is now. Evidently no Christian ideals can control the liver.'

In May Sasha came home completely cured. Worried by the state in which she found her father, and suspecting her mother to be its cause, she reported on it to her sister Tanya who, devoted as she was to her mother, felt the time for candour had come, and wrote to implore her to give up so much needless work and to try to give Tolstoy more tranquillity. Instead of worrying quite so much over his physical health, could she not do more for his mental and spiritual peace? 'You suffer when he does not eat; you protect him from tiring visitors, you make his clothes. You guard him with every possible care. How touched and benefited he would be if you had as much care for his inner life.' Sonya answered this letter reasonably enough:

'You write that I take care of everything to do with Papa's health and material needs. But if he ceased to live materially, how and where would his spirit live? For the manifestation of the spirit a bodily existence is necessary, and must be looked after. Do not, dear Tanya, regard this letter as self-justification, but as an explanation. I feel your love and rejoice in it.'

In June Tolstoy went to stay with Chertkov in his temporary home and, as though at the wave of a wand, his nerves were immediately soothed by the calm, rhythmic existence led there. Concern for Sonya was the only shadow over his content, and anxious to dispel any resentment she might feel at having been left behind he wrote her an almost Darby to Joan letter: 'However fine it may be to visit, home is better; and I shall return as I intended, certainly not later than the 24th. How are you and all your affairs getting on? Are you not worrying too much about them? . . . Goodbye, my dear old wife, I kiss you.' But the 'dear old wife' was in no mood to be placated. Alone with nature, flowers, and her thoughts (her own words) she found the first two inadequate, the third extremely bad company.

She still further exhausted herself sitting up till all hours, working on the new edition; the house, newly repainted, was in chaos, and she dragged all the heaviest furniture about. Overwrought, resentful, she was in no mood to receive a letter from her husband telling her that Chertkov had been granted temporary permission to return to the Province of Tula. Though no doubt Tolstoy had been glad to convey this news by letter rather than by word of mouth, he did not foresee its effect upon a woman already on the brink of complete nervous breakdown. It was catastrophic. Something gave way in Sonya's head; all semblance of self-control collapsed and, with occasional lucid intervals, from now on until Tolstoy's death, she was virtually insane. The ravings of her diary read like passages from a mental case-book. What, she asks, *can* be the matter with her? Is it hysteria? A nervous stroke? Or insanity? Spasms in her throat, pain in her heart, and all the time, day and night, she weeps. 'Where do so many tears come from?' asks her diary.

In this demented condition she harboured, and unfortunately voiced, preposterous suspicions of her eighty-two-year-old husband and the rigidly virtuous Chertkov: 'This senile eroticism for that false hypocrite Chertkov is repulsive. . . . I'm insanely jealous of Chertkov. He has taken from me all I've lived for for forty-eight years!'

Three days after Tolstoy had sent his literally maddening letter he received a telegram from Varvara Feokritova, a friend of Sasha's, now acting as Sonya's secretary: 'Sofya Andrevna intensely nervous attack, insomnia, weeping, pulse a hundred. Asked me to telegraph.' Sasha, rightly suspecting this to have been dictated by her mother, persuaded Tolstoy to reply that it would be more convenient for him to come two days later. 'More *convenient*!' stormed Sonya's diary. 'That's Chertkov's inhuman style!' She describes how she has prepared poison. But will she have the courage to swallow it? 'Yet, isn't it much worse to *live*?' Meanwhile she sent a telegram in her own name. 'Implore you to come quickly,' and the secretary, now seriously alarmed, sent another: 'I think it necessary.' Tolstoy at once started home. Awaiting his return, Sonya wrote what she called her 'Memorandum before death. (A sick woman's ravings.)' From this pitiable document only a few passages need be quoted:

'Chertkov is our divider, a cunning, despotic, heartless man. . . . Yesterday all the methods of suicide passed through my mind and the best of them seemed to be to sink beneath the waves of the sea. . . . I must ask my husband, who recently visited an asylum for insane women, whether he studied it well, for Chertkov will no doubt find it more "convenient" to put me into it. . . . But no! I won't allow that! I have the opium.'

'With all the intensity of my soul and my love of forty-eight years I yearned to go to Leo. I awaited a summons. I wept alone while he wrote me falsely affectionate letters, but stayed with his handsome idol. . . . My head feels like bursting with pain. What a rumbling of carts laden with hay! And what a rumbling in my head!'

Greatly as Sonya longed for Tolstoy's return she dreaded it too: 'I'm afraid of him. I fear his eyes—those eyes that once so passionately doted on me, but now look at me with hostility!' Crazily obsessed as Sonya was with her husband's supposed unnatural love for Chertkov, she yet found time for that age-old complaint of late-life motherhood: 'The children? Away with all thought of them! There is pain enough in my heart. I loved them very much. Could it possibly have been more? Yet all the same we are now all living apart.'

She intends, she writes, to take the poison a few minutes before Tolstoy's return: 'My revenge on him for deserting me *for a man!*' Hearing the approach of carriage wheels, she did really swallow her poison, but not a lethal dose. Tolstoy had a ghastly homecoming, and not until the early hours of the morning did he succeed in quietening Sonya. 'I had a good explanation and made peace with Leo,' rejoiced her diary. It was a flimsy peace—shattered by one peep into Tolstoy's diary. Tolstoy had begged her no longer to read this, but the habit was too old to break. 'I want to try consciously to resist Sofya Andreyevna by kindness and love,' she read. '*Resist?*' protested her own diary. 'What has he to resist when I love him so much, and my one thought and care is for *his* welfare?' Declaring that her husband was bent on presenting himself to posterity as a martyr chained to a shrew, she railed more fiercely than ever against Chertkov. Besides alienating husband and wife, he had, she averred, extinguished the last artistic spark in a great writer. 'Yes, if there is a devil, he is certainly incarnate in Chertkov. He has ruined our life.' Unfortu-nately her diary did not act as an adequate safety-valve. She had also to shriek at Tolstoy. 'Am I a miscreant that you have to struggle with me?' Desperately afraid of the existence of other objectionable passages about herself, she now clamoured to see the previous volume. Tolstoy had to admit that this and, indeed, all his diaries of the last ten years, were in Chertkov's hands. Appalled at the prospect of her enemy publishing every word against herself, she pleaded all day and most of the night for the diaries.

Next came the news that Chertkov, now settling into his new house, Telyakinki, was once again a near neighbour. Prompted no doubt by Tolstoy, he sent Sonya an olive branch in the guise of a civil, if stilted, letter. Professing himself distressed to hear that she felt hostile towards him, he assured her that any such feeling could be due only to misunderstanding: 'You were so right, dear Sofya Andreyevna, when on his birthday jubilee you told me I was your family's best friend.' At their first meeting everything, he felt sure, would be cleared up. 'So convinced am I of this,' he ended, 'that I now zealously ask you to allow me to kiss your hand and express my unimpaired and sincere devotion.'

On one of Chertkov's now resumed daily visits Sonya tackled him about the missing diaries and demanded their immediate return. At this, as he thought, unwarrantable interference between Master and disciple, Chertkov for the first time flung off his cloak of formal politeness and became openly offensive. Was Sonya afraid that he might use the diaries to expose herself and her family? To do this was, he assured her, already well in his power, and only out of affection for Tolstoy himself had he so far refrained from using his influence. 'If I had such a wife,' he added, as he swept towards the door, 'I should long ago have shot myself or gone to America!'

To improve matters, Sonya overheard him say to young Leo: 'I simply can't understand a woman who spends her whole life murdering her husband!' 'A *slow* murder, seeing that my husband has already lived for eighty-two years,' commented Sonya.

The alleged murderess knew how to coax her victim's appetite. That evening Tolstoy said he did not want any dinner: 'But I asked him at least to come and sit with us, and he ate the whole meal with enjoyment. It had been prepared with very special care to suit his digestion: purée soup, rice, a soft-boiled egg, and bilberries on bread soaked in milk.'

Evidently that well-thought-out meal did suit Tolstoy's digestion, for the next day Sonya wrote rapturously of a 'touching and happy explanation'. 'Thank God, he has *not* been taken away from me. My sufferings and ardent love have broken through the barrier of ice between us. Nothing can disrupt the union of our hearts.' Both their diaries tell of this reconciliation. She went into his room and begged him to promise her that he would never go away secretly. He promised that he would not, and in a trembling voice said: 'I love you!' They talked for some time. Thanking him for lifting a load off her heart, Sonya went to her bedroom. But soon the door opened and there he was again. 'Don't say anything,' he whispered. 'I only want to tell you that our talk has been a joy to me—a great joy,' and, weeping, he embraced her. Wholly reassured, Sonya, poor optimist, wrote: 'I'll be calmer now and come to myself. I'll be kind to everyone, and shall try to behave well to Chertkov.'

Alas for Sonya's hopes for herself and for others, the war over the diaries soon revived. It was feared that if they were surrendered to Sonya she would find allusions to Tolstoy's recent Will, of which she was not supposed to know. The arrival of her partisan, young Leo, violently backing up her demand for the diaries, only inflamed matters, and late on the night of July 10th another violent quarrel broke out between husband and wife. Demented, Sonya flung herself downwards on the boards of the balcony outside Tolstoy's bedroom, that very balcony where, on her first visit to Yasnaya Polyana, enchanted by vague inklings of the future, she had stayed on alone in the darkness rather than break the spell by joining the others indoors. Exhausted, kept awake by her moans, Tolstoy implored her to go away and allow him some sleep. Accusing him of driving her out of the house Sonya, thinly clad as she was, tore madly out into the darkness of the garden. She did not come back. Two hours later Tolstoy, alarmed, awoke Dushan and Leo and sent them to search for her. They found her lying on the wet grass. Wildly sobbing, she told them she had been turned out of the house like a dog and that unless her husband came to fetch her she would kill herself. Tolstoy's diary: 'Barely alive. A terrible night. Up till four. And worst of all was Leo. He scolded me as though I were a child and ordered me to go into the garden and fetch his mother in.'

'He with his "forgiveness" and "non-resistance",' growled young Leo, 'sits quietly in his armchair while Mother lies on the floor ready to kill herself—it's revolting!'

Summoned in the hope that she might be able to soothe her mother, Tanya now came, and was bitterly grieved by what she found. Twenty years older than Sasha, she remembered a mother her younger sister had never known—a young *serene* woman! She tried hard to convince Sasha that their mother was not shamming but really seriously ill, and many years later in her book, *The Tragedy of Tolstoy*, Sasha did generously admit that she had misjudged her mother.

Two days after that ghastly night in the garden Tolstoy gave Sonya a letter promising not only to keep his current diary to himself but to reclaim the others from Chertkov. He also told her that if she was afraid that certain passages, written on the spur of the moment, might be published and give a misleading impression, he would gladly express his true feelings for her either in his diary or in a letter. This was no mere concession to illness but common justice, for he well knew now how misleading some of his entries were. Indeed, some time before he had written, unprompted: 'I re-read my diaries and was revolted by my unkindness and harshness to Sonya and Sergei. I should like them to know that I withdraw everything I wrote about them. As I loved you when you were young,' continued Tolstoy's letter, 'so I have loved you increasingly and still do love you despite various causes of coolness between us.' He added that if his friendship with Chertkov distressed her he would, sacrifice though this would be, give up seeing him. This concession was followed by the warning that if peace did not ensue he would have to take back his promise not to leave her. He would go away. But not to Chertkov. He would even see that he did not come to live near him. But go away he certainly would. 'My dear one,' he ended, 'stop torturing not others but yourself—yourself, for you are suffering a hundred times more than anyone else.'

True to his word, Tolstoy sent Sasha to fetch back the diaries. She had to wait a long time, for before handing them over Chertkov and his industrious assistants took copies of all the passages they thought Sonya would be likely to suppress.

Though the recovery of the diaries was a great relief, there was no lasting improvement in the atmosphere. The mere sight of Chertkov's arrival on his white horse was sufficient to send Sonya into hysterics, agonized by the consciousness that nearly all the people around her believed—or pretended to believe— that her hysteria was put on to get her own way. Besides, she knew how many of them were keeping diaries! With what sort of a reputation would she be left?

Only a deranged mind could have suspected anything per- verted in Tolstoy's relations with his disciple, but, in itself, Sonya's dislike of Chertkov was no evidence of unbalance. Both in his personality and in his treatment of herself there was plenty to provoke even a normal woman, and it should not be forgotten that sooner or later he quarrelled with all Tolstoy's daughters, who at first had been devoted to him, as well as with nearly all his own friends. Even Tolstoy himself was by no means blind to his faults. He was annoyed by his habit of showing manu- scripts to strangers without permission. Still more by his criti- cisms of Sonya, for whatever Tolstoy might himself say or write about his wife, he would never allow others to speak harshly of her: 'Sonya *is* pitifuly ill,' he declared. 'It is impossible not to feel sorry for her, and impossible to be hard on her as Chertkov is, and as I often am myself.'

Goldenweiser's pen recorded a ludicrous quarrel between master and disciple when one day Chertkov told Tolstoy that he ought not to risk being made a fool of by his family. Incensed, Tolstoy retorted: 'You're a fool yourself! Everybody knows that you are an idiot!' and furiously shaking his fist at his disciple he continued to bark out: 'Fool! Fool! Idiot!'

Years ago Masha had said: 'It is my father's weakness that he relies too much upon Chertkov,' and the trouble was that, en- feebled by age, he had now grown utterly dependent on Chert- kov's practical services; gratitude, therefore, made him loyally defend his disciple against anyone else. If only he could occasion- ally have criticized him to Sonya how salutary it might have been. But this he would not do and, well aware of his indispensa- bility, Chertkov had no intention of allowing what he called 'the crazy will of a woman' to oust him from his proud position as the right hand of the Master. And he knew how strongly he was backed up. Wholly on his side, Sasha, though Tolstoy often begged her to be kinder to her mother, did all she could in his support, and her friend Varya invariably backed her up. As for the gentle Dushan, loth as he was to condemn any fellow creature, he now almost hated Sonya for endangering the health of the man he worshipped.

Goldenweiser, a guest in Chertkov's house, came over to Yasnaya every day and reported to his host all that he heard. But he was not unsympathetic to Sonya and did not believe her to be shamming. 'She looks ghastly,' he wrote. 'I feel very sorry for her as she undoubtedly is in an abnormal condition.' Tolstoy's kindly young secretary, V. F. Bulgatov, made every effort to be fair, but he did owe his job to Chertkov.

Secret messages being carried to and fro, eavesdropping, the smuggling in and out of the house of private papers, had long given Yasnaya an ugly atmosphere of conspiracy. Not for the first time in his life Tolstoy complained of the loneliness of his singularity in being sane 'in a madhouse run by lunatics'. The recovery of the disputed diaries had brought no real peace. Convinced that Chertkov would somehow get them back, Sonya on her knees implored Tolstoy to give her a written authorization for their custody. Refusing, and unable to endure another scene, he shouted at her to get up and leave him in peace. Frenzied, she ran to her room, came back, and declared that she had poisoned herself. Terrified, Tolstoy rushed towards her. 'I deliberately deceived you,' she said. 'I haven't really drunk it.' Next moment she was weepingly ashamed of her own behaviour, for which indeed there could be no defence, other than the truth that, as doctors were soon to certify, she was now wholly irresponsible for her actions. Appalled by her own condition, she no longer looked or felt in the least like herself: 'I tried to say something, but my voice was not my own. It sounded like a wild creature's.' And when she looked in the glass the eyes of the stranger who glared back at her were like a maniac's. 'You know,' she wrote to Tolstoy, 'I am very ill, and have to admit—must admit—that I am insane. Forgive me, and *help* me.'

She had not made Tolstoy carry out his promise to give up seeing his friend, but her behaviour whenever Chertkov came made it difficult for him to return. Besides, there were her crazy allegations of homosexuality which, widely repeated, had provoked indignant protest from his mother. This absurd delusion, as well as her uncontrolled behaviour, now made most of the family agree that the time had come to call in doctors. Young

Leo's comment on this tardy decision was, however: 'It's not Mother who needs medical care, but *Father*, who has outlived his mind.'

After twenty-four hours' continual observation, two doctors, one a neuropathist, gave a diagnosis wholly unintelligible to Tolstoy's reeling brain. His wife, they told him, was suffering from 'paranoia and acute hysteria', and at present there was an 'episodic exacerbation'. Summoned later, a third doctor pronounced her 'psychopathic hysteria' to be so acute that for the time being her condition must be accounted 'mental disorder'. Those eager to relieve Tolstoy of his wife's presence remembered that her brother Anton had died in a lunatic asylum. All three doctors agreed on the advisability of an immediate separation of husband and wife, and that this advice was not acted upon was the greatest pity. Had Sonya for a time gone into a sanatorium the tragic curtain to her married life might never have fallen. Instead, she was merely prescribed walking, baths, avoidance of agitation; and to prevent rushes of blood to her head, leeches were applied to the small of her back. The triviality of these measures made her laugh. 'What cures for a morally wounded woman!' She went to inspect the river. 'The Veronka is very low, like my life—and at present it would be difficult to drown in it.' Neither leeches nor medicine gave any physical relief.

Having sat up all night, on the 25th of July she decided to go away for a time to 'give Leo rest from my presence and my "suffering soul".' Leaving him a letter thanking him for past happiness, and not forgetting to take some of her now almost routine poison with her, she drove to the station. But the carriage that took her there had been ordered to meet her son Andrey and, under his persuasion, a few hours later she drove home with him. Conscious of anticlimax, she made an immediate retreat to her bedroom, but Tolstoy hurried to her and with tears in his eyes thanked her for coming back. 'I felt I couldn't possibly live without you,' he said, weeping. 'It was just as if I'd crumbled away and gone to pieces. We are too near to one another and have grown too much together. I'm so grateful to you for having returned, dear one. Thank you.'

Reassured, Sonya immediately reverted to abuse of Chertkov who, she knew, now called her, surely natural, concern for her children 'greed on behalf of her family'. Her tactics, if tactics they

R

were—and no one can dispute that there was method in her madness—prevailed. Tolstoy wrote to tell his disciple that, much as it distressed him, he felt that while his wife was so ill it would be better for them not to meet. With however bad a grace, his 'Black Shadow' had for the time to withdraw. 'The evening passed placidly and peacefully without Chertkov,' rejoiced Sonya's diary in the ensuing lull, and Tolstoy said: 'I assure you I'm not grieving at all. I feel so tranquil, so pleased, and I don't need Chertkov at all if only everything goes lovingly between us, and you are at peace.'

Sonya's diary describes her relief:

> 'Leo himself seemed glad to be free from Chertkov's odious presence. And so with tears we embraced lovingly as of old, and with that happiness in my soul I left him. . . . Now it is night. He is asleep, and I should like to look again at his dear old face that I've loved for so many years, and have studied to its veriest details. But we are not together. We live in separate rooms across the corridor, and all night I listen for sounds of him.'

Scarcely had the strife over the diaries subsided before the war of Tolstoy's Will again broke out. The discovery that the words 'being of sound mind and memory' had in error been omitted necessitated a new draft. For the sake of secrecy this was signed and witnessed, not behind locked doors, but out in the woods, with Tolstoy seated on the stump of a tree. 'What conspirators we are!' he groaned.

But Sonya's suspicions had already been aroused. Shortly before the cessation of Chertkov's visits, an overheard snatch of conversation between him and her husband had made her almost certain that they were discussing a Will. She pestered Tolstoy with questions, but he refused to discuss the matter. Her younger sons joined in the cross-examination. No answer was given. News of this fresh crisis alarmed Chertkov, who dreaded the annulment of the Will he had himself planned. He wrote Tolstoy a hasty letter which made unpleasant reading. It told of a plot allegedly hatched against him by his family. If they came to the conclusion that no new Will had yet been made, they intended, by incessantly watching over him, to prevent him from signing one. If, on the other hand, they discovered that a Will had been made, then they would never let him leave the house until they could get doctors in their pay to pronounce him feeble-minded and thus invalidate the Will. . . .

In anxiety to know whether their children were provided for, quite a few mothers might even, in normal health, be tempted to search for their husband's Will; particularly if, as in Sonya's case, no papers of any description had ever been kept from them in the past: 'All our life long we never concealed anything from one another. We read *all* one another's letters as well as diaries. I read *everything* he wrote.'

But at this juncture the thought of Sonya ferreting amongst his papers had become unendurable to Tolstoy. Nor could he bear the sense of being perpetually spied upon. To satisfy herself that he was not going off to meet Chertkov, Sonya would follow him whenever he left the house. Worst strain of all, unable to sleep herself, at all hours of the night she came into his bedroom. Precipitating their double doom, she was destroying him as well as herself. And at moments she realized exactly what she was doing, and what was happening to them both. 'Have just read over my diary and, alas, was *horrified* both at myself and my husband!'

Unable to endure further tension, Tolstoy decided on the temporary respite of a visit to his daughter Tanya; but to the general dismay Sonya insisted on going with him. For a few days the new cheerful surroundings and the people 'all good-natured, not venomous and secretive as in our family hell' calmed her. She enjoyed, too, the company of her grandchildren and respite from housekeeping cares. She also derived no little acid amusement from overhearing Tolstoy ask Tanya for a light French novel to read. 'How tired he is of his rôle of religious thinker and teacher!' At first all went well, but three days after their arrival Sonya was driven frantic by the news that the Government's ban on Chertkov's living in Tula had been permanently lifted. The only way Tolstoy could find even temporarily to quieten her was to renew his promise not to see his friend. In the agony of mind this news had caused her, Sonya was maddened by the sight of her husband absorbedly playing bridge: 'How he has slackened in old age!' She was exasperated, too, by discovering Tanya's collection of no fewer than fifty-seven photographs of him taken by Chertkov. 'When *I* ask Leo to let me photograph him he refuses!'

The nauseating tone of Sonya's diaries in these demented days, and the failure of his own memory, now enabled Tolstoy to write: 'Today, remembering my wedding, I thought that it was a fatal step. I was never even in love.'

Did the old Leo Tolstoy really forget the young Leo Tolstoy, who had written:

> 'Again a sleepless tormenting night—I, who used to laugh at the sufferings of lovers! . . . If she refuses me I shall shoot myself! . . . I live in bliss for the third year now, and every day makes us more united. . . . She is so incredibly good, so pure, and harmonious. . . . Only one man in a million is as happy as I.'

If Tolstoy had really forgotten the past, Sonya was determined to remind him of it. Sasha has written that in this tragic last phase her mother would compel him to read aloud to her passages from his diary, written nearly fifty years ago, when he was so madly in love with her, and how bitterly she wept as, reluctantly yielding, he read of their lost happiness together. No phrase can have rung more ironically than 'How serene and simple you are!'

Shortly before her own sixty-sixth and Tolstoy's eighty-second birthday, Sonya left Kotchety to go to young Leo, characteristically involved in a lawsuit. Husband and wife parted with kisses, tears, and mutual pleas for forgiveness. 'But our love,' poignantly wrote Sonya, 'having again re-awakened, seemed just like a beloved child who was always being wounded.' Able, in Sonya's absence, to relax, Tolstoy entered in his diary: 'I am very, very lovingly sorry for her,' and wrote affectionately enquiring after her health. All seemed well. But Sonya's halcyon mood did not survive homecoming. 'I had a good letter from my husband,' she admitted in her diary. 'But a letter is not life!' and she perturbed Tanya by writing to say that her father really must now definitely choose between his wife and 'the man he so insanely loves'.

Sasha's alarm at her mother's state was not allayed when, calling in a priest, Sonya, in an attempt to exorcise Chertkov's evil spirit, made him sprinkle holy water over Tolstoy's room. Soon after the performance of this rite, and other vagaries, promptly reported to Tolstoy by the diligent diarists, Sonya, further incensed by a would-be conciliatory letter from Chertkov, returned to Kotchety, a far more advanced mental case than she had left it. Refusing to eat anything, she drove Tolstoy distraught by her tears and screams. On September 12th, insanely sobbing—her own words—because he would not come with her, she went back to Yasnaya. Home was the reverse of soothing— 'The emptiness of the house and my solitude seemed terrible. . . . Tried to play a Beethoven sonata, but could not. A moan burst from my very heart.' The next day came a letter from her husband 'like a douche of cold water. There is not even a proper beginning—less courteous than a letter to a tradesman'. Three days later she complained that he had broken his promise to return for her name day. 'It is my name day, and the day of Leo's proposal to me. And what has he made of that eighteen-year-old Sonichka Behrs?'

Tolstoy did not come home until ten days after she had left. It was the eve of their forty-eighth wedding anniversary. 'Terror seizes me at the thought of what awaits me,' he wrote in his diary. His fears were realized by Sonya's shrilly reproachful reception and Sasha's report. Her mother had torn down from its honoured position over Tolstoy's writing-table the large portrait of Chertkov and put in its place one of herself.

The day after Tolstoy's return Sonya arranged for a photograph of themselves to be taken to celebrate their wedding anniversary. Tolstoy who, as well he might, had come to detest the camera, objected. But Sonya insisted. How many times had he not let Chertkov photograph him? Moreover, a newspaper had recently printed a rumour that they were to be divorced. An anniversary photograph must be given to the Press to refute this scandal. Tolstoy submitted. The result, the last photograph ever taken of Tolstoy, is one of the most painful in existence. Aged misery could not be more poignantly depicted. His hands thrust deep into his belt, Tolstoy, now within six months of death, stands in frozen dejection. His sunken eyes stare straight in front of him. Too tired, too defeated to resist, he looks like some wretched creature being dragged to the slaughter-house. At his side, both hands possessively clutching at him, Sonya, dressed all in white, is evidently trying hard to make him turn towards herself; her face, from which every vestige of beauty and charm has gone, intently searching his, as though dredging it for a smile or any slightest sign of response.

Rebuked by Sasha for his want of firmness, Tolstoy felt he must reinstate the deposed picture of Chertkov, whereupon, weeping and raving, Sonya started to take pot-shots at it with a toy pistol; and then, again ripping it off the wall, tore it into tiny shreds. Clearly Yasnaya had become impossible. What was to be done? Might it be better if Sasha went away for a time? This was a thought worth trying; so she and Varya moved out into a little house in the neighbourhood. To Sonya, at all events, it did seem that the 'old folk', as she now called herself and her husband, *were* better left to themselves: 'In general when we are alone, he is as kind and affectionate as of old.' Clutching at straws, she is deeply touched because twice 'with so much love' he brings a pear. Fortunately for her she had never lost the solace of sentimentality, which Tolstoy called 'that vague, feminine, whimpering emotion'.

Oppressively demonstrative, Sonya now kept Tolstoy under ceaseless supervision. Meanwhile Chertkov, tired of acquiescence, wrote to reproach him for allowing a 'spiritually alien person' to come between them. 'They tear me to pieces!' groaned Tolstoy's diary. 'Sometimes I think I ought to get away from them all!'

Worn out, he did temporarily elude them by once again falling dangerously ill. He was seized with violent convulsions. Sonya, though frantic with terror, did not lose her head, but swiftly filled hot-water bottles and applied mustard plasters. He became delirious, then unconscious. On her knees at his bedside Sonya loudly prayed: 'Lord. Not *this* time! Only not this time!' 'I'm suffering far worse than you,' she said to Sasha. 'You will lose a father, but I'll lose a husband for whose death I am to blame!'

Once again Tolstoy made an astounding recovery—his last; but after a family consultation Sergei warned his mother that if she could not control herself they would really be compelled to separate her from his father and put her under restraint. Chastened into temporary sanity, Sonya not only begged Sasha to forgive her and to return home, which she did, but a few days later even invited Chertkov to call. Her diary tells what this concession cost her. Too agitated all day to settle down to anything, she prepared herself for the hateful visit and, hearing the sound of horses' hoofs, had such violent palpitations that she thought she must 'die on the spot'. Exhausted by her reaction, Tolstoy decided that another visit could not be worth the strain; but any hope of peace ensuing from this decision was shattered by a disastrous discovery of Sonya's. Hidden away in the toe of one of Tolstoy's boots she found his new diary, *For Myself Alone*. Confirmation of her suspicions of the existence of a legal Will brought on more threats of suicide. 'I must end these tortures more quickly, or tomorrow Mr. Chertkov will be carrying off not manuscripts, but *me* to a lunatic asylum.' A letter to her husband implored him not to leave their children penniless by depriving them of all the royalties on his works. Her own share, she assured him, she would willingly renounce. What did she want with money? Would she not soon be dead? But the thought of destitute grandchildren was more than she could bear, and how *could* he violate his own principles by having recourse to the Law? 'I'm appalled,' she rightly predicted, 'by the thought that I may survive to see all the evil that will spring up around your grave!' Only too conscious that in making a Will he had gone against his own principles, Tolstoy was deeply disturbed, but refused to discuss the matter. Afraid that he might slip off to meet Chertkov, Sonya, sweeping herself and him towards their double doom, maddeningly persisted in spying upon him. Standing on the balcony, she watched his every movement through opera glasses; if he went for a ride she followed in a carriage. Had she not been out of her mind she would have realized how fatally, by proving the futility of trying to cope with her by kindness, she was playing into Chertkov's hands, and indeed giving Tolstoy every justification to tell himself that, even for her own sake, it would be better if he did go away.

23
'Come Back, Leovochka! Come Back!'

ON THE morning of October 28th, Sonya, as usual, went to say good morning to Tolstoy. She found his room empty. Aghast, she rushed to find Sasha.

'Where's Papa?'

'He's gone.'

'Gone! Where?'

'I don't know.'

'You don't know! Has he gone for good?'

'He left a letter for you. Here it is.'

'My God!' cried Sonya, snatching the letter.

Two sentences were enough: 'My departure will grieve you. I'm sorry for that, but please understand and believe that I could not do otherwise.'

Rushing out of the house, Sonya tore down the lime-tree avenue to the nearest pond. Sasha, Bulgatov, and several servants ran after her, dragged her out of the shallow water and somehow got her back to the house. She tried to jump out of the window, made another dash for the pond, and wanted to fling herself down the well; and so it went on all through a day that was like an unending nightmare. They had to hold her back and take away her penknife and scissors. How, she demanded, *could* she go on living without her husband? And she would be blamed for his flight! That thought turned her grief to frenzy.

Except for young Leo, who was abroad, all her children came, a mental specialist was sent for, and a trained nurse to keep Sonya under constant watch.

She did not know where Tolstoy had gone, but guessing that he might seek his nun sister, addressed to the Sharmandino

Convent a letter full of love, contrition, and reckless promises for the future:

> 'Leovochka, darling, come home and save me from suicide. Leovochka, friend of my whole life, I'll do everything you wish. I'll give up all luxury, I'll be friendly with your friends; I'll cure myself and become gentle. Dear, dear, come back. Even the Gospel says you must never, in any circumstances, desert your wife. My dear darling, friend of my soul, save me. Come back if only to say farewell before we part for ever.'

No news for three days, during which, according to her diary, Sonya ate nothing whatever. Then a telegram from a newspaper: 'Leo Nikolaevich has fallen ill at Astopovo. Temperature 104.' Sonya at once took a special train from Tula to Astopovo. Tanya, Ilya, Misha, Andrey, and the trained nurse travelled with her.

What after so many years of indecision had at last precipitated Tolstoy into flight Sonya was doomed to learn both from Dushan's lips and from the last pages of her husband's diary which told exactly what had given him the 'final jolt', as he called it.

> 'I heard the opening of doors, and footsteps. Through the crack of the door I saw a light in my study and heard a rustling. It was Sofya Andreyevna searching, probably reading. Day and night my every word and move must be known to her. I don't know why this aroused in me unrestrainable indignation and aversion. I tried to sleep again and could not. I tossed about for an hour, lighted a candle and sat up. The door opened. Sofya Andreyevna came in and asked: "How are you?" and was surprised to see my light. My aversion and indignation grew.'

Suffocated by the sense of being perpetually spied upon, Tolstoy was seized by an impulse, overmastering as the claustrophobia that makes a man leap from a moving train. It was not so much that at last he decided to go, as that, suddenly, he could no longer bear to stay. He awoke Sasha and Dushan, and they helped him to pack a few things. Lantern in hand, he staggered out into the darkness and the deep snow and, stumbling, knocking himself against the trunks of trees, made his way to the stables to see to the harnessing of the horses. At five in the morning, accompanied only by the trembling Dushan, he drove away for ever from the home he had loved for eighty years. He turned his head for one last look at his two earliest memories—the lime trees and silver birches, and at that later memory, the apple orchards he and his young wife had themselves planted.

Sonya's guess was right. A kind of homing instinct drew him towards the Sharmandino Convent, to talk to Countess Marya, the sole survivor of his brothers and sisters.

The train journey to the nearest station to Sharmandino took six hours. Concern and pity could not, like lime trees and apple orchards, be left behind. Soon after the train bore him away Tolstoy said mournfully: 'I wonder how Sofya Andreyevna is now. I am so sorry for her.'

What could Dushan answer?

Needless to say, the fugitive was at once recognized by fellow travellers, and before long headlines were telling the world: 'Leo Tolstoy leaves Yasnaya Polyana. . . .'

Tolstoy and Dushan drove in a cab to a monastery near to the convent and asked for shelter: 'My being here may, perhaps, be disagreeable to you. I'm Leo Tolstoy, excommunicated by the Church.' A monk courteously assured him that all were welcome, and he was given a room. Next morning he hurried to see his sister and at once began to search for the 'hut' in which he hoped to end his life. But this plan was shattered by the arrival next day of Sasha to whom he had telegraphed to let her know where he was, but telling her not to follow until sent for. Unable to wait she had, however, come with all possible speed and brought with her distressing letters from Ilya and Andrey, both condemning their father for leaving their mother. Worse, she told him that Sonya had guessed where he was and intended to pursue him. Whatever sense of escape Tolstoy had gained was lost. Panic seized him. He must go away at once—somewhere—anywhere. But first he wrote Sonya a letter intended to extinguish any hope of his ever coming back. 'A meeting between us and still more my return is impossible.' Imploring her to accept the inevitable, he ended: 'Do not think that I went away because I do not love you. I love you and pity you with all my soul. But I cannot do otherwise than I am doing. . . . Farewell, dear, and may God help you!'

Bent on escape, Tolstoy decided to travel south to stay for a day or two with a nephew. From that point onwards his plans were undecided. Perhaps he would try to get abroad; failing that, possibly go to the Caucasus and live with some of his disciples. Meanwhile there could be no delay. They must leave at once. At four o'clock in the morning the party of three set off for the station.

Leo Tolstoy had started upon his last journey. He was looking very ill, and in the afternoon he began to cough, and his temperature was found to be rising. A long halt at Astopovo gave the terrified Dushan a chance to find the station-master, who at once agreed to put up the sick man in his own little house at the railway station. Reluctantly Tolstoy was taken off the train and put to bed.

Two days later Sonya arrived to take up perhaps the saddest vigil ever kept by wife. It was to last five days. Her husband, she was told, was very ill with pneumonia, and his doctors agreed that, as long as any hope of recovery remained, she could not be allowed to see him. In fact, since emotional excitement might well be fatal, he must not even know that she had come. Arrangements were made for her and the nurse to go on living in the special railway coach, now shifted into a siding, in which they had travelled. Meanwhile Sonya had learned who were already there—Sergei, Tanya, Sasha, and, of course, Chertkov.

It had been agreed that Tolstoy should not know of the arrival of any members of his family. But this plan at once broke down. Sonya had brought with her the little pillow, made years ago by herself, upon which, at home, her husband's head always rested. Believing this to be a talisman, she begged Dushan to place it under his patient's head, and he was too soft-hearted to refuse. Instantaneously recognizing his special pillow, Tolstoy urgently asked how it had come. Dushan told him it had been brought by Tanya. Astonished to learn of his daughter's presence, Tolstoy insisted on seeing her, and at once questioned her about her mother. How was she? What was she doing? Afraid of betraying Sonya's nearness, Tanya was evasive. 'Better not talk, Papenka darling,' she said.

'Tell me, tell me,' he sobbed. 'What can be more important to me?'

Meanwhile, the wife who had nursed him through all his many desperate illnesses—so often dragged him back from death —was shut out. Guarded by two hospital nurses, besieged by reporters, snapped by photographers, she stood for hours in the falling snow or wandered despairingly about the railway station. From time to time she would force her way to the little house to peer through its windows, but at her approach the blinds were always pulled down. Then she would go to the door to enquire after the sufferer's condition, and ask what he had said. Inside that little house, unconscious of the lurid irony of the situation, lay the would-be recluse. His efforts to escape into peace and obscurity had resulted in a blaze of publicity, unparalleled even for him. Swarming with police and journalists, the sleepy, hitherto unimportant railway station (today 'Leo Tolstoy Station') had become the centre of commotion and world-wide suspense. The telegraph wires were humming; the local post-office was swamped; perturbed government officials were frantically conferring with the police as to what precautions should be taken to keep order. Sent by the Holy Synod, an Abbot came to urge Tolstoy to return to the Church before he died. He was not admitted, nor were the Governor of the province and various high officials from Petersburg.

Drifting towards the darkness, Tolstoy coughed and tossed. His speech was very difficult to hear, but mumbled snatches revealed how much the thought of Sonya troubled his clouding mind. He was trying hard to convey something to Tanya and, bending over him, she was at last able to catch the muttered words: 'On Sonya . . . too much is falling. We have managed things badly.'

In pain himself, Tolstoy was haunted by the sufferings of others. On the evening of November the third, as one of his daughters straightened his bed, she saw that his eyes were full of tears, and suddenly he sobbed out: 'And the *peasants*, the *peasants*—how *they* die!' That night, in between spells of delirium, he kept asking those about him to write down what he said, but his words were either inaudible or incoherent. Evidently he was most anxious to impart something; he would try to speak, groan, sigh—desist. 'Don't think,' said Sasha, trying to soothe him.

'Ah, how can I stop thinking? I must, I *must* think!'

In the hope that this might soothe him, Chertkov read aloud passages from *The Cycle of Reading*. Tolstoy gave up trying to talk and listened.

Later there came moments when he could again speak quite distinctly. 'It seems that I am dying,' he said to Chertkov. 'However, I must try just a little longer.' But not long afterwards he was heard to say: 'Checkmate.'

Next morning he seemed better, but towards evening again became delirious and then very distressed because he could not make his daughters understand and write down what he was struggling to say. A few gasped-out words they did hear: 'Seek ... seek. Always keep seeking.' ... 'I love much ... I love much.' ... 'Escape. Escape. ... Let me go.' ... 'How dare you hold me back?' ... 'Let me go.' ... 'I am tired of this world of men.' Otherwise his words were unintelligible until, suddenly, at the sound of an opening door, he strugglingly raised himself in his bed and, opening both his arms, in a loud joyful voice cried out: 'Masha!—Masha!'

Dushan still refused to give up hope. But it seemed that the master was trying to say goodbye to the disciple. 'Dear Dushan, dear Dushan,' he was heard to say in a tone of unforgettable tenderness.

On Friday, the fifth, there was a sharp turn for the worse: 'I don't understand what I have to do. ... I don't understand what is expected of me now,' Tolstoy kept repeating. Later he said: 'Hard to breathe. ... It's time to knock off ... all is over and it doesn't matter.' His last audible words were firmly and clearly spoken to his daughters as they rearranged his pillows. 'This is the end,' he said, his eyes full of tears. 'This is the end, and I give you only this one piece of advice. There are millions of people in the world, and you ought not to think only of this one Leo Tolstoy. ...'

In a recent letter Tolstoy had expressed the hope that he might die fully conscious and so not miss the 'experience of dying, which could be so beautiful'. This hope was not realized. Dim now, the famous, penetrating eyes no longer searched nor questioned; and after the morning of Saturday the sixth he did not regain consciousness. Towards midnight all five doctors abandoned hope, and as their patient was dying as hard as he had lived they gave an injection of morphia. After this, for several hours, Tolstoy lay quite still. Chertkov sat at the head, Sergei at the foot of his bed. Except for his wife, all the rest of the family were in the adjoining room, of which the door was open. At last, at about two in the morning, Sonya was allowed to come in. Chertkov had the grace to leave the room. For a few moments, as though afraid to approach, she faltered on the threshold. Then, hastening to the bed, she kissed her unconscious husband's forehead and fell upon her knees murmuring: 'Forgive me, forgive me.' Afraid that recognition of her might drag the dying man back into suffering, one of the doctors led her away into the next room. An hour later the effects of the morphia had quite worn off. Once again the dying man began to stir and to moan; but his pulse was now a mere flicker, his breathing weak and laboured. Sonya was allowed to come back. Kneeling by the bed she whispered words of love, but, far out of reach of sight or sound, Tolstoy could no longer hear the voice he had so often longed, so often dreaded, to hear. He merely gave three deep, deep sighs. After that his breathing became very feeble. Long since too weak for its task, the heart was giving up the lost battle. For Sonya, all existence now narrowed down into intent listening to the involuntary, but long-drawn-out, struggle for survival. Each fluttering respiration seemed an immense undertaking unlikely to be achieved. Frozen, she counted the ever fainter breaths. At last, at five minutes past six in the morning, she saw the weeping Dushan rise to his feet, approach the bed and reverently close the unseeing eyes. The long, truceless war between the contending Leo Tolstoys had come to its end.

In every large city in Russia thousands had stood through the night watching the frequent bulletins, and when there came the final flash, 'Tolstoy is dead', all hats were swept off and sobs broke out. Next day the leading newspapers were widely bordered with black; theatres were closed and no lectures given in the universities.

Nearly eighty years ago, when Tolstoy was a little boy at Yasnaya Polyana, his eldest brother, Nicholas, had told him that in a certain place quite close to the forest of Zazov he had buried a green stick on which was written a magic message that one day would dispel all evil from the hearts of men and bring about eternal peace. This legendary stick remained to Tolstoy the symbol of his lifelong quest—the ending of war. He had told all his children about it and written in his Will: 'Let my body be put into a wooden coffin, and if it is not too much trouble, bury me at the place of the Green Stick.' This wish was carried out. His plain wooden coffin was borne by his sons from Yasnaya Polyana to the place of the 'Green Stick', a small wooded knoll, in which a grave had been dug.

Had the Government, who sent mounted police to the forest, not forbidden the running of any special trains, the funeral procession would have been even miles longer. It was headed by the peasants of Yasnaya Polyana bearing a banner with the words: 'Leo Nikolaevich, the memory of your goodness will never fade among us orphaned peasants.' It was the first public funeral without religious rites ever held in Russia. No priests were present, but two choruses of students sang the chorale, 'Eternal Memory', and everyone knelt bareheaded. Sonya, it was observed, bore herself with restraint and dignity.

24
Widowhood

THE day after the funeral Sonya fell ill, and for a fortnight had to stay in bed with a high temperature, a racking cough, and torments of neuralgia. Over two and a half thousand telegrams came and innumerable letters. But neither pain nor sympathy could distract her from her grief and the anguish of remorse that overwhelmed her. Struggling into clothes, she tottered to her husband's grave. Despair. Dismay. 'What is solitude going to be like?' asked her diary. 'Terrible! And there is no future.' Why was she still alive—she the mere string from which the great kite had broken away, escaped? 'Nov. 29th. Unendurable anguish; gnawing conscience; and pity for my husband. How he suffered at the end. I *can't* live!' 'Dec. 7th. Unbearable despair the whole day. I couldn't sleep all night, and I wept all the morning.' Three days later: 'No sleep at all. Oh these terrible nights all alone with my thoughts and tormented by conscience. The darkness of these winter nights and the darkness of my soul!'

Sleeplessness became unbearable. The veronal she was given made her feel dazed in the daytime. 'Better so,' she wrote, 'one's sufferings become less acute. The body loses some of its capacity to suffer. But where then is the *soul*?'

In the hour of need, faith in personal immortality deserted her: 'I am tormented by the eternal separation from Leo.' And what spiritual sustenance had he left her to live on? If her faith in orthodox religion had not been destroyed, her happiness in its observances was impaired. On her knees in church she felt guilty of mental infidelity towards him. And no new armour of his forging was any shield to her. *The Kingdom of God is Within You*? She recognized this to be a wonderful book, but could find no heaven within herself. She remembered what his brother

Sergei had said of religion 'purged of superstition': 'Our dear
Leo has licked all the caviare out of the sandwich and he now
offers us the dry crusts.'

A faint ray of warmth reached her heart:

'Today, the fortieth since his death, the entire village
assembled at the grave and covered it with leaves and fir tree
branches. The men all bowed their heads and sang "Eternal
Memory". Grief made me cry, but I was touched by the
peasants' love for him. In that we are all at one, and they are
so sweet to me.'

Every day she walked through the deep snow the three-
quarters of a mile to Tolstoy's grave. 'Each time I feel perplexed.
Can that be he, my dear, dear, beloved Leovochka there under
the ground? And every time I cry, cry, cry till I have a pain in
my chest.'

The glade had now become a place of pilgrimage. Men,
women, and children flocked to gaze at the site of the 'Green
Stick' where the body of Tolstoy lay. Many cut inscriptions in
the wooden balustrade that surrounded the small mound of his
grave. Many more wrote messages on scraps of paper and pegged
them to the ground with little sticks, until far around the earth
was strewn with letters to the spirit of Tolstoy.

Sonya made no further attempt to end her life. Those who
maintained that the motive of her suicidal threats had been to
scare Tolstoy into submission declared that her incentive was now
gone. More probably, the reason was the numbed inertia of
despair; the loss of the stimulus of acute nervous strain. Grief
over death is, after all, the rarest cause of suicide.

The months crawled past. The interminable winter melted
into spring. Instead of the snow, forget-me-nots quilted the
grave. The loveliness of the opening year which Leovochka
would never see again brought its peculiar pain. She remembered his yearly delight in the spring, so often put into words:

'The leaf on the birch has opened like a tender little ker-
chief. There are mounds of pale blue forget-me-nots, yellow
fields of wild garlic. . . . A grey-black bee hums, weaves its
way and feasts. Burdocks, nettles, the pipe-stems of rye push

upward hour by hour. Yellow primroses. The dew is iridescent on the sharp-pointed tips of grass. In the evenings the songs of nightingales, cuckoo birds, and of peasant women.'

She remembered, too, his excitement over the first lilies of the valley, the first mushrooms, the fragrance of the lilac.

> The Spring has come, and the earth has smiled,
> And the dead must be forgot?

That is for the young; not for the old. Yet, with the re-awakening of the earth, memories of long-ago springs came softly winging back, and in retrospect these seemed wholly happy. Grief became more gentle. Less inflamed by remorse too, for her anguish over her own part in the final tragedy had been relieved by a doctor's explanation of Tolstoy's flight. There was, he told her, a certain type of pneumonia that at its onset caused such acute cerebral excitement that, poisoned by the infection from his brain, a sick man might easily run away from his home and wander about, hurrying to get he himself knew not where. Eagerly snatching at this diagnosis, Sonya persuaded herself of its truth. Of course, she assured herself, Leo had been very ill *before* he left her. Separations from one another had always reconciled them. This latest reconciliation would be everlasting.

The slow pageant of the year unfurled. She remembered his delight over the cherries ripening in the sunshine, the apples reddening on the trees they had planted, the corn turning to gold.

Sonya felt sure that whatever time might yet remain to her could seem no more than a mere postscript to her life. But not one of the nine years of her widowhood was to be passed in peace. The struggle went on. Endless strife lay ahead. To the end of her days she had to cope, contrive—endure. To begin with plans had to be made. Soon after Tolstoy's death his family approached the Government to ask if it would buy Yasnaya Polyana for the nation. The question was debated at two sessions. At first it was decided that the place should be bought for the sum, suggested by Tolstoy's heirs, of 500,000 roubles. But at the second session it was decreed impossible thus to honour the memory of one of the greatest enemies of the State, or to enrich his children. The matter was dropped. But two years later Sasha, to whom Tolstoy had left all his copyrights in trust, was paid so large a sum for the right to publish his posthumous works that she was able to buy Yasnaya Polyana from her mother and her brothers. This achieved, she did not lose one moment in carrying out her father's lifelong wish, and only one month later his land was handed over to the peasants for division.

Sonya was allowed to stay on in the house and to keep the apple orchard and the plantations, the creation of which, in their early married years, had given her and Tolstoy so much happiness. Acquired by the municipality, the Moscow house and all its furniture became the Tolstoy Museum and Library, and a new building erected in the courtyard the Tolstoy School.

Efforts to carry out the clauses in Tolstoy's Will that concerned his writings led to endless strife, bitter dispute, and even to litigation; it had not ended when, in 1917, the Bolshevik Government confiscated all literary, as well as all other, property. Sasha had the legal right, given her in Tolstoy's Will, to publish, under Chertkov's editorship, the manuscripts lodged in the Historical Museum. But the bone of contention between mother and daughter was not the copyrights but the manuscripts themselves. The year after Tolstoy's death Sonya suggested that copies of these should be taken and put at the disposal of Sasha and Chertkov; she herself would then present the originals to some museum. Her daughter and Chertkov would not agree to this. Sonya then proposed a Court of Arbitration, but, claiming full ownership of the manuscripts, Chertkov and Sasha would not consent to this compromise. Sonya had already handed over to her daughter the manuscripts found after Tolstoy's death at Yasnaya. All she stipulated was that those she had herself put together and that her husband had given to her should not fall into Chertkov's hands. Not trusting him, she feared that he would tamper with them, and her fears were fully justified. Young Leo Tolstoy's vindication of his mother, *The Truth About My Father*, is too partial for its indictment of Chertkov, whom he detested, to be reliable. There is, however, no possible reason to doubt the truth of M. A. Stathovich's article (published in *The Russian Review*), written in collaboration with Tolstoy's daughter, Tanya Sukhotin, who was extremely truthful and in any case wholly disinterested. Here are her words: 'When my mother would not consent to give my sister and Chertkov the manuscripts from the Museum, they resorted to every means to force her to do this.

They went to her doctor and asked him to certify that she was insane.' To explain why her own faith in Chertkov had been shattered, Tanya quoted from her father's Will: 'In the diary of my married life I ask to have all matter destroyed, the publication of which might give pain to anyone. Chertkov has promised to do this while I am still alive.'

'And,' continued Tanya, 'my father in his last years gave Chertkov his diaries so that everything which might after his death grieve anyone should be cut out. Chertkov did destroy all such passages but, without telling my father, first took photographs of every one of them! Thus, against my father's wishes, all the parts in his diaries written in moments of irritation, and which later he wanted to destroy, remained in Chertkov's possession. After my father's death, when the proofs of some of Tolstoy's letters were sent to Chertkov, he struck out every passage in which my father wrote nice things about my mother!'

Sonya cannot be blamed for all the ugly disputes that followed.

Three years after Tolstoy's death the Professor of Russian Literature at Petersburg University asked Sonya to write her autobiography. She protested that she would find it too difficult, but, partly because she felt it to be a duty and partly because she welcomed an opportunity to present her own case, she finally consented. The short book she then wrote inevitably lacks the spontaneity of her diaries, but it is written with unmistakable sincerity and without overmuch exercise of selective memory. Descriptions of how Tolstoy wrote his earlier books, especially *War and Peace*, are extremely interesting. After that, the book mainly concerns itself with the long-drawn-out domestic drama. Expatiating on the peculiar difficulties of her position as the mother of Tolstoy's children, she harps on the enduring mutual love between him and her. The attempts of his 'intimate friend' (Chertkov) to wreck their married life are bitterly denounced, and naturally she seized this chance to contradict the misrepresentations of herself that, widely circulated by gossip, were seeping into innumerable newspapers and magazines. This purpose, in her autobiography only implicit, was clearly stated in the preface she later wrote to *Leo Tolstoy's Letters To His Wife*, a book published in 1918. 'After my death, which in all likelihood is near, the public will as usual misjudge and distortedly depict my relations with my husband. Let them therefore form their own judgments based upon genuine data, instead of upon gossip, guesses, and inventions.'

If, admittedly, Sonya's book aimed at self-justification, it did not spare herself blame. Many humble admissions were made, for instance: 'The sufferings of my hot and harassed heart clouded my reasoning powers. . . . I lost my mental balance, and because of that I had a bad effect on my husband.'

The end of the book describes her widowhood up to the time, 1913, at which she was writing:

'I live in Yasnaya Polyana keeping the house and its surroundings as they were when Leo was alive, and looking after his grave. . . . I try to occupy myself only with what in some way or another concerns his memory. . . . I feel profound gratitude to the Sovereign Emperor for granting me a pension which enables me to live in security, and to keep the house. Three years have now passed. I look sadly on the havoc in Yasnaya Polyana—how the trees which we planted are being cut down, and the beauty of the place gradually destroyed now that everything has been handed over to the timber merchants and peasants, who frequently have terrible quarrels about the land or the woods. . . . And what will happen to the house after my death?'

Little did Sonya suspect the fate that even before her death threatened the house. Not for much longer now would the 'Sovereign Emperor' have power to enable any family, least of all his own, to 'live in security'. His reign was nearing its terrible end and the beginning of a cataclysm in which the mere cutting down of trees would come to seem very trivial. But before that red horror broke, Sonya had to go through the pain of seeing the destruction of all her husband's hopes for World Disarmament. Less than four years after the death of its most persuasive pacifist, the world was plunged into the greatest war yet known—the war that did not end war.

In 1914 Sasha came to see her mother. She found her greatly changed.

'Grief has aged her,' she wrote. 'She spoke little. Mostly she drowsed in the Voltaire armchair in which Father had so loved to sit. . . . Her bowed head shook. She seemed to have shrunk. Her large black eyes that used to be so brilliant and darting were dulled. Her sight was very bad.'

About to leave for the Turkish Front, Sasha was dressed as a nurse. 'Why are you going to the war, Sasha?' asked the pacifist's widow. 'Your father would not have approved.'

Three years of sorrow, suspense, and strain. Then, in 1917, the revolution that was to change the whole world. Search as Sonya might, nowhere in her husband's teaching could she find the slightest support to help her to put hope in any new order likely to emerge from the existing chaos. He had condemned the autocracy of Czarist Russia. But of the forces beginning to oppose it he had predicted even worse:

'The greatest enemy to mankind,' he had written in 1904, 'is this Social Democracy. It is preparing for a new slavery. It teaches a future good without present betterment. It promises golden streets without the bloody Gethsemane. It will regulate everything. It will destroy the individual. It will enslave him. It will make chaos out of cosmos, breed terrorism and confusion, which only brute force will be able to destroy.'

Nothing in that prediction to fortify Sonya, at the end of an exhausting life, to endure the havoc, terror, and suffering all around her, and to see savagely swept away so much that in her happy youth she had loved and believed to be enduring.

Many alleged that Tolstoy had himself been one of the chief causes of the revolution, amongst them his own son, Andrey, who had openly declared: 'If I were not my father's son, I would hang him!' If this be true, history holds no greater irony. Non-violence being the core of Tolstoy's creed, in his opinion no possible end could justify the means employed. And even could the result of the revolution have been achieved without violence, he would have considered it merely the exchange of one form of tyranny for another. His dread and abhorrence were the State. He wanted it to cease to exist.

.   .   .   .   .

In the ferocity of the revolution countless estates were wrecked and their owners burned out of their homes. Yasnaya Polyana was one of the very few to be spared. The house and the surrounding land, turned into a State farm, were put under the management of Sonya's son-in-law, N. L. Obolensky, the widower of Masha; and thanks to this humane arrangement Sonya was allowed to stay and occupy a few rooms in the house. With her lived that lifelong solace her sister. But Tanya's lovely singing voice had gone, and with it her disbelief that she could ever die. A grandson of hers was with them too, and the gentle Dushan. Obolensky, remarried, lived with his wife in rooms in the adjacent Kuzminsky House and his roof sheltered Sonya's daughter Tanya and her daughter Tanichka.

The safety of this little community was by no means assured. Destruction raged all around. Before the end of 1917 terrifying rumours reached Yasnaya Polyana. Peasants from neighbouring villages had decided to come and destroy it! The rumours proved true. A ravening mob approached—came so near that all hope was given up, and flight determined upon. The horses were being harnessed; Sonya, her sister, daughter, and granddaughter were seated on their packed cases ready to flee. Suddenly news of deliverance came. Armed with spades, pitchforks, scythes, the faithful Yasnaya Polyana peasants had mustered themselves to make a determined stand. The rabble was driven off and Sonya's sanctuary, almost the only house in the district to remain intact, was saved.

Famine followed. In 1918 Sasha again came to visit her mother. She found the dinner-table set and Ilya Vasilyevich, the now immensely old manservant, noiselessly serving a formal meal. The tablecloth was snowy white; the silver brilliantly polished; the aged man wore a heavily patched pair of those white cotton gloves that had so often offended Tolstoy. The food was punctiliously handed round. But there was very little on the plates. No meat. Merely boiled beets, and minute pieces of black bread made of flour copiously mixed with chaff.

For a long time Sonya and her companions were terribly short of food but, some time before her death, special rations were mercifully given by the Soviet Government.

Sonya appears to have endured these closing years of shock, terror, and privation with dignity. Old age, a kindly filter to her memory, enabled her to retreat into a skilfully edited past. Her thoughts perpetually drifted back to cherished memories of 'Leovochka's' courtship, and of their early life together. Discriminatingly read, his diary, once the source of so much pain, became her greatest solace. Knowing which pages to turn to—where to linger, where to skip—she could flit for comfort and pride from phase to phase of her long, loaded life.... Courtship—'I could not have believed I would ever be so much in love.' Early marriage—'No one has had, or will ever have such happiness. She is so incredibly good, pure, and harmonious. Something tortures me. It is jealousy for the man who would be her equal. I am not.... Why does such a being as she love me?' And his letter to 'Granny': 'I live in such bliss now for the third year and every day makes it more united and deeper still.' So many passages gave reassurance. Most valued, because most recent, was the memory of his saying: 'Sonya, you are ill; you do not walk about and, do you know that, not hearing the sound of your step, I can neither read nor write.'

She loved, too, to read well-chosen passages aloud to sympathetic listeners, and tributes from her husband's friends—for example, those long, long-ago words of Count Sollugub: 'You are the skilled nurse of your husband's genius.'

Intermittently Sonya continued to write *The Story of My Life*, begun in 1890. But she was never to finish this book. The last words she wrote were:

> 'Evidently my life is drawing to its close. I am beginning to go blind. I have not the strength to finish my manuscript. But I am still very thankful to God that I was for so many years the wife of Tolstoy. And I regard the sufferings at the end as an atonement for my sins.'

Sonya still walked every day—the distance must often have seemed long—to her husband's grave, near which a plain wooden bench had been placed; and each autumn as the last few frozen leaves of the silver birches, turned now to gold, twirled slowly to the ground, she would remember how directly the long winter set in he had always begun to look forward to the spring.

Sonya would often take callers round the house and show them everything associated with Tolstoy, and never failed to draw their attention to that hard, narrow, leather couch, on which all her children, as well as her husband, had been born. When she was seventy-four Tikhon Polner, author of *Tolstoy and His Wife*, spent several days at Yasnaya Polyana. He described his hostess as calm and weary, with a great deal of dignity. 'Tall, slightly bent,' he wrote, 'the Countess moved through the rooms like a shadow that a gust of wind could waft away. She talked readily, but without a smile. With evident enjoyment she read to me memories of the happy early days at Yasnaya, and recited several poems Fet had dedicated to her. Of Chertkov she spoke quietly, rationally, but with a cold animosity.'

Tikhon Polner questioned Sonya about Tolstoy. After a silence of several seconds, she answered: 'I lived with Lev for forty-eight years, but I never really knew what kind of a man he was.' Tikhon Polner interpreted this as bitterness. It could equally well have been humility. How many women with husbands far less complex than Tolstoy would, were they truthful with themselves, have to give the same reply.

Except for Leo all Sonya's sons had left Russia during the revolution, but until the very last the two beloved Tanyas were with her, and Sasha, with whom she had long been reconciled, was a frequent visitor. This forgiven daughter was there when the end came. In the autumn of 1919 Sonya developed pneumonia. Her two daughters nursed her for eleven days. She suffered, but was, they said, wonderfully patient and kind to everyone.

'Sasha, dear,' said the dying woman, 'forgive me. I do not know what came over me that last year. I killed him, you know.'

'Forgive me too,' said Sasha, weeping. 'I too was very much to blame towards you.'

On November 4th, after confession and communion, Sonya died.

'I was the one to close her eyes,' wrote Sasha. 'She had been so gentle and had borne her sufferings with extraordinary fortitude.'

Not long before her death Sonya was asked whether she still often thought about Tolstoy. 'Oh, but always!' she answered. 'I live with him all the time, and torment myself for not having been good enough to him. But I was faithful to him body and soul. I was only eighteen when I married him, but I never loved anyone but him.'

BIBLIOGRAPHY

The Works of Tolstoy.
The Diary of Countess Tolstoy.
The Later Diary of Countess Tolstoy.
Autobiography of Countess Tolstoy.
Tolstoy's Diaries.
The Private Diary of Leo Tolstoy (1847-57)—edited by Aylmer Maude.
Life of Tolstoy (First Fifty Years)—Aylmer Maude.
Life of Tolstoy (Later Years)—Aylmer Maude.
La Verité sur Mon Père—Leo Tolstoy.
Leo Tolstoy—Ilya Tolstoy.
Tolstoy, A Life of My Father—Alexandra Tolstoy.
The Tragedy of Tolstoy—Alexandra Tolstoy.
Recollections of Tolstoy—Stepan Behrs.
The Tolstoy Home—Tatiana Tolstoy.
Tolstoy As I Knew Him—T. A. Kuzminsky.
Leo Tolstoy—Ernest Simmons.
Tolstoy, His Life and Work—Derrick Leon.
Life of Tolstoy—Paul Birukov.
Tolstoy's Love Letters (to Valérie Arseneu)—Paul Birukov.
Autobiographical Elements in Tolstoy's Works—Paul Birukov.
Journal Intime—Preface and notes by Paul Birukov.
The Final Struggle—Aylmer Maude.
The Last Days of Tolstoy—Vladimir Chertkov.
Tolstoy, His Life and Works—Steiner.
Tolstoy and His Wife—Tikhon Polner.
The Letters of Tolstoy to His Cousin—Alexandra Tolstoy.
Count Leo Tolstoy—E. J. Dillon.
Grandeur et Infamie de Tolstoy—Jean Cassou.
The Inconstant Genius—Nazarov.
Tolstoy, His Life and Works—Edward Garnett.
Tolstoy—Romain Rolland.
Talks With Tolstoy—A. B. Goldenweiser.
Tolstoy—Fansset.
Life of Tolstoy (By Deeds of Truth)—Modest Hofman and André Pierre.
Turgenev—Abraham Yarmolinsky.
Turgenev—David Magushack.
Literary Reminiscences and Autobiographical Fragments—Turgenev.
Reminiscences of Tolstoy, Chekhov and Andreev—Maxim Gorky.
Letters of Chekov—edited by Lillian Hellman.

INDEX

D